War Brides & Rosies

Powell River and Stillwater, B.C.

Barbara Ann Lambert

Yorkshire
March 1944

Zella Stade RCAF WD and Sid Clark RAF,
Yorkshire, England 1944.
Sid came to Canada in 1947 as WWII war bridegroom
(male war bride).
Photo: Zella Clark collection

Order this book online at www.trafford.com
or email orders@trafford.com

Most Trafford titles are also available at major online book retailers.

Printed in the United States of America.

ISBN: 978-1-4669-5187-7 (sc)
ISBN: 978-1-4669-5189-1 (e)

Library of Congress Control Number: 2012915100

Trafford rev. 08/25/2012

 www.trafford.com

North America & international
toll-free: 1 888 232 4444 (USA & Canada)
phone: 250 383 6864 ♦ fax: 812 355 4082

This book is dedicated to my parents, Margaret and Ernest Rathbone, and my sister Joyce Stapleton. Together we survived the rationing and bombing in England during WWII.

<u>Cover Photographs:</u>
Front Cover:

Left: *Wedding of WWII war bride Phyllis Kornyk and John Kornyk CAO, Epsom, England 1946. Photo: Phyllis Kornyk*

Right: *Rosie of the North: Freda Stutt (Bauman): Freda worked for Boeing of Canada and the Powell River Company during WWII. Wedding of Freda and Bob Stutt CAO, January 1946, Winnipeg. Photo: Freda Stutt collection*

Back Cover:

Left: *1970 – 50th wedding anniversary of WWI engaged war bride Alice May Sikstrom and Ingve Sikstrom CEF. Photo: Evelyn Sikstrom collection*

Right: *Wedding of WWI war bride Barbara Lee and John Lee CEF, Orkney Is., Scotland – January 1919. Photo: John Lee Jr. collection*

Acknowledgements:

My thanks to the following:

- All the "Rosies", mill workers, war brides and families, interviewed for *War Brides & Rosies* – your stories and photographs made this book possible.

- My daughter, Ann Bonkowski, for her support and technical assistance.

- Teedie Kagume at the Powell River Museum for her continued help with the research of my local history books. My appreciation to the Powell River Historical Museum & Archives for the use of their archives, especially the Powell River Company *Digesters* and WWII newsletters, and their online website "A Record of Service" compiled by volunteer researcher Lee Coulter.

- Glacier Media Group for permission to publish items from *Powell River's First 50 Years* (published in 1960 by the *Powell River News*), the *Powell River News*, and *Town Crier*.

- Karen Crashley for the use of her scrapbook "Powell River During WWII", a collection of articles from the Powell River *Digesters*.

- Bev Falconer, Rosemary Entwisle M.Ed., and Elisabeth von Holst for their written contributions on WWII Child Evacuees.

- Harold Hardman for permission to quote from the document "My Life" by his uncle Don Dunwoodie CEF, a veteran of the Great War 1914-18.

- John Bosher for permission to quote from *Our Roots: The Families of Bosher, Marsden, Readings, and Simister* with reference to his aunt Charlotte Simister, a WWI Belgian war bride.

- Jack Christian for his help and support.

Errors and Omissions
Errors and omissions are due to the passage of time:
2014 -100th Anniversary of the start of WWI, 75th Anniversary of the start of WWII. Time has passed. Two World Wars were fought during the first half of the Twentieth Century.

The Powell River Company 1910-59

The primary focus of this book is to record the social and economic history of the pulp and paper town of Powell River, B.C.

In 1910 the Powell River Company mill was under construction; two years later, when the first rolls of paper were produced, the Powell River Company mill was the largest paper mill west of the Great Lakes. In 1957 the Powell River Company mill was the largest single unit producer of newsprint in the world.

The Powell River Company created a model Townsite for its employees and families; in 1995 the Powell River Townsite was declared a National Historic District of Canada. In 2010 Powell River celebrated 100 years of Townsite history.

The Powell River Company was a patriotic company. The company, after both world wars, hired veterans as exemplary employees and model citizens for the model company Townsite. In 1946, 500 veterans worked for the Powell River Company and an additional 100 veterans worked in the adjacent villages and districts.

During WWII, out of a population of 8,000 (Powell River & District), 1,000 men and women (55) volunteered for the Canadian Forces. For the first time in its history, the Powell River Company hired women to work in the mill plant.

From 1943-44, Boeing of Canada employed women on the Powell River Company mill site to assemble the PBY, a search and rescue plane; these women were known as the Rosies of the North. Rosie the Riveter was, at first, the symbol for women working in the U.S. aircraft industry; however, she later became the iconic symbol of all U.S. women working in war-related industries.

With a large veteran workforce employed in Powell River & District, it is not surprising that many war brides made Powell River home; however, with no local War Bride Association, no record was kept of Powell River's war brides. The war bride story became a "lost chapter" in Powell River's history.

As the decades passed, the names and stories of war brides faded into local history. In 2011-12 for the first time, the story of Powell River's war brides has been researched and published in *War Brides & Rosies*. A WWI war bride, Barbara Lee, made Stillwater home in 1930; from the 1950s Alice May Sikstrom, a WWI engaged war bride became a Powell River summer resident. Over 40 WWII war brides made Powell River & District home in the postwar period.

This research was only made possible with the help of WWI descendants, WWII war brides (in their 80s) and their families, the Powell River Company publications – the *Digester* and the Powell River Company newsletter. The Powell River Company received letters from service men and women around the world. The company compiled the information and sent out a monthly newsletter to 1,000 Powell River service men and women. This letter included information about overseas marriages – war brides. The Powell River Company had created, unknowingly, one of the first social networking systems in the world.

1930 Powell River Company pulp and paper mill, B.C. Canada.
Photo: G. Russell

1943 Invasion! Landing barges hit the Powell River beach
in the Powell River Townsite, near the mill.
A training exercise by Canadian soldiers from Comox, Vancouver Island.
Bags of flour were used to mark the "dead".
A memorable experience for Powell River residents.
Photo: Powell River Museum & Archives

WWII pulp and paper industry information advertisement: Powell River Digester.

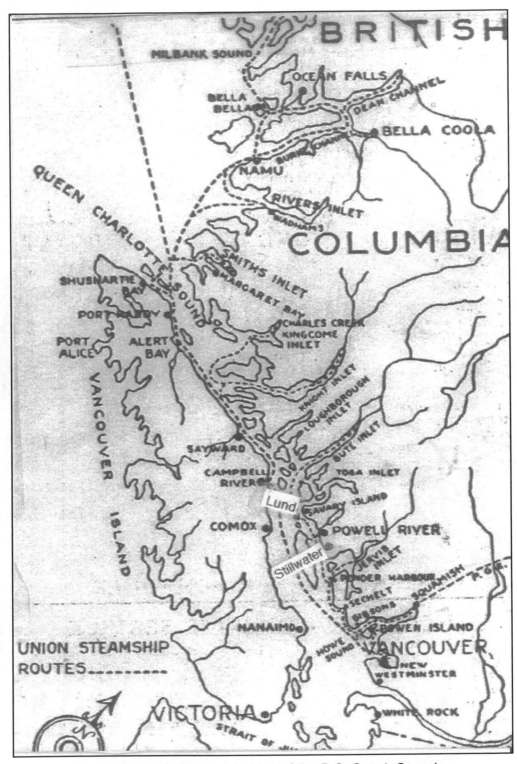

(c. 1938) Union Steamship Map of the B.C. Coast, Canada.
Powell River and Stillwater have no direct road access to other mainland communities.

War Brides & Rosies:
Powell River and Stillwater, B.C.

Contents:

1

For King and Country – Two World Wars

September 1940, Vancouver, B.C.
Lieutenant Colonel John MacGregor, VC MC DCM of Powell River
(WWI—Canada's most highly decorated soldier) in
Vancouver with Johnny Williams, a Powell River Company employee.
Photo: Digester Sept. 1940.

The famous Princess Patricia's Canadian Light Infantry reviewed at Aldershot, England by their Honorary Colonel Patricia Ramsay in 1919 after Armistice Day.
Photo: contributor Charles McLean, Powell River Digester Feb. 1940.
Charles McLean CEF was an original member of the Princess Pats and was the first Powell River man to reach French soil with the Canadians in 1914.

In 1916 the three Lang brothers (L to R) Thomas (Tom), Henry (Harry) and Frederick (Fred), volunteered to join the Canadian Expeditionary Force. Tom and Fred were wounded at Vimy Ridge April 9, 1917. Harry saw action at Passchendaele July 30, 1917. All three brothers returned to Canada—against the odds. Wolfsohn Bay, near Stillwater, B.C. was renamed Lang Bay in their honour. Photo: Muriel Fee

1914, Vancouver, B.C.
As soon as war broke out the four Lee brothers volunteered to fight for King & Country.
Against the odds, all four brothers, after seeing action on the
Western Front, returned to Canada.
(L to R) John, Henry, James and Charles Lee CEF. Photo: John Lee Jr. collection

Left: John Lee CEF and Scottish WWI war bride Barbara Lee, Orkney Is. 1919
Right: 1939 John Lee Veteran Guard WWII and Barbara Lee, Stillwater, B.C. 1939
Photo: John Lee Jr. collection

Two World Wars

The Great War (WWI) 1914-18

The Great War (1914-18) was the largest war known to date, in the history of the world. With the advent of WWII, it became known as WWI.

The assassination of Austrian Archduke Franz Ferdinand on the 28th June 1914 led to a series of events which sparked the start of the war between Germany, the Austrian-Hungarian Empire, and Turkey, known as the **Central Powers**, and the **Allies** – France, Russia, and Great Britain and Empire (Canada, Australia, New Zealand, India, South Africa and the West Indies). Japan initially sided with the Central Powers but in May 1915, joined the Allies. In 1914 Italy was a nominal member of the Central Powers, however she had made a secret treaty with France to stay neutral if France was invaded by Germany; on May 23, 1915 Italy joined the Allies. The United States of America joined the Allies on April 6, 1917; the U.S.A. looked upon Germany as a threat to democracy.

A major war of attrition was fought on the Western Front in France and Belgium. The war was fought on three levels: the air, with the technologies of flight and photography, resulting, for the first time, in aerial surveillance mapping; the ground, bloody trench warfare fought from fixed dug-in positions, filled with mud and water; and a secret underground war of dug-out passages under the Western Front.

An underground army of Royal engineers and miners used the old technology of mining below enemy positions, setting explosives and blowing up selected targets. Thousands of miners lived deep underground, under the Western Front, for many months while digging tunnels. They lived in underground villages with their own sleeping and eating quarters, and received mail deliveries. Their greatest achievement was digging 30 metre tunnels under the Messines Ridge, a task which took over a year. They produced 20+ simultaneous explosions on 7th June 1917, which killed hundreds of Germans, and allowed the Allies to make a major breakthrough and secure the high ground of the Ridge.

The Great War ended on the 11th November 1918. There were tremendous losses, wiping out a whole generation of young men. There were 10 million military deaths: two-thirds were lost in battle, one-third by disease (which included the Spanish Flu). Seven million civilians died in the conflict.

World War II 1939-45

The invasion of Poland by Nazi Germany, September 1, 1939 triggered off the Second World War. In response, the United Kingdom declared war on Germany September 3, 1939. In support of the United Kingdom, Canada declared war on Germany September 10, 1939.

The major **Axis Powers** in WWII were Nazi Germany, Fascist Italy (invaded Albania 1939) and Imperial Japan (attacked Pearl Harbour, December 7, 1941). The major **Allies** were the United Kingdom and Empire, the Soviet Union (declared war on Germany June 22, 1941) and the United States of America (declared war on Germany December 8, 1941). Italy, formerly a member of the axis, switched sides and joined the Allies on October 13, 1943.

Adolf Hitler was the leader of the Third Reich in Germany in WWII. Hitler had served four years in the trenches in WWI. He rose to the rank of Lance Corporal and was awarded two Iron Crosses for bravery. **Winston Churchill** had prominent positions in the United Kingdom in both world wars. In the Great War he was Minister of Munitions and First Lord of the Admiralty; in WWII he was again appointed to the First Lord of the Admiralty as well as becoming Prime Minister of Great Britain on May 1, 1940.

Adolf Hitler, a veteran of WWI, decided to invade European countries in 1939, with swift military strikes called blitzkrieg. Advances in flight technology, since the Great War, resulted in the formation of large Air Forces on both sides of the conflict. WWII engaged countries around the world and was fought on the ground, the sea, and in the skies. Submarine warfare played a large part in the Battle of the Atlantic.

In WWII civilian populations were targeted in countries on both sides of the conflict. The Germans bombed London, in what is known as the London Blitz. Later in the war, V1 and V2 rockets were also used on London. The Allies carpet bombed German and Japanese cities in order to break morale, and end the war.

Radar and code breaking helped win the war for the Allies. At Bletchley Park, Milton Keynes, England, codes and ciphers of Axis countries were decrypted; this intelligence was crucial in winning the war. British counter-intelligence used deception tactics to win the war. The creation of a phantom army in southern England, directly across from Calais, was meant to deceive; the Allies were planning the invasion for the Normandy beaches. Dropping phantom parachutists and radar-jamming devices in strategic locations, away from the Normandy beachhead, gave the Allies the time to make a successful landing on D-Day, 6th June 1944.

In 1942 American troops and a new vast supply of war materials helped the Allies win the war in Europe. After the success of the D Day landings in Normandy, and the capture of the port of Antwerp, the end of the war was in sight. V-E Day (Victory over Europe) was celebrated on May 8, 1945. WWII officially came to an end with victory in the Pacific, three months later. Two atomic bombs were dropped on Japan: Hiroshima on the 6th August 1945 and Nagasaki 9th August 1945. Japan signed a surrender document on 2nd September 1945.

In WWII, military deaths were over 22 million. Civilian deaths were over 60 million. Civilian deaths included: death by bombing, death by starvation, Holocaust deaths, and Japanese P.O.W. deaths. WWII was the deadliest war in the history of the world.

Canada at War – For King & Country

Great Britain relied on its Empire during both world wars for troops and supplies. Canada provided troops, ships, weapons, munitions and food in both wars for the "mother country".

The British Monarchy played an important rallying point for pro-British sentiment. In WWI, King George V declared war in 1914 on behalf of all British subjects in Britain and the Empire. If Britain was at war, then the Dominion of Canada was also at war.

In advance of WWII, King George VI and Queen Elizabeth made the first tour of a reigning monarch to Canada, in May and June 1939. This tour was planned to gain support for "King & Country" in the advent of war against Germany.

Men at War

Canada, a Dominion of the British Empire, automatically supported Great Britain, the "mother country" in declaring war on Germany. All provinces, with the exception of Quebec, gave their full support to the Federal Government. Quebec saw the wars involving Great Britain and Germany as European wars and it had no political will to send Quebecers to Europe. This posed a delicate, political negotiating problem for the Federal Government.

In both world wars the Canadian Government was reluctant to introduce conscription. **Recruitment relied on a voluntary system of military service** which, in the initial years of both wars, worked well. Immigrants from Great Britain saw it as their patriotic duty to fight for "King & Country". Eventually, with so many men being killed overseas, the Canadian Government, in order to keep the forces at full strength, was forced to introduce conscription. **In August 1916 a program of national registration was passed by Parliament, this was later followed by conscription on October 11, 1917.**

During WWII all provinces, except Quebec, gave their approval for conscription "if necessary". **On November 22, 1944 conscription was approved by the Canadian Government.**

The Canadian Expeditionary Force in WWI participated in the following battles in France and Belgium: Ypres (1915), Somme (1916), Arras (1917) which included Vimy Ridge, Messines (1917), Ypres (1917) which included Passchendaele, Somme (1918), Lys (1918), Amiens (1918), second battle of Arras (1918) and battles of the Hindenburg Line (1918). From a total of 620,000 men of the CEF 67,000 were killed.

In WWII over a million men and women joined the three branches of the Canadian Forces: Army, Air and Navy. Over a thousand men and women from Powell River & District (population 8,000) served in the Armed Forces.

Powell River Company *Digester* September 1944:
"To date, 1012 Powell Riverites are in the Armed Forces, and over half of them are with the overseas forces in Italy, France, or with reinforcements in England. Over a hundred others are on the Atlantic convoys or in operational bases on the Atlantic coast, and still others are completing their pre-overseas training."

In WWII Canadians participated in the Battle of the Atlantic (from 1940), Dieppe Raid (1942), Sicilian and Italian campaigns (1943-45), Normandy campaigns including the Normandy Invasion on D Day (6ᵗʰ June 1944), Battle of the Scheldt (October – November 1944), and the Liberation of Holland (1945). 42,000 Canadians died in WWII, 55 from Powell River & District.

A Patriotic Duty

Patriotic WWI veterans volunteered to participate in World War II – often lying about their age. WWI veterans of Powell River & Stillwater: John Lee, James Lloyd and John MacGregor volunteered to re-enlist.

John MacGregor VC MC & BAR, DCM, ED
Canada's most decorated soldier in WWI

John MacGregor VC MC DCM, born in 1889 Cawdor, Scotland came to Canada as an immigrant in 1909. He volunteered for the Canadian Expeditionary Force in WWI. Sergeant MacGregor became Canada's most decorated soldier, winning his first medal (the DCM) at Vimy Ridge in April 1917; nine months later he won the MC for leading a trench raid and capturing prisoners. He was then promoted to Captain. Later, in the same year, Captain MacGregor won the VC when he single-handedly attacked three German installations. At the end of WWI, November 1918, Captain MacGregor was awarded a bar to his MC for capturing two bridges from the retreating German Army.

After WWI, John (Jock) MacGregor married Ethel Flower, a nurse he met in Prince Rupert. Ethel persuaded John to live in Powell River, B.C. and work as a carpenter for the Powell River pulp and paper company.

Captain John MacGregor volunteered to serve in WWII. After the authorities realized that the applicant was Canada's most-decorated Great War soldier, he was promoted to Major, and later Lieutenant-Colonel. He served in a military camp in Vernon, B.C. After the war John MacGregor returned to Powell River and established the MacGregor brick factory in Cranberry Village. Producing concrete bricks for the postwar building boom was a successful business venture.

John's oldest son, Captain James MacGregor, served with distinction in the Air Force during WWII. He wrote his father's memoirs "MacGregor VC".
Barbara Ann Lambert 2009 "Powell River 100"

November 1943 Powell River.
Zella Stade RCAF WD on leave before travelling overseas to the Linton-on-Ouse,
Canadian Air Force bomber squadron base, Yorkshire, England. During WWII
women had the opportunity to volunteer and serve in Women's Divisions of the Canadian
Armed Forces. 45,000 volunteered—5,000 served overseas.
Photo: Zella Stade (centre) with cousins Mavis (L) and Myrna Goddard (R).
Photo: Zella Clark collection

Mrs. T. Green of Powell River, B.C., one of 3,000 nursing sisters who worked in casualty
stations, military hospitals and hospital ships during the Great War. It was partly due to the
sacrifices of the nursing sisters (14 were killed when the Llandovery Castle was torpedoed, 27th
June 1917) that Canadian women gained universal suffrage in 1918.
During WWII Mrs. Green volunteered for the Powell River ARP and IODE.
Photo: Powell River Digester January 1942.

*WWII Powell River Subassembly Plant Boeing Workers (Rosies of the North)
and Powell River Company mill workers:
(L to R) Freeda Mohr (Parsons), Jean Northey (Thompson), Mildred Ross (Dice),
Dodie McGillivray (Anderson), Lynette (Sis) Hayes (Toll), Barbara Manwood, and Isobel Aubin.
The "girls" ran the Powell River Company mill while the "boys" were fighting overseas.
Photo: Powell River Museum & Archives*

*Rosie of the North (1945): Betty Thornton (Harris) off to work at the Boeing of Canada
factory on Sea Island, Vancouver. High wages paid by Boeing attracted Betty
to go into war work and leave her job as a librarian.
Photo: Betty Thornton*

WWI war bride: Barbara Lee of Stillwater, B.C.
John Lee CEF and Barbara Gray, Orkney Is., Scotland 1918
Photo: John Lee Jr. collection

WWII war bride: Hanna deWynter of Powell River, B.C.
Joe deWynter CAO and Hanna Tymstra, Oosterwolde village, Holland 1945
Photo: Hanna deWynter collection

1945 the Canadians liberated Holland. May 13, 1945 Oosterwolde village, Holland.
Liberation parade with the Tymstra sisters: Ge, Simy and Hanna
on a horse-drawn wagon (no gasoline).
Photo: Hanna deWynter collection

Liberation Festivities May 13, 1945 Oosterwolde village, Holland.
Members of the Dutch underground from Oosterwolde village
impersonated Hitler and his henchmen.
Hitler: Lou Somer, Hanna Tymstra's brother-in-law. Photo: Hanna deWynter collection

Women at War – WWI women win the vote for their sacrifices

In the Great War thousands of men left their jobs on the farms, in banking, government services, teaching, factories and transportation (conductors on trams etc.), to volunteer to fight overseas. It was Canadian women who filled in for them, without them, the economy of the country would have faltered.

Women joined patriotic organizations in both world wars. They knitted socks, sent hampers overseas, rolled bandages and raised money for the Canadian Red Cross, Independent Order Daughters of the Empire, and the Canadian Patriotic Fund. Thousands of women worked in war-related industries.

Posters urged women to encourage their men to fight in the war; it was a patriotic duty to fight for "King & Country".

Traditionally, women were homemakers looking after husbands and raising children. They did "women's work": cooking, washing, ironing, mending, cleaning and dress making; and if they were farmer's wives, raising chickens, milking cows and goats, making butter and cheese. The majority of women had a basic elementary education before filling their destiny: marriage. A few, with a higher education, became teachers and librarians. They worked while they were single; however, after marriage, their services were terminated.

In WWI a number of wives and mothers journeyed to Great Britain (often with children) to be near loved ones, who were in army camps and hospitals. Prior to WWI a large number of British families had immigrated to Canada, thus many women returned to stay with relatives for the duration of the war. After the war, these women returned to Canada with **WWI war brides**, their passage paid for by the Canadian Government.

Canadian nurses, known as "nursing sisters", were attached to the Canadian Army Medical Corps in WWI. Over three thousand Canadian women worked in casualty stations, military hospitals and hospital ships during WWI. Fourteen nurses were killed on the HMHS *Llandovery Castle*, 27th June 1918 when the hospital ship was torpedoed by German submarines while returning to Liverpool, England from Halifax, Nova Scotia. It was their supreme sacrifice which helped achieve universal suffrage for Canadian women.

The **Federal vote** was given in 1917 to female relatives of military men under the Wartime Elections Act. All females, 21 years and over, were given the Federal vote on the 24th May 1918. A year later, in July 1919, women were given the right to stand as Members of Parliament. Ten years later, it was the Persons Case of 1929 which gave Canadian women the right to be Senators.

Women at War: WWII Canadian Armed Forces form WD'S (Women's Divisions)

The Second World War led to the mobilization of Canadian women on a huge scale. The National Selective Service Act was passed by the government in 1942 to mobilize and organize the work force. At first only those women who were single and between 20-24 were to register; however with the shortage of labour, in 1943 older single women and married women were registered for part-time work in war-related industries.

Women worked in industry: paper mills, making bombs, assembling aircraft etc. The Powell River Company pulp and paper mill hired women to work in the mill plant, and on a one-year Boeing subcontract assembling the PBY search and rescue plane. Women who worked as riveters, welders, etc. in the Canadian aircraft industry were called **Rosies of the North**, after Rosie the Riveter, the iconic poster woman of U.S. industry.

As in WWI there was a shortage of farm labour. With the men overseas many married women had to run their own farms, besides doing traditional "women's work" on the farm (feeding chickens etc.); women were now operating and repairing farm machinery in the fields. A quarter of a million Canadian women, during WWII, worked on the land.

During WWII, newspaper advertisements encouraged women to join the Women's Divisions of the Armed Forces. The WD of the Royal Canadian Air Force was created in July 1941, the Canadian Women's Army Corps in February 1942, and the Women's Royal Canadian Naval Service (known as the Wrens) in July 1942. Forty-five thousand women served with the Armed Forces, some served overseas.

In Powell River & District 55 women became WD's in the Armed Forces: 35 joined the RCAF, 17 the CWACs and 3 the Wrens. Ten Powell River WD's served overseas. Zella Stade, a teacher in Powell River, joined the WD of the RCAF because it was her "patriotic duty".

For the first time, in WWII, married women were hired to teach. Mrs. Ingrid Cowie was hired to replace Zella Stade who joined the Canadian Forces.

Nurses, with rank of a commissioned officer, served in all three branches of the Armed Forces. The majority, 3,500+ served in the Royal Canadian Army Medical Corps, 450+ served with the Royal Canadian Air Force, and 325+ served with the Royal Canadian Navy.

Ingrid Cowie 2002 (Wildwood School, Powell River 1942-46)
"Women didn't work outside the home before the war. The war really changed things for women. They got a taste of leadership, and being in charge of things. It was a different world to the one they had experienced in the Depression". (Rusty Nails & Ration Books B.A. Lambert 2002)

WWI & II War Brides

After both wars, thousands of war brides and their children, mainly from Britain, made Canada their home: 20,000+ after the Great War, 43,500+ after WWII. The arrangements for free travel for war brides after WWI were duplicated for those travelling to Canada, after WWII. The war brides travelled by train to a port of departure in Britain, across the North Atlantic in converted troop ships, and by train to a destination in Canada. The organization of moving large numbers of wives, some pregnant, some with small children, was huge. It was organized by the Canadian Army, with the support of the Red Cross, IODE, the Salvation Army, and various patriotic organizations.

A number of engaged war brides came to Canada after both wars, at their own expense. WWI engaged war bride from Wales, Alice May Sikstrom, had to wait until her fiancé Private Ingve Sikstrom saved up the fare before she was able to travel in 1920 to Edmonton, Alberta.

In Western Canada, the numbers of WWI bride accounts are few. In British Columbia there is only one self-published book: *Lone Cone* by WWI war bride Dorothy Abraham. There are two accounts published by historical societies: *A War Bride's Journey in 1917* the story of Flora Gould published by the Okanagan Historical Society, and *Mary Jane Yates, WWI War Bride* published by the Crowsnest Pass Historical Society.

Recently three WWI war bride stories have been researched through family histories: Barbara Lee of Stillwater, B.C., Alice May Sikstrom of Hay Lake, Alberta and Charlotte Simister (a Belgian war bride) of Victoria, B.C.

After WWII a few war brides came privately, at their own expense, by plane to Canada. In 1947, Hanna deWynter, a war bride from Holland, flew over to Canada with her young son, to Vancouver; the long journey included five changes at Prestwick, Gander, New York, Toronto and Calgary. In 1947, Zella Clark (Stade) RCAF WD flew by BOAC from England to Canada with her British war bridegroom, Sidney Clark RAF, and child, to Canada. War brides and bridegrooms who travelled privately to Canada were not tallied in the official numbers.

Due to War Bride Associations and the advent of the Information Age in the second half of the 20th Century, there are many books and articles published about the lives of WWII war brides. Recent research, published in *War Brides & Rosies* (2012), pays tribute to the 40+ war brides that made the pulp and paper town of Powell River, home.

2
<u>Powell River Company</u> 1910-59 - A Patriotic Company

- 1910 Powell River Company mill and model Townsite under construction – Italian workforce send for wives and sweethearts from Italy – "Little Italy" at Riverside.
- 1912 #1 and #2 machines in production - **first newsprint west of Ontario**.

The Great War (WWI) 1914-18

- 1914 - 600 employees. Employees (numbers unknown) left to volunteer for King & Country. Severe labour shortage in company mill.
- 1918 Spanish Flu epidemic in Townsite.
- November 8, 1918 (3 days before the Armistice signed) telephone call at the mill – "The War's over!"
- 12 employees killed on the Western Front.
- Postwar period – company policy – hire veterans, exemplary employees and model Townsite citizens: hired John MacGregor VC, MC & BAR, DCM, ED; Joe Falconer DCM; Robert Taylor DC MM and others.
- 1922 *Powell River Digester* 1st publication

The Great Depression 1929-1939

- 1930 **Barbara Lee WWI war bride,** Stillwater, B.C.
- 1930 – 1,300 mill employees: 680 construction workers, payroll $2,256,437
- 1931 Census: Canada 10,000,000; B.C. 700,000; Powell River & District 4,953
- Powell River Company in production 4 days a week: Townsite rents pro-rated
- No Depression in Powell River – area an economic miracle
- 1933-34 The Great Purge: 350 workers fired for voting CCF: blacklisted
- Powell River Company anti-union: Pinkerton agents hired.
- Robert Taylor DC MM blacklisted – left Canada for New Zealand.
- Robert Wilson blacklisted – left Canada for Britain – daughter Dot Riley (Wilson) returned to Powell River as WWII war bride.
- 1937 – 80% of company employees voted for Union.

World War II 1939-45

- 1,000 men and women (55) from Powell River & District volunteered for King & Country out of a population of only 8,000. WWI veterans John MacGregor, Jack Dave, John Lee, James Lloyd and others re-enlist. Young men of Italian ancestry volunteered: Albert & Marino Mitchell, Gino & Aldo Bortolussi, Dino Aprilis and others. Aldo, an airtail gunner, was shot down and killed over Germany. 55 Powell River service men gave their lives for King & Country.
- 1939 Powell River Company in full production 7 days a week.
- 1940 June 10th - War Measures Act: everyone in Canada of Italian ancestry declared "enemy aliens". The Powell River Company manager interceded with the Canadian Government to keep its Italian workforce. Restrictions eased after October 13, 1943 when Italy joined the Allies.
- 1940 – June 26th "the cream of the crop" of Powell River Company employees departed on the *Princess Mary* to join the Canadian Forces.

- ❖ 1940 – August 9th to 11th National Registration Day
- ❖ 1941 November – Jean Banham first Powell River girl to enlist in the Forces.
- ❖ 1941 December 7th - Pearl Harbour – everyone of Japanese ancestry declared "enemy aliens".
- ❖ 1942 All Japanese removed from the B.C. coast, including employees of McNair Shingle Company (Stillwater), and the Shingle Mill at Powell Lake.
- ❖ 1942 Food rationing of sugar, honey, tea, coffee, jam and meat followed by liquor and gas (petrol) rationing.
- ❖ 1942 July 26th – historic reunion of 72 Powell River "boys" at the Canadian Beaver Hut in London, England. Idea came for Corp. "Tish" Schon RCAF and arranged by Canadian officials in London. The Powell River Company sent airmail letters to commanding officers of overseas units asking for cooperation in arranging leave for Powell River boys in Europe. Powell River was the first district in Canada to officially organize reunions abroad.
- ❖ **1943 February publication of 1st Powell River Company Newsletter. The Powell River Company established a 1940s world-wide social networking system which shared information with 1,000 service men and women.**

Female Employees hired by Powell River Company 1942-46

- ➢ For the first time in its history the Powell River Company hired women to work in the mill plant; some were from the Italian community (Rina Dalla-Pria and others).
- ❖ 1942 September – Miss Mary Cavanagh 1st female employee in the mill plant.
- ❖ 1943 March – Mrs. Grace Johnston and Mrs. Wilfred Paul 1st women on ARP patrol.
- ❖ 1943 June 6th – "Invasion" of Powell River – military training exercise.
- ❖ **1943 November 1st – 1944 November 1st Boeing of Canada subassembly plant located in Powell River warehouse: employed 121 women known as Rosies of the North.**
- ❖ 1944 January 23rd Second Powell River Overseas Reunion at the Beaver Club, London, England attended by over 100 men and women in uniform. The Powell River Company organized a historic movie film to be taken of the reunion – later shown at the Patricia Theatre, Powell River Townsite.
- ❖ 1945 May 8th **V-E Day** – the war in Europe is over.
- ❖ 1945 September 2nd - Japan signed a surrender document. WWII is over.
- ❖ 1945-46 Female employees given notice by Powell River Company, with the expected return of former male employees from the war. Widows of veterans hired for office jobs.

Post War Powell River

- ❖ Powell River Company – largest postwar expansion 1,700 employees, $5 million payroll.
- ❖ Post WWI policy continued: hire veterans as valued and loyal employees.
- ❖ Powell River Company encouraged former employees who had served in the Canadian Armed Forces to return to Powell River. With a large postwar expansion, veterans from other areas also hired.
- ❖ **1946 – 500 veterans employed by the Powell River Company** (plus a further 100 veterans worked in the Villages and Districts).

War Brides

- ❖ A cluster of 40+ war brides made Powell River & District home.
- ➤ WWI & II veteran Jack Dave married the Scottish sweetheart he left behind after WWI, and brought her back to Powell River as a WWII war bride.
- ➤ No War Bride Association in Powell River – no records kept of war brides.
- ❖ 1944 December – Margaret Long 1st war bride to arrive in the area.
- ❖ From 1950s to 70s – **WWI war bride Alice May Sikstrom** summer resident.
- ❖ 1955 Powell River Company sold the Townsite houses to sitting tenants (mill employees). Municipality of Powell River formed from the Townsite, Cranberry & Westview Villages, and Edgehill & Wildwood Districts.
- ❖ **1957 Powell River Company mill largest single site unit producer of newsprint in the world.**
- ❖ **1959 Powell River Company merged with MacMillan Bloedel – known as MacMillan Bloedel & Powell River Ltd.**
- ❖ **1964** New company known as MacMillan Bloedel.
- ❖ From 1980: War brides (seniors) from other areas came to live in Powell River's retirement community.
- ❖ **1995 Powell River Townsite declared a National Historic District of Canada.**
- ❖ **2005** Catalyst Paper owner of Powell River paper mill.
- ➤ (2012 – 3 machines and 400 employees)
- ❖ **2010 Townsite Centennial**
- ❖ 2012 Celebration of 100 years of papermaking (1912-2012). April 1912, #1 paper machine produced the first roll of paper at the Powell River Company pulp and paper mill.

1911 Powell River Company Townsite—a construction zone.
Photo by Rod Le May: Frank Haslam collection

1945 Powell River Company mill and model Townsite.
At the forefront of the picture is Riverside, known as "Little Italy"—
demolished and sold for lumber 1950s.
1995—Powell River Townsite declared National Historic District of Canada.
Photo: Alice Johnson (Dice) on rock.
Photo credit: Jack Dice

Powell River Company (1910-1959) – A Patriotic Company

Dr. Dwight F. Brooks and Michael J. Scanlon planned the development of the area near Powell Lake as the first pulp and paper mill west of the Great Lakes. With hydro-electricity from the lake, the potential for the site was far-reaching.

The site they chose, near the mouth of the river from Powell Lake to the ocean, was the site of the best fishing in the area. A large winter village, Tees Kwat (big river) was located there. Tla'Amin (Sliammon) First Nations had fished from this area for over thousands of years. Powell Lake was used by First Nations to reach Jervis Inlet for fishing and hunting. In the 1880s, B.C. First Nations were confined on small Indian Reserves, losing vital traditional territory which supplied food from the ocean and foreshore. Sliammon First Nations were confined to a small reserve north of Powell River and Powell Lake.

Powell River was named after Dr. Israel Powell, Superintendent of Indian Affairs in 1880 by Lieutenant-Commander Orlebar, who saw a river tumbling over a rocky ravine, when sailing along the B.C. coast in the HMS *Rocket*. In 1885 Powell Lake and Powell River appeared, for the first time, on the official maps of B.C.

Canada World Youth Student – Heather (2001)
"Long before anyone heard of Mr. Isaac Powell, the Sliammon people inhabited the land which is now home to the Powell River Townsite residents. It was also home for the Homalco and Klanoose tribes. The Sliammon had used the entire Powell River area. Travelling in different kinds of canoes, the Sliammon explored the immediate areas around Powell River."

****

Brooks-Scanlon formed the Powell River Paper Company with a working capital of one million dollars. In 1910 the model company town of the Powell River Townsite was under construction. In 1912, two years prior to the beginning of the Great War, the Powell River Company started up #1 and #2 machines. It was an historic moment for the company as the first rolls of paper, produced west of Ontario, rolled off the machines. One year later, in 1913, #3 and #4 machines started up.

By 1957, with #9 machine in operation, the Powell River Company mill was the largest single unit pulp and paper mill in the world.

The Townsite was built on the philosophy of the English Garden City movement – creating a town with all the amenities which gave the workforce a pleasant place to live: excellent schools (Henderson and Brooks), the magnificent Dwight Hall for community events, the Patricia Theatre for the latest films, the Powell River Hotel (Rodmay) for meals and drinks in the pub, a "modern" hospital, three churches (United, Anglican and Catholic), and recreational facilities (sports ground, golf course, bowling green, tennis courts and parks).

At the heart of any company town is the Company Store. Remember the 1960s song, "I owe my soul to the company store"? It is simple arithmetic: in Company towns, employees pay rent to live in company houses, and they shop at the company store; thus the wages earned by the employees flow back to the company. Jack Pearson, a company employee living in Edgehill, near Cranberry Village, received a letter from the Powell River Company encouraging all employees to show their *loyalty* to the company, by shopping at the company store.

Merve Wilkinson (2002)
Vancouver Island (employee of the Powell River Company – 1930s)
    "Everything was expensive at the company store – about 30-40% higher than Woodward's and Eaton's in Vancouver. I saw one man's cheque for two weeks of work. He only got 20 cents; the rest of the pay had been taken to clear his slate at the company store. The company could not prevent any employee from buying through the catalogues, as the goods came in at the government wharf as opposed to the company wharf. The company used a tactical way of getting employees to shop exclusively at the company store; those who were regular shoppers (and spenders) were given promotions in the mill!"

Rusty Nails & Ration Books (2002)
B.A. Lambert

Frontier company towns, with single men, were well known for their drinking, gambling, brawls, and "loose" women. The Powell River Company wanted to attract married men with families, families that attended church, and contributed to social civility in the community; employees who were loyal to their country and employer. The Company saw these qualities in returning veterans of the Great War.

Mainly American, British, and Canadian born Caucasians (many were WWI veterans) lived in the main area of the Townsite. European Nationals lived across the river in Riverside (known as Little Italy). A move to a more senior position in the mill resulted in a bigger house, and a better location in the town.

The rented houses were built in the Craftsman style, to encourage neighbours to talk to neighbours from their open porches, in pleasant tree-lined streets. The largest homes, with an ocean view, were constructed for mill management and were located on "Bosses' Row".

Graeme Cooper (2009) (son of Russell Cooper, General Manager)

"Powell River was a model community of company-owned residences. The General Manager's family occupied a home overlooking the mill and situated very near the company guest house, whose staff consisting of a cook and his wife, reported to the manager's wife. The manager's house was also equipped with servant's quarters. Professionals resided in a specific area, merchants in another, and everyone in the Townsite rented from the Powell River Company."

The location of the Riverside accommodation was not ideal. The houses were not insulated, and on the dam side of the houses icicles formed in winter.

Jim Silvestrini (2009) (born 1923 Townsite/lived in Riverside)

"The houses at Riverside were very damp. Every time the dam gates were opened to lower the lake level, a thick cold mist permeated over the area."

Martin Rossander (2009) (mill employee 1948):

First I lived in the bunkhouses at the east side of Riverside. They were cold, drafty, and uninspiring. I was at the bottom of the social ladder at Riverside, and working in the labour gang. Within the mill itself was a social structure."

Powell River 100 (2009) B.A. Lambert

As the mill expanded into world markets, so the Townsite grew. The Powell River Company added more Townsite houses, but there was a limit to the number that could be built, and maintained on company-owned land Lot 450. The Townsite houses were well built with the best of materials, houses that were built with modern amenities – running water, electricity and sewers. Houses with reasonable rents for the employees – houses which could never keep up with the demand for rental accommodation from an ever-growing workforce. The turnover on Townsite rental housing was extremely low. Many Townsite employees stayed in their comfortable, attractive houses, in walking distance of all amenities, for decades until they retired from the mill, and were forced to move.

Due to the lack of available rental accommodation in the Powell River Townsite, the villages and districts surrounding the company-owned land grew rapidly. The economic growth of the villages of Cranberry and Westview, and the districts of Edgehill and Wildwood, were directly connected to the economic growth of the Powell River Company mill. The majority of male householders in the villages were employees of the Powell River Company. Villages and Districts became self-contained mini-communities with their own shops, elementary schools and churches. Village children walked the trails to attend the high school, and the movie theatre in the Powell River Company Townsite.

As the populations in the villages and districts grew, they started to match then overtake the Company Townsite. The Townsite figures remained essentially the same at 2,000 as its growth was limited to Lot 450 and the limited number of houses (500+) it was prepared to maintain.

In 1955 the Townsite houses, with their own individual lots, were sold by the Powell River Company to any sitting tenant who wished to buy. The prices varied, depending on the size and location of the house, from a low of $5,000 to a high of $8,000. The houses at Riverside were sold off for lumber.

The Corporation of the District of Powell River was formed from the Townsite, Cranberry and Westview Villages, Edgehill and Wildwood Districts in 1955.

In 1959 the Powell River Company merged with MacMillan Bloedel and was known as MacMillan Bloedel & Powell River Ltd. In 1964 the new company was known as MacMillan Bloedel Ltd. The good old days of the Powell River Company were over.

The Powell River Townsite was declared a National Historic District of Canada in 1995.

In 2010, the Townsite celebrated its Centennial.

The Powell River paper mill has continued to remain the economic hub of Powell River & District; however, the work force has shrunk from a high of 2,500 in 1973, to 400 employees in 2012. In its 102 year history, the mill has had many different owners; the present owner is Catalyst Paper.

In 2012 the Powell River mill celebrated 100 years of papermaking.

Looking Back: Memories of the Powell River Company Townsite

Bev Falconer (Carrick) (2008) Townsite resident from 1937
"When I grew up here, it was not called the Townsite, it was Powell River, and it was the hub of the universe. The Townsite was a big model community."

Martin Rossander (2009)
"After two days of indoctrination (1948) by a Powell River Company supervisor I was assigned to the labour gang. I was told once you were employed by the Powell River Company you

were secure for life. In the two years I worked for the Powell River Company — it was the most mind-stifling thing I ever encountered."

Jim Silvestrini (2008)
"Yes, looking back, the Powell River Company was good to its employees. We didn't realize how good we had it back then."

Norma Smith (Flett) (2008) Townsite resident
"After the Powell River Company sold out, and subsequent owners did not support the pipe band and community events, the word got out,
"Father Christmas has left town!"

Frank Haslam (age 104) (2009) Townsite resident since 1911
"The Powell River Company was a d---- good company!"

For King & Country

WWI 1914-18 Powell River Company B.C.

During WWI the Powell River mill site and Townsite was a construction zone. The men, who volunteered to join up to fight for King & Country, were mainly construction workers.

Victory Loan campaigns were held in the community. In 1917 a progress clock was used to show the amount raised. After the war, a memorial was erected for the 12 Powell River men who were killed on the Western Front: Ralph Birkenshaw, Alex Black, R. Bryanton, E. A. (Harry) Carter, Gordon Cole, Tommy Lant, C. Moodie, Tommy Simmons, W. (Bill) Stanley, S. Stewart, George Washington, R. (Dick) Welch.

The following Powell River & District men volunteered for the CEF and returned safely home: Don Dunwoodie (Stillwater), Tom, Harry & Fred Lang (Wolfsohn Bay), Joe Rolandi (Myrtle Point), Joseph Gustave Courte (Powell River Townsite), and Joe Falconer (Powell River Townsite).

Arthur C. Dunn:
"Powell River in 1914 was not much more than a clearing in the bush. It must be remembered that in August 1914, when the war began, Powell River was very young. It was passing through the transition period between construction camp and industrial town. Many employees stayed for only brief periods and so many men who joined the armed forces were not well known.

About 600 men were employed here in 1914. Then came the World War and a severe shortage of men. The permanent gang was only about 14 men. All except mill shift workers worked the 60-hour week in those days. All was hand labour too (on the dock). We were promised electric machines but they were a long time coming."

Armistice 1918

It was on November 8, 1918, three days before the actual signing of the Armistice. A premature news flash, but near enough for we around here to realize the end was near.

Just on 11 a.m. Jack Short was called to the phone in my office. He spoke a few words and then called to his men: "The war's over!" Just then the mill whistle blared out. The three carpenters simply picked up their tools and walked off! The end of the day for them! We on the dock couldn't quit so suddenly, so had to carry on for a time.

It was a time which called for rejoicing, celebrating and thanksgiving, but was also the period of Powell River's greatest gloom. **The little town of those days was just recovering from the ravages of the terrible Spanish Flu.** *Social gatherings of all kinds had been forbidden for some time, and many people were very sick, although the crisis of the terrible epidemic had passed. An impromptu meeting was called in the old Ball Ground, and a good crowd gathered in the early evening. The Mill Manager and several others made speeches, but it was a quiet and orderly gathering."*

Powell River's First Fifty Years (1960)

After the Great War, the Powell River Company hired many returning veterans. Veterans made ideal, exemplary citizens for the model community of the Powell River Townsite.

John MacGregor VC MC DCM ED, Canada's most decorated soldier in WWI, was hired by the Powell River Company.

Robert Taylor DCM MM was also hired by the company.

The Role of Women in Powell River
during the construction years and the Great War

During the early years of construction of the mill and the model Townsite, Powell River's population was mainly composed of single men.

A few single women (teachers and nurses) lived in the Townsite. Some single teachers lived at the Powell River hotel (The Rodmay).

First Nations women visited the emerging Powell River Townsite and villages. They traded or sold fresh salmon and beautiful cedar baskets.

A small number of married women had joined their husbands by the time the Great War started in 1914. It was traditional for the Powell River Company to pay their employees cash. It was also traditional, for many years before the company went to direct deposit, for the men to buy liquor and gamble away their hard-earned wages on card games. Married women, aware of this tradition, waited outside the mill on pay days to obtain cash from their husbands to pay household bills before they went to the beer parlour.

In 1911 Teresa Michelus travelled from Italy with two children and her brother-in-law to join her husband Pietro Michelus (Mitchell), who was working on construction in the Powell River Company mill. On arrival, she went into shock at the primitive living conditions, and refused to unpack her trunk for a year!

Josie Mitchell (1987)
"I was born in a tent. We moved from a tent to a bunkhouse and then when the house was built, we moved to Cedar Street. We were the first occupants."

During WWI there was a severe labour shortage at the mill. Women living in the Townsite were not considered a viable alternative because they were few in number, and had domestic responsibilities.

The role of married women in Powell River, during the Great War, was that of providing the necessities of daily life for workers in the mill: food, a place to stay (as boarders), and a laundry service (washing and mending clothes). Food was cooked in tents and bunkhouses and delivered directly to the men, on the mill site, by wives and small children.

Italian husbands and single men, working on construction, saw the opportunity of long-term employment with the Powell River Company, and sent for wives and sweethearts to join them.

Married Women and Sweethearts left Italy to join husbands in Canada

Italian women, with great courage, travelled across oceans and countries, often with young children, little money and unable to converse in English, to join husbands and fiancés in Canada.

Ann Piccoli (Zorzi) made the journey from Italy in 1913 with two young children, Gagliano and Mafalda, in order to join her husband, Giuseppe Piccoli in Powell River. Guiseppe had worked on construction, in the Townsite, from 1911.

Dora Buse (Piccoli) 1987:
"Mother (Anna Piccoli) came out in 1913. Can you imagine a woman, who didn't speak the language, had hardly any money with two little kids, to come all the way from Italy to go to Powell River? All on their own, with no house to live in. They lived in a tent when they first came here, down by the old cemetery (golf course).

Mother told me how she used to cook for the Italians in one tent because as soon as they (the bachelors) knew an Italian lady was there, they wanted Italian food. We slept in another tent, and she served in another. We had three tents. She had 16 boarders.

My father had the first bank because he used to keep all the Italians' money. He made a little safety box with a combination lock and he had all their money in envelopes."

Children delivered hot lunches to the Italians in the grinder room:

Fides Prissinotti (Brandolini) 2008:
"We had a wicker basket with a lid. We'd put everything there — the dish, fork and knife, and a glass (for wine) — just like they were eating at home. We had to get down there fast — so it was hot!

We all stayed in that big, long bunkhouse in the Townsite. She (Ermina Brandolini) had five or six boarders. When we moved to Riverside (known as Little Italy), five or six boarders slept upstairs. My mother worked hard, everything was done from scratch — all these Italian dishes. She cooked spaghetti, stews and roasts. The men always had a glass of wine with their meals."

Ida Toigo travelled on her own from Italy to Powell River, B.C. to marry her fiancé Luigi Scarpolini.

Ida Scarpolini (Toigo) 1924 *Digester*
"*I know this sounds strange, and people would think it a very unconventional thing for a girl to go running around the world to marry a man. But the world is changing. Girls are doing things today that would have shocked their mothers!*"

First Nations Women

Sliammon First Nations had an economy based on fishing. Women from the Sliammon Reserve went door-to-door, in the villages and the Powell River Townsite from 1910-1950's (including both World Wars) selling fresh salmon and cedar baskets.

Ingrid Cowie (2002):
First Nations, from Sliammon, came around Wildwood with fish and baskets. We were always told, "Caught this morning!" The fish were 25 cents each in the 1930s. On one occasion I traded a good coat for a beautiful cedar basket.

Roy Leibenschel (2002):
"*First Nations brought salmon and baskets around in the 1930s and 40s to Cranberry Village. My mother used to can it. I remember buying a great big chunk of salmon for 75 cents in the 1940s.*"

Mary Masales (2002):
"*The men at Sliammon used dugout canoes and brought in large quantities of salmon. The women smoked them for the winter. The clams were collected in large gunny sacks. Rakes were used to get at the cockles under the sand.*

I used to see the women searching, by the washed out areas of Sliammon Creek, for the fine long cedar roots. Some were peeled and dyed with berry juice. The roots were used to make baskets."

Barbara Ann Lambert (2012):
"*First Nations used to come around to the old Lambert farm in Paradise Valley (Powell River Regional district) in the 1930s. My mother-in-law, Gertie Lambert, exchanged farm produce for salmon and cedar baskets.*"

Elsie Paul "Elder in Residence" Vancouver Island University 10/08 Powell River Museum presentation:

1915 Powell River Company mill saw room.
During the Great War (1914-18) and until the early 1920s, women and children delivered
homemade hot meals directly to the men working in the mill.
Although the mill was desperately short of labour during WWI, women were not hired.
Photo: far right: Mary and Tom Higgins
Photo credit: Brian Crilly collection

1920s Piccoli family, Wildwood District, Powell River, B.C.
In 1913 Anna Piccoli made her way from Italy to the Powell River Townsite
with her two children Gagliano and Mafalda.
The family lived in one tent; in another Anna fed 16 Italian bachelors.
Front row: Mary/Middle row (L to R) Amalia, Angelina, Isadora
Back row: Seated: Giuseppe & Anna Piccoli/Standing (L to R) Mafalda, Gagliano
Photo: Amalia Gustafson (Piccoli)

1924 Brandolini family Powell River Townsite. Erminea had six Italian bachelors as boarders.
As a child, Fides Prissinotti delivered hot meals directly to the Italians in the grinder room.
(L to R) Ottavio & Erminea Brandolini/Ligia/Echara/Fides/Asswero
Photo: Fides Prissinotti (Brandolini)

Display of cedar baskets of the Tla'Amin (Sliammon) First Nations at Spirit pole tour North
American Indigenous Games May 6, 2008, Willingdon Beach, Powell River, B.C. During the
first half of the 20th Century (including two World Wars), First Nations women went door-to-
door in the Powell River Townsite and villages, selling fresh salmon and cedar baskets.
Photo: B. A. Lambert

"My grandmother gathered materials for basket weaving. I watched her weave baskets. She would go into Powell River (from Sliammon) to sell her baskets — I helped her pack them in. She traded for part — cash, food, blankets, men's clothes, etc. There were times when she sold a basket for $5 — today they are worth thousands. Sometimes my grandparents would walk to Wildwood, and they'd trade fresh salmon for meat, chickens and beef at a farm there."

Powell River & District WWI war brides

Lance Corporal John Lee CEF, who lived at Stillwater, worked for Kelly Spruce, a division of the Powell River Company. His Scottish wife, Barbara Lee was a WWI war bride. Barbara Lee's story, told by her youngest child John (79), is published for the first time in *War Brides & Rosies*.

After WWII, a WWI war bride, Alice May Sikstrom from Hay Lake, Alberta, was a frequent visitor to Powell River. Alice's story, told by her youngest child Evelyn (81), is also published for the first time in *War Brides & Rosies*.

Because of the high number of WWI veterans living in Powell River & District, it is possible there were other WWI war brides who lived in the area; however, their names and stories have vanished into history.

For King & Country

WWII 1939-45 Powell River Company, B.C.

The Powell River Company was a patriotic company and fully supported the 1,000+ men and (55) women from Powell River & District in uniform. At this time Powell River had a population of only 8,000. All male employees, who gave up their jobs to go to war, were promised back their jobs on their return.

As soon as the war started, employees were leaving the mill to join up. In December 1939 Norman Hill, Dave Jack and George Harris proceeded overseas. June 26, 1940 was an outstanding day that went down in the history of the town, when a mass migration of Powell River Company employees left to volunteer for the Canadian Forces. The "cream of the crop" were given a royal send-off on the old *Princess Mary.*

A Royal Send-off

"The war became of first importance to Powell River last night when the first body of recruits left on the night boat to enter training. A turn out that eclipsed anything ever seen here was at the wharf to give the lads a royal send-off. Both the pipe band and the Union Band joined in a parade from the recruiting station to the boat. Members of the Powell River Ex-service men's association and the Canadian Legion formed a guard of honour for the new soldiers making their departure."
Powell River News June 27, 1940

Entire shifts left from the Powell River Company, all it would take was one man to call out *"Let's go tomorrow, boys!"* and the entire shift left on the boat the next day.

War Contracts

The Powell River Company mill was an integral part of Canada's war industry. Harvested high grade spruce lumber went into the making of the Mosquito and other British planes. The largest percentage of aeroplane spruce, cut on the Pacific Coast, passed through the Powell River plant.

Pulp and paper products were produced for the war effort – **Powell River Digester** September 1943:

"Paper and cardboard made in Powell River packs food and medicine for the Armed Forces and carries their shells and ammunition. How many of us know that pulps are used in the nitrating into explosives, making plastics, substitutes for metal, component parts of electrical apparatus, military radios, Air Force housing etc. And in the manufacture of such wide and varied essentials as synthetic fibres (rayon), fragmentation bombs, cargo chutes, aerial delivery chutes, mosquito nettings, powder bags, gas protection capes and helmets, various types of clothing for the Services, including paratroop jump suits, shirts, uniform linings, identification badges, hospital wadding and surgical dressings, etc.; pulp is an integral ingredient."

The Powell River Company machine shop filled many special war orders: December 1942 - steering bases for cargo ships; February 1943 – acetylene tank buggies; March 1943 – steam valves for ships' auxiliary equipment, and truck wheels for industrial use; May 1943 – valves for auxiliary engine room equipment on Canada's Merchant Navy; and July 1943 – machine parts for diesel engines for Canadian shipping.

The largest contract was the one-year Boeing of Canada Contract, November 1, 1943 – November 1, 1944 to assemble parts of the PBY, a patrol and rescue plane.

Italian Workforce

On June 10, 1940 after Italy's Declaration of War and alliance with Germany, Canada's Italian population became subject to the War Measures Act; they were declared "enemy aliens". Camps (men only) were set up in Kananaskis near Banff, Alberta, and at Camp Petawawa in Ontario for those persons deemed sympathetic to Mussolini and/or Hitler.

In 1939 Powell River was an integrated community with all its citizens loyal to Canada. The Powell River Company manager interceded with the Canadian Government to keep its Italian workforce. Italians who came to Canada after 1924 (when Mussolini came to power), those without the correct papers – including children without a registered birth in Canada ("born on the boat" or in Italy) had to register with the RCMP. After Italy surrendered in 1943 these restrictions lifted. Italian men and women worked in the mill during WWII.

Young men of Italian heritage from Powell River joined the Canadian Armed Forces (Albert and Marino Mitchell, Gino and Aldo Bortolussi, Dino Aprilis and others). Aldo Bortolussi, an air tail gunner, paid the ultimate price for his loyalty to Canada; he was shot down and killed on a bombing raid over Germany.

Female Workers in the mill and Rosies of the North

For the first time in its history the Powell River Company was forced to hire women to work in the mill plant.

The first woman to be hired was Miss Mary Cavanaugh who became a mill employee September 1942. Two-hundred plus women, from Powell River and District, worked in the mill plant, and on a one-year Boeing subcontract assembling air plane parts. Women who worked for Boeing were known as Rosies of the North. Rosie the Riveter was the iconic poster woman for U.S. women working in the aircraft industry.

Boeing of Canada operated a sub-assembly plant #185 in #3 Warehouse at the Powell River Company site. It operated for one year from November 1, 1943 to November 1, 1944. Twelve squads were formed from 121 women and 32 men, their job was to assemble parts of the PBY, a patrol and rescue plane. During the contract time, 16-25 aircraft were completed per month. The wages were good: trainees made 47 cents an hour, 4th class workers 54 cents an hour, and 1st class workers 70 cents an hour. One enterprising Boeing worker scratched the names of the Boeing employees on a small piece of scrap metal from the project; it is presently displayed in the Powell River Museum.

Initially, the company management were somewhat hesitant at employing women, and looked upon it as a "novel" experience, and a necessity. Initially the male workforce were shocked at the mill becoming "sissified" when female washrooms were installed, and doors put on existing male toilets!

Powell River Digester September 1942:
"The question of employing women was anticipated some time ago by the company, and a thorough survey made to determine in what departments they could be employed. To date the beater room, sulphite plant, finishing room and pulp testing departments have employed a number of women."

Prior to WWII, apart from a few well-paid positions in teaching and nursing in the Company Townsite at $75-$80 a month, the only other job available for women was housework at $5-$10 a month. The majority of stores in Powell River and area generally employed men, with the exception of female relatives. There were a few successful business women in the district: Madame Loukes ran the profitable 5th Avenue Dress Shop in Westview, a different Madam operated a House of Ill-Repute in Wildwood District, and Olive Devaud was a property owner and philanthropist in Westview Village.

For the first time in Powell River, female mill workers were earning good union wages. For Ruth Allan, a widow with children, it meant she could purchase a modest house in Westview Village and have a decent standard of living.

Women went to work during the war for patriotic reasons, however many enjoyed the wartime experience of having a good paying job in a society which generally paid women very low wages. When the boys came home, the women lost their jobs; by the time they had finished working in the mill, they had gained the respect of male supervisors in the mill for their adaptability, reliability, and flexibility.

Powell River Digester August 1943
"The experience of the Powell River Company with women employees has been very satisfactory. They have, for the most part, shown unusual alertness and surprising adaptability. They have responded to the careful instruction given by experienced workers and have proved themselves efficient replacements for our employees who are serving their country on the war fronts of the Empire."

In the February 1944 edition of the *Powell River Digester*, management stated that few women, if any, intended to work after the war. In reality, wartime work performed by women in the Powell River Company mill plant was always considered temporary until the men came home and assumed their old jobs.

An assumption was made by management, the government, and 1940s society that all women were willing to give up their jobs and return to their traditional role as homemakers and childrearers. In postwar B.C., married female teachers, who taught for the first time during WWII (due to the shortage of male teachers), won the right for employment with school districts, regardless of marital status. Gradually the role of women changed from 100% homemaker to that of persons who had the choice to work or not. WWII changed the perception of women's role in Canadian society.

WWII – House of Ill Repute

There was no House of Ill Repute in the company-controlled Townsite. During WWII freighters and tugs docked at the company dock and sailors found their way to the only House of Ill Repute in the area, in the nearby District of Wildwood. One small boy recalled, while playing out on the street in the Townsite, a taxi drawing up and a sailor calling out of the window, *"Boy, which way to the Hook House?!"* World War II brought increased business to the women who worked in the only House of Ill Repute in the area.

Eunice Sawchuck remembers the Wildwood "cathouse":
"Sometime in the late 1950s my husband bought a house in Wildwood. We were informed later, after the sale, that it was a "cat house". The house had a large entrance hall and main room plus nine small bedrooms."

According to Frank Haslam (2008, age 103) the Madam in charge was called May and there were four or five young women living there. May told Frank not to make coal deliveries in the morning as her girls liked to sleep in! The young women were checked regularly by the town's doctor, Dr. Marlatt, during daytime visits.

The girls wore beautiful expensive gowns bought from Madame Loukes 5th Avenue Dress Shop in Westview Village. They visited the shop "after hours" to choose their dresses and accessories. Madame Loukes, who was originally from New Orleans, saw selling expensive dresses to the ladies of the House of Ill Repute as good financial sense.

Dorothy Loukes (related to Madame Loukes by marriage):

"All the girls in the House of Ill Repute came to Madame Loukes for their clothes, which she bought especially for them. The dresses that the girls on the hill wore were really gowns. The girls had the pick of the stock at Madame Loukes' store. They chose only the very best and only had the best of the makeup from the drugstore. They were all lovely girls, one was exceptionally beautiful. The Madam of the house on the hill was a very gentle lady."

The Madam of the "cat house" sent all the washing from her business to Emil Gordon's laundry at the Shingle Mill near Powell Lake.

Angelina MacMillan (Piccoli) 1987:

"There was a bag that was taboo and that came from a special house in Wildwood (the "cat house") and no one was allowed to touch that bag and it was put in the wash by itself!"

The Powell River Company wartime publications

The *Powell River Company Digester* and monthly Newsletters played an important part in the sharing of wartime service information, and news about wartime romances!

During WWII the Powell River Company printed articles and photographs of "our boys and girls" in the services, in the monthly *Powell River Digester*. It became a 1940s Facebook with many photographs of service weddings and Powell River service reunions in London, England.

In February 1943 the Powell River Company, with resources around the world, created a 1940s social networking system for 1,000 men and women in Powell River & District Armed Forces with the issuing of the Monthly Company Newsletter which shared information.

Powell River Company Monthly News Letter to Our Employees in the Armed Forces Vol. 1 No. 1 February, 1943

"This is the first issue of our Monthly News Letter to all Powell River men in uniform. The officials of the Company thought you might be interested in hearing news of your friends and chums in the Service; and accordingly our News Letter will be partly composed of extracts from letters received from Powell River boys in all branches of the Armed Forces and partly of quick flashes from the Home Front.

If this idea of a monthly letter appeals to you, please drop us a line and tell us all the news the censor will permit -- what you are doing -- information about any other boys --- your furloughs etc. These will be printed in future News Letters.

Harold S. Foley/R. Bell-Irving/D.A. Evans

1917 Gustav Courte (1886-1969) CEF
Gustav worked for the Powell River Company before WWI 1911-16
and after the war, 1918-1930s.
Photo: Teedie Kagume

1914 Joe Rolandi (1885-1977) CEF.
Joe came to Canada from Missio, near Milan, Italy.
For reasons unknown, Joe joined the Regiment of the Scottish Highlanders and wore a kilt.
Joe logged at Myrtle Point (near Powell River) before WWI,
and after the war in Olsen Valley, near Powell Lake.
Photo: Vi Rolandi

1944 January 23rd Beaver Club, London, England.
The second historic Powell River Overseas Reunion,
attended by over 100 Powell River men and women in uniform.
The reunion was organized by the Powell River Company and Canadian officials in London.
Centre, second row, behind the Powell River sign, Zella Stade RCAF WD.
Photo: Powell River Museum & Archives

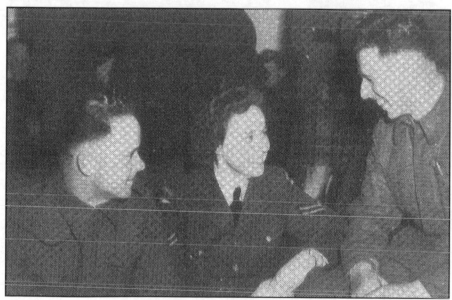

1944 January 23rd Zella Stade at the historic Powell River reunion,
Beaver Club, London, England.
(L to R) R. H. Daly CAO, Zella Stade RCAF WD, Albert Mitchell CAO
Photo: Digester April 1944

1945 V-J Day. Powell River Company employees rejoice that WWII is finally over.
Hubert Rushant blowing the donkey whistle. Photo: Powell River Museum & Archives

1945 V-J Day.
Agnes McPhalen (Boeing of Canada and Powell River Company mill worker)
and Joyce Hassell (mill worker) blowing the mill whistle. WWII is over!
From 1945-6 the female mill site employees were let go with the return
of former male employees from the services.
Wives of service men, killed in action, were offered mill office jobs.
Photo: Powell River Museum & Archives

Under the inspiration of Flying Officer Tish Schon, and with the cooperation of the Powell River Company, the Canadian Legion, and residents at home, Powell River personnel staged two successful overseas reunions at the Beaver Club in London, England. The first was held on July 26, 1942 and the second on January 23, 1944. A sound film was made by the Powell River Company of the second one, and shown in the Patricia Theatre to over two thousand residents.

V-E and V-J Days in Powell River – celebrating the end of WWII

In 1945 WWII came to an end, first in Europe, and a few months later in the Pacific. On May 8, 1945 Germany surrender unconditionally. Ruth Allan, a mill worker, having missed the news on the radio, went to board the bus from Westview village to the Townsite. The bus driver yelled out:

"Lady, you won't be going to work today. The war is over!"

The mill and schools were closed for the day. A few days later the three inch headlines of the *Powell River News* said it all:

THANK GOD

"The news flashed over the radio and heralded by the wail of sirens caught Powell Riverites as they awakened to a day of apparent normal activity. Before many minutes passed, however, excited residents came to the realization that it was the most momentous day since that Sunday in September 1939 when Chamberlain announced to the world that Great Britain was at war with Germany. At 7:08 the air raid sirens blared forth the victory signal."

May 11, 1945 *Powell River News*

Powell River residents greeted the end of the war in Europe with joy and sadness:

"V-E Day in Powell River was greeted with mixed feelings of thankfulness and restrained rejoicing. The long five-and-a-half years campaigning had bitten heavily into the lives and happiness of this closely knit community. Over a thousand of our citizens were in the Armed Forces. Fifty-one of these had answered their last roll call. Another 50 had been wounded or disabled. A half-dozen were still prisoners of war.

All these boys were intimately known to almost everyone in the community. These boys — those killed, the missing and the prisoners of war — were all Bill and Harry and George and Dick to us."

Powell River Digester June 1945

The end of the war in the Pacific was greeted with joy, relief and thankfulness by Powell Riverites. A deep blast of the mill's whistle brought the news to everyone in the mill and Townsite.

Sergeant Allan Todd was in London, England when the news broke. His recollections of that day were printed in the September edition of the *Digester*.

Sgt. Allan Todd RCAFO:
"Instinctively the people of London, as if pulled by an invisible cord, converged on Buckingham Palace where the King and Queen with the two Princesses waved at the crowds from the balcony of the Palace.

Everybody was gay, happy and excited. They had good reason to be as they had been in the front line for nearly six years under conditions of almost intolerable strain. They had a right to celebrate."

Bev Carrick, a schoolgirl living in the Townsite, recalls how her block celebrated V-J Day.

Bev Falconer (Carrick):
"Finally V-J Day happened. Such celebrating! People meeting on the street shouted excited greetings to each other. And we young people had our own celebrations. The houses across the street had long front porches so the kids on our block congregated on the Robertson's' porch. I took my most precious possession – my windup portable record player which played 78 RPM records. We played my records over and over again! And we banged pot lids like we did on New Year's Eve. This is how "our gang" on the 900 block of Maple Avenue celebrated the end of the war!"
Rusty Nails & Ration Books: Great Depression & WWII Memories 1929 -1945
Barbara Ann Lambert 2002

Night time street lighting came on again in London, England; the lights also came on again in Powell River. The war was finally over: no more blackout at night or ARP patrols, no more digging for Victory, no more wartime shortages, and for Canadians an ending of wartime rationing was in sight (due to food shortages, rationing in Britain continued until 1954).

As soon as the "boys" came home, the "girls" lost their jobs in the mill plant.

WWII war brides

A "cluster" of 40+ war brides came to Powell River & District in the post war period of WWII.

News about "our boys" getting married, in Canada and overseas, were published in the *Digesters* and Powell River Company monthly newsletters throughout the war years.

The Powell River Company encouraged its own veterans to return home, and take up their old jobs in the mill in a January 1945 newsletter:

Powell River Company Newsletter No. 1 1945

"We know from your letters and from talks with the men who have come back, that most of you are pretty keen to get back to Powell River. We, too, are looking forward to that day, and we want to have a suitable job with security and prospects for advancement ready for you.

… there are today over 1,000 from the Powell River District who are on active service, of which well over 700 are Company employees – a record of which we are intensely proud of and which we are sure is unequalled in Canada.

Why are we doing this? First in gratitude for what you have done for us. You volunteered to fight for the security of Canada – we feel it is our duty to provide security for you in return. Our second reason is a purely selfish one. We think Powell River is a good community now, but we want to make it still better, and **we can think of no finer group of citizens to settle in our town than you who have fought for us.**"

According to the *Digester* nearly 100 of "our boys" married overseas; some returned to Powell River with their war brides.

With a huge postwar expansion, veterans from other areas were offered employment by the Powell River Company. According to the "Welcome Home" publication, published by the *Powell River News* July 1, 1946, 500 veterans were employed by the Powell River Company, and a further 100 worked at other jobs in the district. In 1947 the Powell River Company mill, with a payroll of five million dollars, employed 1,700 men.

Thus a second group of war brides, married to veterans from other areas, came to Powell River in the postwar era.

Some war brides in Powell River returned to Britain, others relocated with their veteran husbands to larger and less isolated communities in Vancouver and Vancouver Island.

From the 1980s, a third group of war brides (seniors) joined Powell River's retirement community.

3
WWII Women in Uniform

Traditionally, Canadian women were seen as wives, mothers, and homemakers. Many supported their husbands and brothers overseas by working for organizations such as the Red Cross, YWCA (Young Women's Christian Association), and IODE (Imperial Order of the Daughters of the Empire). Historically, the perception of women at war, were of camp followers to provide "comfort" to the troops after each battle. This perception, and the role of women in war, was to radically change with WWII when Canadian women were given the opportunity to join WD's (Women's Divisions) of the Canadian Army, Air Force, and Navy.

Britain had led the way in the mobilization of the nation's women for "essential work". In the spring of 1941 all women from age 18-60 had to be registered; a few months later, December 1941, the National Service Act was passed. Initially only single women from age 20-30 were called up, however, by 1943 eight out of ten women, single and married were involved in war work. Women worked on the land (WLA-Women's Land Army), cutting down trees (Women's Timber Corps), driving ambulances (WVS-Women's Voluntary Service), putting out fires after air raids (ARP-Air Raid Precaution), and dangerous work in munitions factories. Women were members of the different women's branches of the Armed Forces: WAAF (Women's Auxiliary Air Force), ATS (Auxiliary Territorial Service), and WRNS (Women's Royal Naval Service). British women in the Armed Forces, unlike Russian women, were not trained to be battle ready. Russian women fought as equals with the men in battles against the German invaders, many gave their lives for "Mother Russia".

Canadian women were as enthusiastic as their British sisters to join the Forces; many felt it was their patriotic duty. There was reluctance within the Canadian "top brass" to endorse the idea of Women's Divisions, and, at the beginning of the war, a general reluctance by the Canadian public to change their perception of women's traditional role in society as homemakers, to independent women serving their country in the military. However, the Canadian Government, and the top generals in the Canadian Forces, could not ignore the precedence set by the British Government in mobilizing women for war. Other Allied countries had organized women's auxiliary units: South Africa – November 1939, New Zealand – February 1941, and Australia – March 1941.

In July 1941, the Canadian Government gave permission for the Air Force to enroll women. In August 1941 the Army received the green light, and lastly, in July 1942, the Navy. The following women's divisions (WD's) were formed: RCAF WD

(Air Force), CWAC (Army), and the WRCNS – Wrens (Navy). Possibly the Canadian Government was influenced by the knowledge that the Canadian Forces, a volunteer force, would benefit from women taking over non-military tasks (telephone operators, clerks, etc.) in the military, and this would release additional men for active overseas duties.

Women across Canada (45,000) were accepted into the WD's of the Canadian Forces. They responded to recruitment posters and advertisements in newspapers. Their acceptance depended on a successful medical. Once accepted, they were given an identity card, and a uniform. Each service had a smart and distinctive uniform. They were trained for a variety of positions: clerks, cooks, hospital orderlies, drivers, mechanics, weather observers, and telephone and radio operators.

After the successful initial training of WD's, some overseas postings became available (5,000); they were eagerly sought after. These postings were not without danger; the journey across the North Atlantic was hazardous with German submarines attacking Canadian shipping. Life in Britain was not easy, with severe rationing and the constant danger of bombing.

Powell River & District WD'S

Fifty-five young women from Powell River & District volunteered to serve in the various Women's Divisions of the Canadian Armed Forces. 35 joined the RCAF WD (Air Force), 17 joined the CWAC's (Army), and 3 joined the WRNCS – Wrens (Navy). Ten volunteered for overseas service:

6 Air Force (RCAF WD): Jean Banham, Doris Humphrey, Elsie Foster, Hazel Clapp, Marjorie Fairgrieve, and Zella Stade.

4 Army (CWAC's): Doris Bailey, Mary Loukes, Mrs. Gladys MacIntyre, and Phyllis Simmonds.

Going from civilian life to life in the services (wearing a uniform, living in barracks, eating cafeteria style, and drill marches) was a shock.

Julia McGuffie RCAF WD (Manning Depot, Rockcliffe, Ontario), Powell River Company Newsletter May 1943:
"Well, here I am in the Air Force at Rockcliffe. When we arrived here the four of us from Powell River: Bette Parkin, Frances Haigh, Edith Taylor, and myself all had our own ideas of sleeping in bed by each other. They changed all that. They sent us to bed in alphabetical order, and I found an

POWELL RIVER DIGESTER

INVEST IN VICTORY

Corporal Frances Haigh RCAF WD Digester cover photo
for the Powell River 7th Victory Loan. Dec. 1944
Frances was presented to HRH Princess Alice at Dartmouth, England.
Photo: Digester Oct. 1944

Jean Banham

A.W.I Eileen Heavenor

1942 Alfreda Lee RCAF WD from Stillwater, B.C., daughter of Barbara Lee WWI war bride.
Far right (top): Jean Banham RCAF WD, first girl in Powell River to volunteer for the
Forces, and (below) Elaine Heavenor RCAF WD.
Photo: John Lee Jr. collection

Edith Taylor RCAF WD enjoying life in the Forces on an eastern Canadian Air Force base.
Far right (top): Ada McLean RCAF WD. Far right (below): Elsie Foster RCAF WD.
Photo: Digester Oct. 1945

AW. Doris Humphrey   AW. Gerry Doran   L.A.W. Mary Loukes,   L.A.W. Joan Simmonds.

AW2 Marjorie McPhalen   AW Beverley Scott   Wren Frances Hughes   Pte. Verna Arnold

Powell River WDs in the Canadian Forces: Top row (L to R) Doris Humphrey RCAF,
Gerry Doran RCAF, Mary Loukes CWAC, Joan Simmonds CWAC.
Bottom row (L to R) Marjorie McPhalen RCAF, Beverley Scott RCAF,
Frances Hughes WRNCS, Verna Arnold CWAC.
Photos: Digesters 1942-45

"MC" girl from the east beside me. Guess it will work out alright. In the drill hall here, there is basketball, badminton, indoor softball and every gym convenience. On Saturday night, dances are held in the drill hall. There are 140 girls in our squadron; 19 from B.C. and 4 from Powell River."

The first Powell River girl to enlist in any of the Forces was Jean Banham, November 1941. Jean joined the RCAF WD and was later selected for an overseas posting in the UK. In June 1943, when her unit was being inspected, she was presented to **Her Majesty, Queen Elizabeth** (later known as the Queen Mother).

Jean Banham persuaded her friend Violet Rolandi to join up. Vi enjoyed being a nurse's aide in the RCAF WD. However, after her marriage to Walt Liebich (May 1943), Vi became pregnant and resigned from the RCAF. Pregnancy immediately ended the career of any woman in the three services.

The first to enlist in the CWAC's was Doris Bailey. In December 1943 Doris went overseas and served in the UK, and after D Day, in Belgium.

Only three Powell River girls joined the "Wrens", Frances Hughes, Grace Scott, and Bea Sutton. Frances, after training at Galt (Cambridge, Ontario), served in HMCS *Givenchy*. Grace was attached to HMCS *Bytown*, Ottawa, and later served on HMCS *Givenchy*, at Esquimalt (Victoria, B.C.).

Six Powell River & District Service women met and married men in the Canadian Services: Bette Parkin, Alice Oster, Marjorie McPhalen, Violet Rolandi, Edith Taylor, and Mrs. Ernie McLeod. With the exception of Bertyne (Betty) Parkin, who married James Henry Bryan RCNVR from Toronto, the other girls married boys they had previously known in Powell River.

Zella Stade RCAF WD, while overseas in the UK, fell in love and married Sidney Clark RAF British Forces. After the war was over, Sid a **WWII war bridegroom** flew over to Canada with his wife and child. He made British Columbia his permanent home, and raised six children, with Zella.

All the girls enjoyed receiving newsletters and parcels from the Powell River Company. Excerpts from their thank-you letters were printed in the Powell River Company monthly newsletters:

Frances Haigh RCAF WD
January 1944 RCAF Station Admin. Building, Dartmouth, Nova Scotia
"Thanks for the lovely present the Company sent. I really appreciated it, and when the kids saw the chocolates they made one concerted dive for them. Dinner was served in the mess and as we went in they handed everyone a quart bottle of beer."

Pat Hughes RCAF WD
February 1944 RCAF Station Mountain View, Ontario
"Thanks for the Powell River Company's swell Xmas gift. It was a grand surprise and really made me feel remembered —funny how getting away from the home town makes a person really appreciate it. The weather is cold and crisp here with some snow."

Peggy Fraser RCAF WD
December 1944 #7 Equipment Depot, Winnipeg, Manitoba
"Please thank the Company for the lovely Christmas gift. It is nice to be remembered by the people that you used to work for. I went to Montreal for my New Year's leave, and in one of the movie shorts a picture of good old Powell River flashed on the screen. I am sure everybody in the show must have heard me yell, "Hey, that is my Home Town!" – I sure felt proud of Powell River then."

Louise Craigen CWAC
January 1945 RCEME (Royal Canadian Electrical and Mechanical Engineers) Queens Park, London, Ontario
"Thanks for the lovely Christmas gift and for the newsletters. Am stationed at Meredith Barracks here and am in the Orderly Room of the RCEME and like it fine. Haven't seen any P.R. people yet but hear there are some around."

Kay MacLean RCAF WD
January 1945 East Camp RCAF Station, Patricia Bay, B.C.
"Thanks a million for the newsletters and for the Company's super Christmas gift. Am still at Pat Bay, and after 14 months, a posting anywhere looks pretty good – Spent a few days in P.R. at Christmas, and it is hard to believe a town could change so much."

Doris Humphrey RCAF WD
March 1945 RCAF Pay and Records Department, London, UK
"Thanks again for the cigarettes and newsletters which arrive regularly."

Prior to Christmas 1944, Frances Haigh was honoured by being presented to **HRH Princess Alice** in Dartmouth barracks:

Digester January 1945 "----- a group of visitors invaded her quarters. In the forefront was a charming lady in Air Force uniform, who smiled and walked over to

60

Frances and said, "Why, hello, how are you?" They chatted for some time and the Princess was obviously amused at catching Frances off guard (out of uniform, resting on her bunk). There is no evidence that Frances was the least bit flustered."

Jean Dunlop, and later Frances Haigh, graced the covers of the Powell River Company *Digesters*:

September 1943   "Miss Jean Dunlop CWAC was employed in the Powell Stores. Today with 35 other Powell River girls, she is helping release men for front line service."

October 1944   "This month's cover picture is our own Cpl. Frances Haigh, RCAF WD, daughter of Mr. and Mrs. Joe Haigh of Powell River. Frances is one of 46 local girls who have enlisted for service.

These girls, as much as our boys, have "Invested in Victory" by joining the colours, and relieving men for front line service. Seven of our girls are already overseas, and others are doing their duty in widely spread stations throughout Canada."

Powell River Girl in Uniform Marries Overseas

Clark, Sidney RAF
Clark, (Stade) Zella Sergeant RCAF WD

Powell River Company Newsletter

May 1945   *"As promised in our last issue, here is the list of Powell River girls now serving in the forces ------------ (including) Zella Stade RCAF."*

February 1944 A.L. Rorke letter:

"Out with Zella Stade the other night. My gosh, what a relief to go out with a Canadian girl again. They don't ask you to marry them the second time out."

"The first pictures of the Beaver Club Reunion have just come in ----- rather taken with the one of Corp. Zella Stade gazing soulfully into Albert Mitchell's large brown eyes."

March 1944

"There were many sighs of envy as Doris Humphrey and Zella Stade, appeared and reappeared surrounded by hopeful swains."

May 1944   *"It's three stripes for Zella Stade and a seat in the Sergeant's Mess."*

November 1944

"A few weeks earlier (to Martin Naylor's marriage to Sandra Cadman), Sgt. Zella Stade married an RAF officer in England, which sort of squares things up, but which will be received with groans from most of the gang who know Zella."

January 1945 Jean Banham letter: *"Sgt. Zella Stade was in to pick up her discharge."*

July 1946

"The Air Force attracted the larger proportion of Powell River girls. Twenty-three of them served their country in the air branch, and a considerable number proceeded overseas. Sgt. Jean Banham ---- Doris Humphrey, Elsie Foster, Hazel Clapp, Marjorie Fairgrieve and Zella Stade were all in the overseas group,"

WW II Bride Groom

A Journey for Love
Sidney (Sid) Clark RAF (1920-1998)

During WWII Sid Clark RAF worked as meteorologist, providing up-to-date weather information to a Canadian bomber squadron at Linton-on-Ouse in Yorkshire, England. It was in the "ops" (operation) room where he met Zella Stade, a pretty, bright young woman in the Canadian services. They fell in love, and after a seven-month courtship (this was long by wartime standards), the couple married in Woodhorn church, near Newbiggin-by-the-Sea, on Halloween October 31, 1944. After the war was over, they flew to Canada with their young son Ian in 1947.

Sid Clark was part of a small group of English WWII war **grooms** who left their own country after WWII **to make a new start in a new land with a Canadian bride**. Like the thousands of English war **brides** who came to Canada, they **made the journey for love**.

Sidney Clark, born 1920 in Newbiggin-by-the-Sea, the youngest of eight children: - Lillian, Harry, Molly, Leslie, Joe, Reavely, Jack and Sidney.

Sidney's father was manager of the underground workings at the Newbiggin coal colliery. Sid won a scholarship to Morpeth Grammar School. In 1939 Sid passed the British civil service exam and qualified in the Meteorological division. During WWII Sid served as a meteorologist and airborne weather observer, first as a civilian, and from 1942, as a member of the RAF. Later in the war Sid became a meteorological flyer, sending back the latest weather reports to HQ.

Sid met Zella Stade, a member of the Women's Division of the Canadian Air Force at the Linton-on-Ouse airfield in Yorkshire in 1943. The Linton #62 bomber squad air base was part of the Canadian Six Group which took its orders from Six Group HQ.

In July 1944 Sid was transferred to Blyton airfield in East Anglia. This transfer was probably made because Sid (a commissioned officer) was developing a serious relationship with Zella, a non-commissioned officer. This was frowned upon by those in command.

1943 RCAF WDs on overseas postings at the Linton-on-Ouse,
Canadian Air Force bomber base, Yorkshire, England.
(L to R) Margot, Tommy, Paddy, Beverly and Zella Stade
Photo: Zella Clark (Stade) collection

Zella Stade RCAF WD at the Linton-on-Ouse,
Canadian Air Force bomber base in Yorkshire, England, 1943.
With no motor transport (reserved for military use only) bicycles were used
as an alternative. Photo: Zella Clark collection

*Zella Clark RCAF WD and Sid Clark RAF wedding October 31, 1944 at Woodhorn church
near Newbiggin-by-the-Sea, England. Zella borrowed a wedding dress in exchange for a pair
of nylons! Butter and sugar for the wedding cake came from the kitchen at the Canadian air
force base. Photo: Zella Clark collection*

*After WWII Zella Clark RCAF WD and her husband Sid Clark RAF
(a WWII war bridegroom—male war bride) made their permanent home in British Columbia.
The Clark family, Vancouver, B.C. Christmas 1965. Back row: Ian (19), Keith (14), Peter (17)
Front row: Stephen (5), Zella Clark, Sid Clark with Pixie the dog, Valerie (13), Gerry (8)
Photo: Zella Clark collection*

Sgt. Zella Clark (Stade) RCAFO WD

Zella Stade came to teach in the **Powell River** area in the late 1930s.

Zella spent her childhood in the Chilliwack farming area. She was an exceptional student and skipped a couple of grades. Zella was connected to the Powell River area with two maternal aunts living here, Aunt Miron (Goddard) and Aunt Vinie (Maggs).

Aunty Miron was married to George Goddard, a pharmacist who had worked in the Townsite, for the Powell River Company, from 1926. He managed the Townsite pharmacy until 1965. The Goddards had two children, Zella's cousins Myrna and Mavis.

Not wanting to nurse, Zella chose teaching as a career and attended Normal School in Vancouver. She received her teaching certificate at age 18. With a reference from her Uncle George, Zella was able to obtain a temporary four-month replacement for a teacher at the Cranberry Lake school, in Cranberry Village, for a teacher who was on leave in Europe. Fortunately for Zella, the teacher on temp leave did not come back, and Zella was given her fulltime position. She taught a total of four years in the Powell River area from 1938-42 (Cranberry Lake, Southview and Wildwood).

Zella Clark January 2011 (age 90):
"When I taught at Southview school I boarded with the Uzzells who lived in a small house, without any running water and electricity, on the Southview beach. Billy had been a prospector on Texada Island and was quite a character. He had been a soldier in WWI and when war broke out in September 1939, he insisted on me taking drill marches! I knew Mary Powell (Masales), we went walking at weekends.

*I later taught for a year in Wildwood, however, when a job came up at Westview I applied for it. It was fate that I didn't get it because I then applied for a position with the Canadian Forces. I could have stayed at Wildwood but **I was ready for a change and I felt it was my patriotic duty to do something for the war.***

*After war broke out there were ads in the **Vancouver Sun** for the Women's Division of the Canadian Air Force. They were general duties which included kitchen work. I didn't want that but later the ads were for women with senior matriculation for specialized training. I knew this was what I wanted, so I applied and was accepted."*

Zella completed her basic four-week training at Rockville. This was followed by a second four-week clerk-ops course, also at Rockville. Her first posting was a six-month stint at Eastern Air Command HQ in Halifax. Part of her duties included aircraft plotting. After Halifax, in 1943, came a six-month posting at Dartmouth.

Just as Zella was considering taking officer's training, a chance came up for an overseas posting. For Zella this was an opportunity of a lifetime as she had always wanted to travel.

Before sailing to England on the *Mauritania*, Zella was given leave in November 1943 to visit family and friends in Chilliwack and Powell River. The *Mauritania* docked in Liverpool, December 1943. Her first overseas posting was at the Linton-on-Ouse Canadian air base in Yorkshire.

Zella Stade RCAF WD overseas posting #62 Canadian bomber base at Linton-on-Ouse, Yorkshire, England

Zella:

"I worked in the ops (operation) room. I was at a high desk which overlooked the table where the COs met to discuss the bombing raids. Large maps of England and Europe were located on the wall. It was my job to scramble the messages going out. Besides the Canadians there were only a couple of Englishmen on the base, the intelligence officer and the meteorological officer. This was how I first met Sid who brought in the weather reports. He would stand at my desk chatting while he waited to give his report.

I had been going out with a number of Canadians on the base, nothing serious, they were all good fun and the friendships were strictly platonic. I then started going out with Sid, and we went on bicycle rides into the countryside. We visited old abbeys. After a few months of dating, Sid asked me if I would like to go and visit his family at Newbiggin-by-the-Sea. I was somewhat hesitant as I did not want a serious commitment; however, Sid anticipated my hesitation and had the right words to say:

"Zella, this is just hospitality to the troops!"

When initially meeting Sid's family, I had difficulty in understanding their Geordie accent. Sid's mother showed me a photograph of Sid receiving an award from the Duke of Northumberland at Morpeth Grammar School. He was chosen to accept the reward because of his high academic achievement. I was impressed by Sid's academic record. I then started to take our relationship a little more seriously! I remember being told at Normal school that intelligent parents had intelligent children. I wanted intelligent children, and I wanted six of them!"

In Canada, Zella had a number of boyfriends, and Harry Webster was the one she admired. He was her yardstick for any man she would eventually choose to marry. They had some general understanding that they would eventually be together, however Harry had never formally declared himself. Harry's immediate goal was to work a few years to pay off debts from Normal school, and Zella, an independent young woman, wanted to teach six years, and travel before getting married. During the war Zella and Harry wrote to each other.

Due to their wartime meeting in the "ops" room at a Canadian air base in Yorkshire, Zella and Sid had fallen in love. Just as their commitment to each other was growing, Sid was transferred to Blyton airfield in East Anglia; however, Sid found innovative ways to meet up with Zella. They were engaged July 1944.

Zella:

"Before accepting Sid's proposal I told him I had two conditions he had to accept; the first was that **we would live in Canada**, *and the second being that I wanted to have six children. Sid agreed to both!*

Sid wrote to my father, asking his permission to marry me. It was my mother who replied – to me! She wanted to know why I wasn't marrying one of the nice Canadian boyfriends I had back home – like Harry Webster. Mother was also annoyed she was not arranging the wedding. This made me even more determined to marry in England.

We were married on Halloween, 31st October 1944 in Woodhorn church near Woodbiggin-by-the-Sea. My wedding dress was borrowed from a recently married friend of Sid's sister-in-law Lorna. For the loan of the dress I gave the girl a pair of nylons!

The service was taken by the Reverend Medd; he was very deaf and used a large trumpeter to hear with. I did not want to say "I obey" so he omitted it from the service. Sid's family organized the reception, not easy because of the rationing. The cake was made with butter and sugar from the Canadian Forces' mess hall at Linton-on-Ouse.

For our honeymoon we stayed at the Borrowdale Hotel by Lake Windermere in the Lake District. Later we had two wonderful holidays in Scotland at Alastrean house in Aberdeenshire, home of Lady MacRobert. She had lost three boys in the war and she opened up her residence to officers for recreational use. The war was now nearly over and I requested the Canadian Air Force administrations to be discharged in England so that I could accompany Sid to his RAF postings (Tiree, Aldergrove and Kinloss). Our first child Ian was born in 1946 in a hospital near Aldergrove."

In 1947, independently of the Canadian Government, the Clarks travelled as a family by BOAC (British Overseas Airways Corporation) from Prestwick via Iceland to Montreal (there was a six-month wait for tickets). They proceeded to cross Canada by train, staying over at various stops along the way to visit with service friends.

Throughout the war, Zella kept in contact with her Powell River friends in the Services. It was Zella's good friend Doris Humphries who passed on the information about the 1944 Powell River reunion in London. Zella attended the reunion and had her photo taken with the "boys".

From an Overseas posting in England, Zella Clark (Stade) RCAF WD returns permanently to Canada with her husband, Sid Clark RAF

Zella:

"Jobs were not easy to get after the war in Vancouver. There was discrimination against servicemen from England. Jobs were posted with a disclaimer:

NO ENGLISHMAN NEED APPLY

Sid tried to get a job in meteorology but that didn't work out. In desperation to feed his family he worked for one year on the green chain in a sawmill. After a number of different jobs he became a successful salesman working for Van & Rogers for 33 years. He worked his way up the company and retired in 1985 as President.

Sid had no regrets in leaving England. *He liked the **Canadians**, New Zealanders, Australians, and South Africans he met on the different bases **for their open way of communicating with each other.***

Sid did not like the English class system.

His mother wanted the best for her boys, however, she did not want her "baby" (Sid was the youngest of eight) to leave England. She felt she would never see him again. My mother was not happy that I married an Englishman (What happened to those nice Canadian boys? What happened to Harry?) She was shocked when she found out Sid smoked!

It was 20 years before we were able to get back to England for a visit. We were raising our six children: Ian, Peter, Keith, Valerie, Gerry and Stephen, and we didn't have the money."

After retirement, Sid and Zella moved to the BC Gulf Islands. Sid became involved in farming. He died in 1998. In 2010 Zella celebrated her 90th birthday with her six children, and many grandchildren.

Local Girl in the Air Force Marries Childhood Sweetheart in the Army

Liebich (Rolandi), Violet   RCAF WD
Liebich, Walter   CAO (Canadian Army Overseas)

Violet (Vi) Rolandi, a Powell River girl, joined the RCAF WD in 1942 at age 18 after being encouraged by her friend Jean Banham who was already in the services. Jean Banham RCAF WD was the first Powell River girl to join the Forces in November 1941. Vi's three brothers Ray Rolandi, Bob and Bill Christie joined the Army. Ray and Bob went overseas.

Vi had spent her childhood in beautiful Olsen Valley, Powell Lake, B.C. The postal address for Olsen Valley was Foch, and Vi's birth certificate notes she was born in Foch, B.C. Foch was named after the famous leader of the Allied Forces in WWI, Marshal Ferdinand Foch.

Joe Giuseppe Rolandi (1885-1977)

Joe (Giuseppe) Rolandi, Violet's father, logged at Myrtle Point (Powell River Regional District) as early as 1907. He was one, of a number of Italians, who came to the coast in the early part of the twentieth century. His descendants continue to live in the area.

Joe had left Italy (Missio near Milan) in 1906 to join John, an older brother in the U.S.A. For one year, Joe made his way up the west coast of North American until he reached Vancouver, B.C.; it was here that Joe heard of a logging job at Myrtle Point.

In 1914, while logging at Myrtle Point, Joe volunteered to fight for "King & Country" in the Canadian Expeditionary Force in the Great War (1914-18). For reasons unknown, Joe joined the Regiment of the Scottish Highlanders, and wore a kilt as part of his "uniform". He fought in France and survived the terrible conditions in the trenches. After the war, while Joe was still in France, Joe was given a two-week furlough to visit his family in Italy. He had not seen them for 11 years. Joe travelled by train to Italy. He was wearing his kilt when he arrived at his mother's house. On first seeing him, she exclaimed:

"My son, my son, you spend all those years in Canada,
and you come back to Italy without any pants!"

Rolandi family near Milan, Italy 1905
Middle of the back row: Joe Rolandi Centre of the front row:
Joe's parents, Mr. and Mrs. Rolandi
Photo: Vi Liebich (Rolandi) collection

Joe Rolandi and children, Olsen Valley, Powell Lake B.C. 1930
Driver: Joe Rolandi/Passenger: Catholic priest from Powell River.
Back: Mrs. Johnson (neighbour), Jean, Flora and Vi (sitting on lap).
Front: Ray, Art, Bob, John and Bill.
Joe volunteered for the CEF in WWI, four children:
Bob and Bill Christie, Ray and Vi Rolandi volunteered for the Canadian Forces in WWII.
Photo: Vi Liebich collection

1942 Powell River B.C. Vi Rolandi RCAF WD
Lower left hand corner: Vi and Walt Liebich's wedding, May 1943 Powell River.
Photo: Vi Liebich collection

1944 summer Texada Island: Vi Liebich and baby
Photo: Vi Liebich collection

After the family reunion, Joe rejoined his regiment, and travelled by troop ship from England to Canada in 1919.

Joe made his way back to the Powell River area, looking for a job in the logging industry. In 1920 Joe logged in Olsen Valley; it was here that Joe met his wife Flora Christie, a widow with four small children: John, Jean, Bill and Bob. They married and homesteaded in Olsen Valley. Joe and Flora had four children: Raymond, Violet, and twins Margaret and Arthur. On the birth of the twins, Joe remarked it was "a poor man's luck", meaning there were two mouths to feed instead of one.

In 1925 Joe built the second Olsen Lake schoolhouse on the old Simard property in Olsen Valley. He was one of the workers who built the first Wildwood bridge.

On July 1st every year, Joe escorted his family to the celebrations in the Powell River Company Townsite. They all dressed up for the occasion in their best Sunday clothes. It was a lot of fun with races etc. The highlight of the day was a delicious ice cream treat.

One Christmas Eve, Joe and Flora had a terrifying time when they were stranded on Powell Lake in a storm. The engine of their boat had broken down. Tony Bauman, a neighbour in Olsen Valley, found them on Christmas Day. After that experience, Joe said, "*I'm getting out of this country!*" and bought 40 acres of land in Paradise Valley, Powell River.

Vi Rolandi RCAF WD

After Vi enrolled in the WD of the RCAF, she spent six weeks of basic training in Rockcliffe, Ontario at an Air Force base. This was followed by specialized training for a nurse's aide at Deer Lodge Military Hospital, Winnipeg and Yorkton, Saskatchewan.

Vi went on leave, Christmas of 1943 and stayed with her family in Powell River. While on leave, Vi met up with an old school friend, Walt Liebich. Walt was an engineer with the Army, and he was also on leave. They immediately fell in love, and became engaged. Walt wanted to get married before going overseas, so Vi and Walt married May 1943.

Vi returned to Yorkton, however, after a few months had passed, she found she was pregnant. Immediately she had to resign (Air Force regulations).

After the war, when Walt came home, the couple decided to live at Van Anda on Texada Island because Walt's family lived there. The first home they lived in was a shack in Van Anda. Not long after they arrived, there was a knock on the door, and a voice called out, *"Do you want a job, Walt?"* Walt immediately went to work for Cap Harrison at H&H Logging. He worked for the same outfit, driving machinery from the late 1940s to early 1970s.

Vi and Walt had four children: Judy, Douglas, Wendy and David.

After the kids had grown up, Vi and Walt lived in logging camps up the coast, first they had two years at Minstrel Island, and then a few years at Loughborough Inlet for Art & Ray Rolandi Logging Company. Vi was the camp cook.

While they were away from Texada, they just locked up the house, knowing everything would be safe until they returned. In those days everything was safe and secure in a small community.

In the 1980s, Vi ran the concession for five years at Shelter Point. In the late '80s Vi worked in the kitchen at the Texada Hotel.

At age 87, Violet Liebich (Rolandi) now lives in Powell River. She lived on Texada Island for 62 years, in the same house, at Van Anda. Vi remembers with pride her time in the WD of the RCAF.

Powell River & District WDs (Women's Division) Canadian Forces WWII 1941-1945

The following 55 names have been researched in 2011 from the Powell River *Digesters* 1939-46, the Powell River Company WWII monthly newsletter, the 2011 Stillwater service list, and private sources.

Aquilin, Evelyn	Pte CWAC
Arnold, Verna	L/Cpl CWAC
Aster, Alice	RCAF WD
Bailey, D.E.M(Doris)	Private CWAC Overseas
Banham, Jean	Sgt. RCAF WD Overseas
Black, D.	Pte CWAC
Bryan (**Parkin**), Bertyne (Betty)	RCAF WD

(Bryan, James Henry RCN VR (from Toronto)/married Vancouver, B.C. 1944)

Clapp, Hazel	LAW RCAF WD Overseas
Clark (**Stade**), Zella	Sgt RCAF WD

(Clark, Sidney RAF married 1944 England – Sid Clark came to Canada as a WWII war bridegroom)

Craigen, Louise	Pte CWAC
Donkersley, E.E. (Betty)	Pte CWAC
Doran, A.W. (Gerry)	RCAF WD
Dore (**Oster**) Alice (Sis)	Sergeant RCAF

(Dore, Earl CA/married 1943 Powell River)

Dunlop, Jean	Cpl CWAC
Evans, Marjorie	Sgt CWAC
Fairgrieve (**McPhalen**),Marjorie	RCAF WD Overseas

(Fairgrieve W.C. (Bud) RCAFO/married Halifax, Nova Scotia 1943) killed in action 1944

Foster, Elsie	LAW RCAF Overseas
Fraser, Margaret (Peggy)	AW1 RCAF WD
Haigh, Frances	Corporal RCAF WD
Hassell, Joyce	CWAC
Heavenor, Elaine	RCAF WD
Hembroff, Margaret	Cpl RCAF WD
Hughes, Frances	L/Wren WRNCS
Hughes, Patricia	Sgt RCAF WD
Humphrey, Doris	Cpl RCAF WD Overseas
Hunter, Brisbane	RCAF WD
Ingram, Joyce	AW1 RCAF WD
Irwin, Jean (Teddy)	RCAF WD

Kielty, Margaret	RCAF WD
Lee, Alfreda (Freda)	LAW RCAF WD (from Stillwater)
Liebich (**Rolandi**), Violet (Vi)	RCAF WD
(Liebich, Walt - CAO from Texada Island/married 1943 Powell River)	
Lloyd, Belle	RCAF WD (from Stillwater)
Loukes, Mary	Pte CWAC Overseas
McGuffie, Julia	AW2 RCAF
McGuire, Gwen	RCAF 2D
MacIntyre, Gladys	L/Cpl CWAC Overseas

(MacIntyre, Battleman (Batt) Lt. Col. Canadian Army Overseas – Proprietor of the Rodmay Hotel, Powell River – married 1935 Powell River)

MacLean, Kay	LAW RCAF WD
McLean, Ada	LAW RCAF WD
McLeod, E.V., Mrs.	CWAC
(McLeod, Ernie RCN, married 1945 Powell River)	
Nutchey (**Taylor**), Edith	RCAF WD
(Nutchey, Tom RCAF married 1945)	
Peteske, Nancy	RCAF WD
Price, Mollie	LAW RCAF
Roberts, Aleda	RCAF WD
Scott, Beverly	Cpl RCAF WD
Scott, Grace	Leading Wren WRCNS
Simmonds, Phyllis	Sgt. CWAC Overseas
Sivertson, Ann	CWAC
Smythe, Mary	RCAF WD
Staniforth, Hilda	RCAF WD
Sutherland, P.M.	AW1 RCAF WD
Sutton, Bea	RCN
Tomlinson, Joan	RCAF WD
Tomlinson, Patricia	Pte CWAC
Williams, Mrs. J.H.	CWAC
Wilshire, Thora	Pte CWAC

March 1943
Mrs. Grace Johnston and Mrs. Wilfred Paul: first women in Powell River on ARP patrol,
wearing ARP marked armbands with hardhats. Photo: Digester March 1943

1943 Powell River Red Cross Women's Corps in uniform marching down
Ash Street, Powell River, B.C.
Photo: Powell River Museum & Archives

Junior Red Cross Grade 3 girls, Malaspina Cranberry Lake School,
Cranberry village, Powell River 1941-2:
Back (L to R) Gloria Daly/F. Garret/
Front (L to R) Rita Negrin/Vera Daly/Joan Gibson/Lucy Culos/Betty Harding.
Photo: Gloria Riley (Daly)

WWII Red Cross project: Jam for Britain: wild blackberries picked by local children from Powell
River & District made into jam and sent to Britain in large cans. Jam for Britain committee:
Left of photo: (L to R) Eva Dice, Jean Foot/ Far right: Mrs. Marlatt/rear:
Brenda Cooper, Carolyn Taylor & others.
Photo: Powell River Museum & Archives

WWII Powell River Women Volunteer for the ARP, IODE, Canadian Red Cross, and St. John's Ambulance Brigade

Hundreds of women, of all ages, from Powell River & District volunteered their services for the Canadian Red Cross, St. John's Ambulance Brigade, IODE (Imperial Order Daughters of the Empire), and ARP (Air Raid Precautions) during the Second World War.

ARP (Air Raid Precautions)

Soon after war was declared, the Canadian Government readied its coastal defences. The local Powell River ARP, composed of many veterans of WWI, ensured local residents abided by the blackout regulations. Two prominent members of the ARP were nursing volunteers, Mrs. T. Green and Mrs. W. Brown. Mrs. T Green had served overseas in the Great War as a nursing sister.

During 1942 a Junior ARP was formed for boys and girls over the age of 12. Brenda Cooper, daughter of Russell Cooper, the general superintendent of the Powell River Company was an active participant.

Graeme Cooper (2002)

"One had to be 12 years of age before being accepted as a full member of the Junior Air Raid Patrol. Graeme's sister Brenda reached the age of 12 in 1942 and was the envy of her brother as she went out on Junior ARP duty with her steel helmet, gas mask, ARP arm band, and whistle. When she had other commitments, Graeme was permitted to borrow her arm band and helmet, and went out on patrol with his father. He wasn't permitted to borrow either the gas mask or the whistle.

The duty of the ARP's was to patrol the sidewalks, looking for light escaping through doors and windows. If a light should show around the covering of someone's window, it was the ARP's responsibility to knock on the door of the offending house and inform the resident that his home was clearly visible to an enemy airplane, should one be nearby. In addition to the window coverings, which were usually gray blankets, Powell Riverites were encouraged to keep pails of sand strategically placed throughout the house."

It was March 1943 before the first women were appointed ARP wardens, and patrolled the Townsite streets at night.

Powell River ARP Goes Modern; Leads the Way in New Wardens

New Wardens

"Powell River's ARP organization is keeping abreast with modern trends. The two trim wardens, Mrs. Grace Johnston and Mrs. Wilfred Paul are the first two local women to join the wardens' ranks. We don't profess to know much about the business, but certainly if most of the male wardens we have seen looked as snappy as the latest female recruits, there would be a lot more zip in these "emergency" practices. We have a feeling that half the male population of Powell River would be frantically looking around for that pail of sand or bucket of water they have forgotten."

Imperial Order Daughters of the Empire (IODE)

Described in the January edition 1943 of the *Digester* as "the most active and energetic war organizations in Powell River are the two branches of the IODE." The two branches were the Lukin Johnston chapter in the Powell River Company Townsite, and the Sara Blain chapter in the fast-growing area of Westview Village. Both groups had a large membership of women eager to contribute to the war effort. The membership of the IODE Westview branch quickly jumped to a membership of 50 during the war and "the entire chapter threw itself vigorously into war work."

The IODE members knitted heavy seamen's sweaters, scarves and socks for those in the services, including service men in POW (Prisoner Of War) camps. They also stitched items of clothing for women and children of bombed-out areas in Britain. In the month of March 1940 the IODE sent a large shipment to the Provincial chapter.

Powell River News April 4, 1940
"A summary of war work given by Mrs. J.T. Fullerton, war work convener and sent to the Provincial chapter for distribution: 6 sweaters, 9 scarves, 3 blanket helmets, 4 fully fitted hold-alls, 3 pneumonia jackets, 31 pairs of socks, and 17 hospital night gowns."

A Sister Susie Club was attached to the IODE; this was a group of school girls who also worked for the war effort:

Powell River News February 8, 1940:
    "A much admired collection of sewn and knitted garments were on display, the work of a group of school girls under Mrs. E.A. Hansen's leadership. The garments are for distribution to refugee children."

    POW parcels were assembled by the IODE and given to the next of kin to mail. November 1942, the local chapters of the IODE mailed 105 Christmas parcels overseas; November 1944, 400 parcels were sent overseas to "our boys and girls".

Ina Lloyd 2011 (90)
    "My mother was a member of the IODE. We lived at Stillwater, and she couldn't get in for meetings. She made boys' pants from old suits, and they were sent over to Britain for bombed-out families. Mother also sent into town lilac, from her garden, for the IODE to sell for funds."

    Men and women, in isolated air and naval stations along the Canadian coast, were most appreciative of the regular shipments of newspapers and magazines by the IODE. Over 2,000 magazines and hundreds of books were sent out each month.

    Mrs. Hugh McPhalen was the Regent of the Powell River IODE. The following were officers: Mrs. K. Macken, Mrs. Barrett Leonard, Mrs. T.W. Green, Mrs. C. Manwood, Mrs. S. Purvin Good, Mrs. J.T. Fullerton, Mrs. H. Slade, Mrs. L. Schon, and Mrs. F. Egan.

St. John Ambulance Brigade

    The women's division of the St. John Ambulance Brigade was formed in 1942 and attracted a number of local women:

Digester September 1942
    "Another important group of the women's auxiliary war emergency army is the WD of the St. John Ambulance Brigade. This branch, formed early this year, had made splendid progress. All ranks are taking their training seriously, attending regular parades, and studying hard. The women are given special hospital training, and in an emergency will take over as auxiliary nurses. Mrs. Howard Jamieson heads the women's division of the brigade, and their smart appearance on recent parades has been commended."

    April 1944, the first Women's Industrial First Aid certificate "C" was passed by seven women in the community: Mrs. Lew Griffith, Mrs. A. Harding, Mrs. Eva Scott, Miss Mildred Dill, Mrs. Riley Etner, Mrs. Amy Bull, and Miss Tanya Hof.

Canadian Red Cross

The Canadian Red Cross attracted women of all ages from the Powell River & District; over 300 women were engaged in Red Cross activities. Red Cross classes included: first aid, home nursing, motor mechanics, ARP, sewing, knitting, jam making, food and office administration. With so many young men away in the Forces, it was an organization where many young women met and socialized. A Junior Red Cross was formed for younger members in the community.

Mildred Ross (Dice) 2011 Powell River Company mill worker
"I started working for the Powell River Company in 1942 as a pulp tester, later in the beater room, shovelling paper into beaters. My father was in the Home Guard for the duration of the war. My mother and I trained in first aid through the Red Cross. The Red Cross was a place to go and meet other young people. Most young men were away in the Forces. There were dances in the community but the married women did not want their husbands dancing with single girls."

The Canadian Red Cross Corps was formed in Powell River, March 1942, and attracted many dedicated young women. They wore uniforms and attended regular parades. The detachment was affiliated as an auxiliary to the local Reserve Unit, and had a total strength of about 40, active and reserve. The CO was Mrs. Staniforth who had worked for the Red Cross in the Great War; other officers were: Mrs. J.A. Lundie and Noreen McSavaney.

A food conservation class was headed by Mrs. C.R. Marlatt, with the help of Mrs. Eva Dice and Mrs. Jean Foote. Jam making classes were held at Brooks' school kitchen. The Red Cross sponsored **A Ton of Jam for Britain** project in the summer of 1941. Everyone in the community, from Powell River to Stillwater picked the local wild blackberries. In the summer of 1942 – 2,1112 lbs. (pounds) of blackberry jam was made and poured into 4 lb. cans. The recipe used was a special recipe, for the tropics, from Eva Dice's cookbook. The jam was shipped to Britain via the Panama Canal.

Bev Falconer (2002)
"One big community effort was the 'Ton of Jam for Britain' project. It was also a ton of fun. Dozens of boys and girls were taken out in big open trucks to pick blackberries. We stood up in the back, hung onto the wooden sides, and sang at the top of our lungs, 'Alouette', 'Off we go into the wild blue yonder' etc. A cloud of dust followed our noisy convoy and when we picked berries at Myrtle Point, they were covered with dust. The pails of berries were taken to the Home Ec. room at Brooks, where another team made them into jam. One year I was part of that team. I think some of the jam was overcooked as one of the teachers made the comment that we could dispense with the tins, and just cut the jam into blocks!"

4
Women on the Home Front

Rosies of the North

All the day long, whether rain or shine,
She's part of the assembly line.
She's making history,
Working for history,
Rosie the Riveter

The iconic recruiting poster for women in the U.S.A., during WWII, was of **Rosie the Riveter** – a young woman wearing a bandana and uniform with a clenched fist showing her muscles. She symbolized a patriotic war heroine on the home front – a song, movie and comic strip were made about her.

As Canadian men left their jobs in industry to go to war, women were employed to do their jobs. Canadian women, working in the aircraft industry for the war effort, were called **Rosies of the North**.

Boeing of Canada Ltd. had a large factory at Sea Island (Vancouver International Airport site) and employed thousands of workers.

Betty Thornton (2002) Powell River
   "The war brought opportunities for women to obtain good paying jobs. The men were away in the forces and there was a desperate shortage of labour for the war effort.

   My sister was the first in the family to work at Boeing. She was earning three times the amount I was earning as a librarian. So, I quit my job and went to work for Boeing.

   In order to get to the Boeing factory on Sea Island, a company bus met the Inter-urban car at Marpole. The company bus had no seats! This was all part of the war effort as 100 people could stand in the company bus, saving gas and drivers. If we were late for a shift, our pay was docked.

   We wore overalls and scarves around our head to prevent our hair catching in the machines. I worked in the supply department, handing out tools etc. The noise was terrible in the factory and everything had to be written down. A whistle went for a coffee and lunch break. Everything stopped. There was no hot lunch canteen. We all took a thermos of coffee and sandwiches to work. On the factory washroom door was the following notice:

IS THIS TRIP NECESSARY?

This was a reminder that it was our patriotic duty to be as fast as possible, and that every minute contributed to the war effort."

WWII Powell River Rosies and Mill Workers

The Powell River Pulp and Paper Company, was forced, for the first time in its history, to employ women to replace men who had volunteered to go in the Services.

Local women worked in the company plant in the following areas: the beater room, sulphite plant, finishing room, screen room, wet machines, machine room, machine shop, Kelley Spruce division, pulp and paper testing offices.

For one year, from November 1, 1943 to November 1, 1944 **Boeing of Canada Ltd.** employed women in a subassembly plant, which produced the PBY, a patrol and rescue plane, at the Powell River Company mill site. A female supervisor, from the Sea Island factory, periodically came to check on the girls at the Powell River Boeing plant. The women working for Boeing were called **Rosies of the North.**

September 1942 *Powell River Digester*

Women Fill Many War Time Jobs in Powell River Plant

"War of necessity brings many changes. To Powell River, perhaps the most novel is the spectacle of women entering and leaving the plant, and punching time cards, side by side with male employees. The shortage of manpower, felt throughout the Continent, has brought about the utilization of female labour for the first time in the Powell River plant.

Necessary rest room and other facilities have been installed, and a satisfactory solution worked out with the local trade unions regarding wages and working conditions. Many of the women being employed are wives of Powell River employees now in the overseas forces, in some cases, in the same department as their husbands were, and possibly may even take over their husband's jobs for the duration.

"The girls are shaping up good", one foreman remarked.

The honour of being the first woman ever employed in the Powell River plant belongs to Miss Mary Cavanagh who took over as a pulp tester."

December 1942 *Powell River Digester*

The Girls Carry On – women employees help keep the wheels turning

"Women employed in the Powell River plant now number about 75. This figure had gradually increased over the past two months as men leave for military service. Surprisingly the transition of women taking over men's work during the war period had been accomplished without friction or dislocation."

September 1943 *Powell River Digester*

New War Work for Powell River – bomber parts now being assembled locally

"Following the policy of utilizing to the fullest extent their facilities at Powell River for war work, arrangements have now been made with **Boeing of Canada Ltd.** to carry out assembly work on bomber parts. In order to prepare for this work, the Company has started a training school, under supervision of the Government War Emergency Training Schools. Approximately 25 employees, most of them women, are now undergoing preliminary training. The work is being carried out in one of the Company paper storage sheds, which is being refitted to provide suitable accommodations for both men and women employees. Many applications are being received by local women for employment in this new war contract, and these will be absorbed as fast as they can be trained."

October 1943 *Powell River Digester*

Women Employees Pass Century Mark –
Girls build plane parts; work on machines, and run beaters

"Just over a year ago, in September 1942, the hitherto unchallenged male supremacy of the Powell River plant was shattered when Miss Mary Cavanagh of Cranberry dropped the first card ever punched by a woman employee into the Time Office rack. Thirty-two years of unquestioned masculine supremacy received its first challenge.

As we go to press the number of women employees has swelled to 130, and the end is not yet in sight. The girls are penetrating every nook and cranny."

February 1944 *Powell River Digester*

Minimum of Present and Post-War Problems
– Employment of Women in Powell River not a "Problem Child"

"At the time of writing, 150 women are employed in the Powell River plant, 76 in production, and assembling of aeroplane parts, and 74 in other departments throughout the plant.

Few, if any, of these women intend to continue working after the war. They are quite willing, now that they have demonstrated their ability to fill in during national emergencies, to give up their jobs to husbands, sons or men returning from service."

Memories:

Mary Carlson (Douglas) 2002
"World War II changed everything. My two sisters found work in the mill. Due to the shortage of men, the Powell River Company employed women for the first time in its history.

Mildred Ross (Dice) 2002 & 2011
"The boys left for the war and the girls were left behind. We all went to work in the mill.

I started working for the Powell River Company as a pulp tester and later, in the beater room shoveling paper into the beater. I worked in the mill until April 1946, by this time the war was over, and I helped men who were returning. The women, who had lost their husbands in the war, were given jobs in the Company offices.

We all knew that after the war, when the men came back, they would take over our jobs in the mill."

Stella Saunders (Hall/Hewson) 2007
"I worked at the Boeing Subassembly plant on the Powell River Company mill site. I was a fitter, and I learned to handle a drill.

I knew Joan Tomlinson; she worked in the mill offices. She quit her job with the Powell River Company and joined the Women's Division of the RCAF."

Ruth Allan (Fear) 2002 & 2011
"I was a widow living in Turner Valley, Alberta. In 1943 I came out west with my children to visit my sister Pearl Lang at Douglas Bay, Powell River. Pearl advised me to go down to the Powell River Company and apply for a job at the mill. The Powell River Company was hiring

women for the first time in its history due to so many workers volunteering to fight in the war overseas. I had no previous experience but I got a job in the mill.

I worked in the mill plant, and on the one-year Boeing contract. When I worked on the Boeing contract I was at the business end of a drill, drilling holes into metal parts of the airplane. Over 100 women worked for Boeing, building spare parts for the aircraft. We were paid 59 cents an hour, the same wages as men. Before I finished the base rate was 64 cents an hour.

I also worked in the mill plant in the cutting room with another woman, Beatrice Rabie. Our supervisor was Roger Hart. One of the jobs was to put a marker, one every 42nd sheet (42 sheets made a ream of paper). The rolls of paper were brought into the cutting room and stacked three tiers high and four rolls long. The men adjusted the cutting machine for different orders; our job was to cut the rolls into bundles. The men packaged the bundles, two reams package.

Men supervised the women but women did all the work men had previously done. The women gained the respect of the men for the dirty, difficult jobs they did.

I had no idea the war had ended until I went to get the bus from Westview to the Powell River Townsite. I was boarding the bus when the driver called out:

"Lady, you won't be going to work today. The war is over!"

The men who had volunteered to go overseas were given their jobs back. Of course, some sadly did not return. Gradually, the women were let go. It did not happen all at once. If there were vacancies, men were hired to replace the women. Hiring women had just been a wartime measure, the exception being women who lost their husbands in the war; they were offered office jobs.

One of the last jobs the women did was to clean all the soot and banana oil off the hundreds of windows around the mill. During the war the mill had been blacked out so as not to attract the enemy."

Freeda Parsons (Mohr) 2002 & 2011

"I went to work in the mill in 1942. The mill was hiring women because so many men had volunteered to join up. We wore white overalls, hair nets and caps. I worked for Boeing. I learned how to rivet. I had no previous experience. The female employees had an on-site male supervisor. Every so often, a lady supervisor from Boeing in Vancouver came up to Powell River to check on how the girls were doing.

I met my husband at the mill. His name was Walter. The girls used to tease me and call out every time they saw him coming, 'Walter, Walter, lead me to the alter.' We had a good time in the mill."

Freda Stutt (Bauman) 2002 & 2010

"During the Depression the only work available for women in Powell River was housework at $5-$10 a month. The war changed all that. I was able to get work at the mill. My sisters Lilly and Ruby also found work with the Powell River Company. Lilly worked on the Boeing project and Ruby worked in the finishing room. We belonged to a union, and were paid the same wages as men.

In 1942 I worked for the Powell River Company at the staff quarters in the Townsite. I waited on tables, cleaned rooms, and occasionally cooked. In 1943 I was transferred into the mill.

From 1943-44 I worked for the Boeing Company which subcontracted parts for patrol and rescue planes, at the Powell River Company plant. All the girls working on this project were given a 10-day training course. I worked on assembling the pilot's enclosure on the aircraft.

After the Boeing contract expired on November 1, 1944, I was transferred to the finishing room. My job was to help prepare the rolls of paper for shipment. Two "cappers" worked on each paper machine. All together there were 18 cappers working shift work, around the clock, on three machines. The rolls which were sent overseas were capped with heavy wooden discs. It was physically hard work but all the girls did an excellent job and never complained.

I married Bob Stutt CAO, just after the war. Bob worked for the Powell River Company from 1941-2. He volunteered for the Canadian Forces in 1942."

Rhoda Auline (Hatch) 2011

"Yes, I worked for a short time in the finishing room for the Powell River Company during WWII. I married during the war, later became pregnant, and immediately had to quit my job."

Eddie Needham 2008

"My mother, Ina Needham, worked for Boeing for one year, and then in the beater room until the war was over — then it was back to the kitchen sink!"

Nancy Crowther (Cougar Queen of Okeover Arm) 1987

"I was working in the mill capping and sheet laying. I worked for three years and three months in the mill. I lived in Powell River during the week, but bicycled home to Okeover at the weekends. At first I walked home, and it took six hours each way. Yes, I worked in the mill during the war, until the boys came home — and out I went!"

September 1942 Miss Mary Cavanagh first female employee
of the Powell River Company plant.
August 1943 Mary left the mill to train as a nurse at St. Paul's hospital, Vancouver.
Photo: Digester Sept. 1942

September 1943: Fifteen of the first female employees to enter the service
of the Powell River Company.
Top row: Elizabeth Cameron, Beatrice Raby, Agnes Johnson, Anne Macaskill
Row 2: Ada Graham, Margaret and Barbara Manwood, Ruby Entner
Row 3: Gen Waugh, Audrey Bissett, Arline Huxter
Bottom row: Ruth Cattermole, Florence Douglas, Margaret Bestwick, Betty Smith
Photo: Digester Sept. 1943

Mildred Dice (Ross) Powell River Company mill worker WWII
Photo: Digester Dec. 1942

January 1945 WWII female employees Freda Bauman (Stutt) (L) and Irene Pauling (R) with
Alex Graham (supervisor of the Powell River Company finishing room)
with rolls of paper recently capped and ready for shipment.
Photo: Freda Stutt collection

January 1944 WWII finishing room shift, Powell River Company paper mill:
Back row: Vi Desjarlies, Freda Bauman (Stutt), Irene Pauling
Front row: May Wards, Olida Fee, E. Beami
Photo: Freda Stutt collection

WWII 1942 female employees working for the Powell River Company:
(L to R) _____/Irene Pauling/Pam Johnson (Cloke)/Barbara Manwood/May Wards/
Hanna Johnson/___ / Olida Fee (Simard)/_____ /Elizabeth Cameron (Evans)/
Verna Harper/Arlene Huxter
Photo: Powell River Museum & Archives

September 1943 WWII Rosies of the North enrolled in the first instructional school for female aircraft workers, Powell River Company plant.
Photo: Digester Sept. 1943

WWII February 1944 Rosies of the North working on the assembly line of the Boeing PBY search and rescue plane in a Powell River Company warehouse on the mill site.
Photo: Powell River Museum & Archives

1940 The Mohr farm, Blue Mountain, Powell River: a photo of friend Charlie Robson CEF CAO before he left for overseas duty. Freeda and Maple Mohr became Rosies of the North when they worked on the Boeing subcontract for the PBY search and rescue plane from 1943-44. (L to R) Freeda Mohr, Charlie Robson, Maple Mohr, Clinton Mohr, Garfield Mohr
Photo: Freeda Parsons (Mohr)

February 1944 Subassembly Boeing workers at the Powell River Company plant site.
Supervisor: Mrs. Moriarty—far right, black jacket and hat.
Boeing workers in alphabetical order (surname—given name): Allan (Fear) Ruth, Amos Florence, Bauman Lilly, Bull Amy, Chadwick Jessie, Cormer June, Donkersley Elizabeth, Douglas Irene, Erickson Ada, Farell Grace, Fulton Winnie, Gayton Winnie, Grigg Betty, Hayes Lynette (Sis), Hird Mary, Johnson Dora, Malnick Pearl, Menzies Margaret, McAteer Elsie, McCrossan Jean, McPhalen Agnes, Missio Theresa, Mohr (Parsons) Freeda, Mohr Maple, Monteith Edna, Morgan Irene, Pye Phyllis, Mould Vera, Needham Ina, Palmer Mrs., Radford Emily, Sear Kay, Skorey Marg, Sloboda Jean, Sparrow Bea, Stewart Beaulah, Suffil Vi, Swanson ?, Thompson Elvia, Thompson Mrs.Trevor, Weaver Jean, Wright Mrs., Zeron Amy, and ? Nellie.
Photo: Powell River Museum & Archives

A List of Men and Women Who Worked During WWII for Boeing of Canada at the Powell River Subassembly Plant #185
November 1, 1943 – November 1, 1944

- Abrams, Millicent
- Adams, Edna
- Adams, Jewell
- Allan, Ruth
- Amos, Florence
- Anderson, Bev
- Anderson, Gundren
- Anderson, Nita
- Angus, Myrtle
- Aubin, Isobel
- Baldwin, Swannie
- Ball, Bill
- Baxter, Betty
- Beads, May
- Behan, Win
- Bauman, Freda
- Bauman, Lilly
- Bell, Hazel
- Bernier, Ed
- Bestwick, Margaret
- Belyk, Edna
- Black, Doreen
- Borden, Vernon
- Brown, Kay
- Bryson, Elsie
- Bull, Amy
- Cameron, Agnes
- Caldicott, M.
- Candish, Frank
- Castigen, Elizabeth
- Chadwick, Jessie
- Clarke, Frank
- Cliff, Norman
- Clutterbuck, Glynn
- Collins, Kay
- Cook, Betty
- Cormer, June
- Crighton, Louise
- Cramb, Art
- Cullen, Wm
- deWynter, Pearl
- Dixon, "Dixie"
- Dodsworth, Thelma
- Donkersley, Elizabeth
- Dorman, Blanche
- Douglas, Irene
- Dunlop, J.P.
- Dunlop, June
- Eckman, Mary
- Ellis, Ethel
- Erickson, Ada
- Fahay, Dorothy
- Farrell, Grace
- Fleury, Eileeen
- Finlay, Doreen
- Firbank, D. J.
- Fox, Blanche
- Fraser, Frances
- Frisko, Lloyd
- Fulton, Winnie
- Gayton, Win
- Gilham, Vera
- Good, Eura
- Gray, Mar
- Griggs, Elizabeth
- Griggs, Betty
- Hart, Olga
- Hatch, Ida
- Hayes, Cal
- Hayes, Mac
- Heatley, Daisy
- Helland, Ivan
- Hewson, Stella
- Hird, Mary
- Hof, Tanya
- Houghton, Eliz

- Johnson, Dora
- Johnson, George
- Kent, Ella
- Lang, Myrtle
- Leyland, Lucille
- Littler, Eleanor
- Littler, Albert
- Lloyd, Ed
- MacKay, John
- Malnick, Pearl
- Mantoani, Nika
- Manwood, Barbara
- Mawson, Les "Mayor"
- McAteer, Elsie
- McBurnie, Ruth
- McCrossan, Jeannie
- McCullough, Al
- McDonald, Julia
- McGillivray (Anderson), Dodie
- MacKenzie, Bill
- McLean, George
- MacMillan, Nellie
- McPhalen, Agnes
- Menzies, Margaret
- Missio, Theresa
- Mitten, Rosa
- Mohr, Maple
- Monteith, Edna
- Morgan, Irene
- Moriarty, Mrs. (supervisor)
- Morse, M.
- Mould, Vera
- Murray, Dick
- Nassichuk, Alice
- Needham, Ina
- Noel, Jean
- Norman, Gil
- Northey (Thompson), Jean
- Oliver, Isabell
- Olsen, Helena
- Palmer, Bob

- Palmer, Isabel
- Parsons, Freeda
- Profitt, Garnet
- Profitt, Oakley
- Pye, Phyllis
- Radford, Emily
- Richardson, Norma
- Rochat, Violette
- Rogers, Edna
- Samoyloff, Wm
- Scott, Bonnie
- Scott, Eva
- Sear, Kay
- Skorberg, Gunnar
- Skorey, Margaret
- Sloboda, Jean
- Snowden, Bill
- Sparrow, Bea
- Stapleton, Caroline
- Stewart, Beaulah
- Suffil, Vi
- Swanson, (?)
- Taylor, M.
- Thompson, Elvera
- Thompson, Trevor (Mrs.)
- Thornton, Walter
- Toll (Hayes), Lynette (Sis)
- Tomlinson, Frances
- Townsend, Margaret
- Troup, "Buzz"
- Turner, Jack
- Watt, Dave
- Weaver, Jean
- Whitehouse, K. J.
- Williams, Frank
- Wood, Nelson
- Wright, Enid
- Young, Wm
- Zaccarelli, Wilma
- Zeron, Amy

WWII List of Female Employees at the Powell River Company Mill Plant

*Note: Some names appear on both lists (Boeing and mill)
because employees were transferred between the two work sites.

- Aubin, Isobel
- Auline (Hatch), Rhoda
- Bauman (Stutt), Freda
- Bauman, Lilly
- Bauman (Lambert), Ruby
- Beamin, E.
- Bestwick, Margaret
- Bissett, Audrey
- Cameron(Evans), Elizabeth
- Cattermole, Ruth
- Cavanagh, Mary
- Crowther, Nancy
- Dice (Ross), Mildred
- Desjarlies, Vi
- Douglas, Florence
- Etner, Ruby
- Fear (Allan), Ruth
- Fee (Simard), Olida
- Gayton, Winnie
- Graham, Ada
- Griffith, Lew
- Gustafson, Mrs. Gus
- Harper, Verna
- Harrick, Lena
- Hassell, Joyce
- Hay, Mrs. Jessie
- Heward, Mrs. Rose
- Huxter, Arlene
- Immerson, G. E.
- Johnson, Agnes
- Johnson, Hanna
- Johnson (Cloke), Pam
- Kurutz, Helen
- Le Clair (Sadler), Joyce
- Lundgren (Erickson), Ada
- Lye, Mrs. Bob
- Macaskill, Anne
- Manwood Margaret
- Manwood, Barbara
- McGillivray (Anderson), Dodie
- McPhalen, Mrs. Agnes
- Needham, Mrs. Ina
- Northey (Thompson), Jean
- Parsons (Mohr), Freeda
- Pauling, Irene
- Pye, Mrs. Phyllis
- Raby, Beatrice
- Razzo, Mrs. Elizabeth
- Scott, Eva
- Smith, Betty
- Toll (Hayes), Sis
- Wards, May
- Waugh, Gen

Powell River Company Office Workers (payroll, time & general office depts.)

*Note: 70+ women worked in the Co. offices during WWII.
After the war, widows of servicemen were offered jobs in the mill offices.

- Betts, Jack Mrs.
- Dice (Johnson), Alice
- Evans (Daly), Ruth
- Hayes (Newman), Trudy
- Hill (Richardson), Joan
- Jones, Edith Mrs.
- Parkin (Taylor), Mollie
- McSavaney, Noreen
- Raby (Howard), Norma
- Tomlinson, Joan (1943 RCAF WD)
- Thompson (Mckay), Mable
- Wards (McNeil), Sylvia

5

For Love and War

Just a Thought
By Kathleen Partridge

Young Brides
They've chosen their partners,
They're proud and they're glad
Of their Aussie, their Yank or Canadian Lad.
From parents and friends and their land they'll depart.
What a great step for a very young heart.
Off to a country unknown and untried
To learn other methods and customs beside.
Even their partners at first must be shared with
His people and friends who have waited and cared.
These brides must take courage and kindness along
For they can't rush back home when small matters go wrong.
They will speak for this land by behaviour and deed,
Must earn the acceptance and honour their breed.
Good luck and God bless them,
These pioneer brides, and give them fine children,
The best of both sides.

"Just a Thought" was discovered in Ruth Longacre's wedding album.

War Brides WWI & II

In both world wars there were thousands of war time marriages between Canadian servicemen, and women from Europe. The majority of war brides were British girls. During WWI a small number of war brides came from Belgium and France; in WWII 2,500+ Canadian servicemen married girls from Holland, France, Belgium, and Italy. In WWII, eight out of ten overseas marriages were attributed to servicemen in the Canadian Army.

Canadian servicemen were stationed at various bases in the UK for the duration of the war (four years WWI, six years WWII), and the months afterwards, waiting for transportation back to Canada. On leave, Canadians met British girls in pubs, parks, cinemas, hospitals, tea and base dances.

By the end of both wars, many thousands of Canadian servicemen were stationed overseas and married with children. The estimation of war brides from both wars varies: WWI 20,000+; WWII 43,500+. These numbers did not include engaged war brides who travelled privately at their own expense.

The Canadian Government had the huge problem of transporting, not only servicemen back to Canada, but their dependents. In 1919, after WWI, the Canadian Government passed an Order in Council which authorized free transportation for wives and dependents of Canadian servicemen in the UK. This allowed war brides, and returning Canadian wives, to travel to Canada at the government's expense. These arrangements became the prototype for transporting back dependents after WWII.

Concerned that war brides needed to have some basic information about the new country they were coming to, the Canadian Government printed a handy booklet after both wars; after the Great War, *Information for Wives of Soldiers Coming from Overseas*, and *Welcome to War Brides* after WWII.

Information for Wives of Soldiers from Overseas contains practical information for WWI war brides regarding clothing, travel arrangements, purchasing of food on the train, reception committees, and the estimation of time between the port of entry and various Canadian cities. It stated that all 3rd class travel was free for the war brides and dependents under age 18.

Welcome to War Brides booklet:

> *"Your complete journey from your home overseas to your new home in Canada is provided for by the Canadian Government, with the best accommodation available. Third class accommodation on British Railways and, in Canada, coach class transportation with sleeping car for night travel, is provided together with all meals."*

WWI & II Transportation of War Brides

Free transportation for British war brides and children to Canada, after both wars, was the same: a train journey to port of departure, a sea voyage across the Atlantic, and a journey across Canada by train. After WWII, a small number of brides came to Canada by commercial aircraft, paying their own fares.

WWII war brides, without children, were often sent in small groups (200) in ships containing returning soldiers. Those with babies and infants were sent in war bride ships adapted for taking children; the *Queen Mary* was adapted as a war bride ship with six bunks and attached cribs in each stateroom.

After the sea voyage across the North Atlantic Ocean, arrangements were made by the government to transport brides in war bride trains across Canada to their final destination.

Immigrants had been crossing Canada by train since June 1886, when the first passenger train left Montreal, destination Port Moody, B.C. The Trans-Canada highway was just a pipe dream in 1919; many decades past before it was officially opened as a modern highway, from coast to coast, in 1962 by Prime Minister John Diefenbaker.

After both World Wars, women who were *engaged* to Canadian servicemen, travelled to Canada at their own expense, and made their own travel arrangements. Alice Latchford came out to Canada as an engaged WWI war bride in 1920. Her fiancé, Private Ingve Sikstrom CEF, paid the $200 fare, a huge sum of money at that time.

The Great War (1914-18)

In WWI wives were often on the same ship as their returning husbands. Wives of officers usually travelled with their husbands in 1ˢᵗ class cabins. Wives of "other ranks" were berthed together in a designated section of the ship, their husbands berthed in a different section. They were allowed to meet on deck, during the day.

Dorothy Abraham travelled with her officer husband Ted Abraham aboard the S.S. *Olympic*, from Southampton to Halifax in 1919.

Dorothy Abraham, a WWI war bride published her journal "Lone Cone" sometime during WWII. She wrote of her experiences on board ship:

"I shall never forget the send-off they (the troops) had; the docks were black with people, bands playing, people singing, and speeches, a stirring sight. There were few other passengers so we had plenty of room, amongst them were the Duke and Duchess of Devonshire, the former at that time Governor of Canada, a few army officers and their wives, some nurses and a few civilians. I thoroughly enjoyed the trip. The troops put on some wonderful concerts which we went to, and my husband met some fellow officers he had known in B.C."

Mary Jane Yates, and her husband Private James Yates, travelled to Canada on the S.S. *Melitia*. Although they were on the same ship, Mary Jane was berthed in 3ʳᵈ class with other WWI war brides. Private James Yates was berthed in a different section, with returning soldiers of "other ranks". They were allowed to meet each other on deck, during the daytime. The couple left Liverpool on February 28, 1919 and the ship later berthed at St. John, New Brunswick. While travelling across Canada by train, Mary Jane was impressed by the generosity of the Canadian people. At every major railway station the troops and brides were served with refreshments, which included fresh fruit. Mary Jane's story was published in 1979 by the Crowsnest Pass Historical Society.

Florence Gould, a WWI war bride (wife of Private Arthur Gould), travelled to Canada aboard the *Justica* in 1917. Arthur Gould travelled at a later date. Florence was four months pregnant, and had very little money; this caused a personal financial crisis because her ship was diverted from Halifax to New York, due to the devastating explosion in Halifax harbour on December 6, 1917. Her account, "A War Bride's Journey of 1917" was published by the Okanagan Historical Society, November 1973.

Florence Gould:

"We reached Liverpool during the night, too late to be getting overnight lodgings. A group of us stayed in one of the waiting rooms to await the morning and further direction.

(We were) ----- taken to our cabins. We had a 1ˢᵗ class patronized by officers, wives, and those had a little more cash, but most of us were satisfied with the 2ⁿᵈ class deck. We were told there were 200 infants and small children aboard, and it certainly sounded like it at times.

Many soldiers were returning to Canada for various reasons. They were able to join the other passengers on the decks, and a few romances seemed to blossom. Some soldiers were lucky enough to have their wives aboard. After about 10 days aboard we were told that our destination was New York."

World War II (1939-45) Travel Arrangements

The arrangements for bringing WWII brides across the Atlantic were a duplication of those made after WWI. The Canadian Army was put in charge of organizing the mass exodus of returning servicemen and women, war brides and children.

The Army located the Canadian Wives Bureau at 40, Piccadilly, London, W.1, August 1944. This became the central office to deal with all applications and arrangements for travel of wives married to men in the three services: Army, Navy and Air Force. Applications were sent to the Civilian Repatriation Section to be processed.

Free passage and war bride status was denied to overseas wives of men in Canada's *Merchant* Navy. Doris Gammer, wife of George Gammer (Merchant Navy), was refused a free passage to Canada by the Canadian Government; however her application for travel to Canada was processed through the Canadian Wives Bureau. Doris Gammer paid for a 1ˢᵗ class ticket, but had to share her stateroom with "official" war brides and their children. No assistance was given to Doris on her arrival in Canada.

Doris Gammer (Powell River, B.C.) 2011   "an unofficial war bride"

"Because George (Gammer) was in the Canadian Merchant Navy, I was not an "official" war bride so George had to pay for my travel arrangements to Vancouver. I had to do the same paperwork as other war brides, and have a medical in London. After that I was on my own. I was notified of my sailing from Liverpool, and then had to find my own way there.

I sailed on the "Mauritania" with "official" war brides on March 20, 1946. George had bought me a 1ˢᵗ class ticket but the accommodation was not first class. Yes, I was in a stateroom but I was sharing it with five "official" war brides and their babies. The beds were bunk beds. Some had cribs at the side for babies.

Because I was an "unofficial" war bride I was directed to have my meals with a small group of English businessmen.

There was no Red Cross to greet me in Halifax. I was all on my own."

WWII Powell River War Brides:
Memories of the Journey to Canada

Mildred Adams (89) Powell River 2011

"The boat was outfitted for war brides. I was given a bottom bunk in "the bowels of the earth". There were lots of food such as eggs and oranges; everything was in short supply in England. I was afraid to go near the railings and look down at the ocean. There was some pilfering on board of nappies (diapers)."

Mary Bortolussi (89) Vancouver 2011

"I left England as a war bride in 1946 on the Ile de France. The food was French. It was good. The war brides on board had no children, some were pregnant. The journey took either eight or nine days.

We crossed Canada by train. Lots of wheat fields. Along the way the train stopped to let war brides off. Gino (husband) met me at the station in Vancouver. He was wearing a civilian suit, last time I saw him he was in uniform."

Hanna deWynter (88) Powell River 2011   War bride from Holland

"I flew over to Canada from Holland in 1947 with our youngest son John. It was a terrible journey to get to Vancouver. There were five changes: Prestwick, Gander, New York, Toronto and Calgary. At New York there was a tremendous amount of paperwork even though I was in transit. There was no food on the planes; it was included in the airfare but had to be picked up at airports. I was too airsick to care.

Flying over the prairies I saw a vast landscape, and what seemed to me a few small towns. Poor Joe (husband), when I landed in Vancouver, I looked a mess. I was ill with airsickness. For the first time I saw Joe in civilian clothes. I recognized him, but did he recognize me?"

Elizabeth Hindle (Powell River)
2011 memories by her daughter Georgia:

"My father Harry Hindle was shipped back to Canada and Powell River before we sailed in November 1946 on board the T.S.S. "Letitia" from Liverpool. My mother was devastated at leaving her sister Kathleen – they were very close.

For the entire voyage my mother was very ill with severe malnutrition and home sickness. I was only four years of age but I had to look after my mother and baby sister Kathleen during the voyage. Other people on board were very kind. The food on board the ship was wonderful but my mother was unable to eat anything.

Mother and Kathleen continued to be ill on the train across Canada. A black steward was very good to us. Some nice things my mother had brought with her were stolen on the train — even Kathleen's diapers were stolen; when we arrived in Vancouver, Kathleen was wearing the only diaper she possessed. Poor mother, after the train ride, one extra boat ride to Powell River!"

Phyllis Kornyk (87) Powell River 2011

"I sailed with a couple of hundred war brides on a troop ship that sailed from Liverpool. Some brides were pregnant; however, there were no children on board. Pregnant women got the bottom bunks. There were six brides to a room. We were all excited. The meals were wonderful — bacon and eggs! I piled my plate high.

I shall never forget crossing Canada by train. I nearly freaked out -- going, going, going. I kept my fingers crossed to see a city.

The train stopped at various locations to let small groups of brides off, sometimes it was only one on an isolated track with no houses in sight. Some war brides simply could not get off the train. These brides were then put in a special compartment at the end of the train. They returned to Halifax and were put on a boat to return to England."

Joan Mansell (89) Powell River 2011

"I shall always remember crossing the Atlantic on the "Queen Mary" with the other war brides and their children in 1945. It was the "Queen Mary's" first war bride voyage.

I had two boys with me, and the three of us shared a cabin with one other war bride and her child. I think we had good accommodation because of our husband's rank (Sergeant Major).

I was sick the whole way across. Two sailors were near the dining room door ready to grab any of the girls who were about to throw up.

The Red Cross and the Salvation Army helped with the children. There was a special play area for the children."

Ann McKenzie (87) Powell River 2011

"All the war brides without children gathered at Hyde Park house, then we went by train to Liverpool. We were on a ship with returning soldiers. There were about 200 war brides on our ship. Some girls, even though they were married, had romances on board.

The food was marvellous compared to what we had on rationing during the war. I piled my plate up, some girls went back for two or three extra sittings, however I only went to one. We docked in Halifax. It was all very exciting. We (the war brides) came across Canada in a big, long train. It was slower than the trains in England. I spent a lot of time in the observation room. All I could see was grass to the horizon, not a house, not a home, not a hut in sight, no people, no towns, no nothing!

We had a two-hour stop in Winnipeg. We took taxis to the Hudson Bay Company and shopped for clothes. At last, new clothes without coupons!"

Margaret Morrissey (Powell River)
2011 memories by her son John:

"I was just 7 years old when we left Southampton on the "Queen Mary". For me, going to Canada was an adventure. It was exciting to explore the "Queen Mary". The three of us, my mother and my baby sister Theresa, had our own cabin. It was amazing – there was electricity, and water that came out of a tap! We had lived in a cottage with well water and oil lamps. The first thing I did was to stick a pair of scissors into an electric socket. Of course, I got a shock. I was in and out of the bathtub two or three times a day."

Doris Gammer (88) Powell River 2011 "an unofficial war bride"

"When I first meet George (Gammer) of the Canadian Merchant Navy, I was a bottle blonde. All the time we were in England I never told him I was actually a brunette. Even when we got married I never told him.

I let my hair return to its natural colour for the journey to Canada. I met George in Vancouver. I recognized him in his civilian clothes, but he didn't recognize me, because he was looking for a blonde!"

A Return Voyage for Two Powell River Brides

Part of the war bride story is the excitement of a voyage to a new land. For two Powell River war brides they were returning, not only to Canada, but the same area they had grown up in! Both families had returned permanently to Britain before the war, thus the brides were granted official war bride status.

The Baker family, originally from England, settled in Wildwood village (Powell River) in 1929; however, they returned in 1936 because Mrs. Baker was homesick for the "old country". Mary had attended Wildwood school and was 14 years of age when she returned, with her family, to England. At age 18 she joined the ATS. Gino Bortolussi also attended Wildwood school, he knew Mary as a school girl. With the outbreak of WWII Gino joined the Canadian Army and went overseas. Feeling lonely, he visited the Bakers – a neighbour had given him their address. Mary and Gino fell in love and were married in England, October 1943. Mary left England as a war bride in 1946 on the *Ile de France*. With their daughter in Canada, the Baker family joined her in 1947 in the village of Wildwood – the same village they had left in 1936.

The Wilson family originally from Yorkshire, England, came to Canada in 1922 and lived in a rented house in the Powell River Company Townsite. Robert Wilson worked for the Powell River Company. In the political purge of 1933-34 he was fired with approximately 350 mill workers. With no hope of getting a job in Canada (all fired workers were blacklisted), Robert returned to England with his wife Agnes and their two children, Dorothy and Ken. Dorothy (Dot) was 16 years of age when they returned; she left behind her old school sweetheart, Eddie Riley. It was WWII that brought them together again; Eddie joined the RCN and when on leave in England, looked up his school sweetheart, Dot Wilson. The meeting rekindled their love, and they were married in Wakefield, Yorkshire in 1942. A pregnant Dorothy returned to Canada as a war bride in 1943 on a ship with British evacuees. In 1947 the entire Wilson family returned to Powell River, B.C., the town they had left 14 years before, in order to be with their daughter Dorothy, and grandson Robert (Bob).

WWII war bride grooms

A few **bridegrooms** (numbers unknown) came to Canada after WWII. These were men from countries other than Canada. They married Canadian servicewomen who were overseas during a time of war.

Zella Stade, a teacher in the Powell River area, joined the Women's Division of the Royal Canadian Air Force, after seeing an ad in the *Vancouver Sun* for women with senior matriculation, who were required for specialized training.

After training, Zella was posted overseas. She met Sid Clark in the "ops" room at a Canadian Air Force base in Yorkshire, England. Sid, who was in the RAF, worked at the base as a meteorologist. They fell in love, and were married in the UK.

Zella Clark (90) 2011
"Before accepting Sid's proposal, I told him I had two conditions he had to accept; the first being we would live in Canada, and the second that I wanted to have six children. Sid agreed to both conditions! We were married on Halloween, 31ˢᵗ October, 1944 in Woodhorn church near Woodbiggin.
The war was now nearly over and I requested the Canadian Air Force to be discharged in England so that I could accompany Sid to his postings with the RAF.
We travelled to Canada in 1947 with our first child Ian, on BOAC. There was a six-month waiting list."

WII War Bride Associations

Many War Bride Associations sprang up across Canada. They were initially support groups; in later years, a place to share memories: life in war torn Britain (the rationing and the bombing), the adventure of travelling to Canada by ship and train, and the challenge of a new life in Canada.

In the computer age, the collecting and publishing of war bride stories was made possible with the help of War Bride Associations. From the end of the 20th century, with diminishing numbers, many associations had to close. Some kept open by allowing children of war brides, in memory of their mothers, to become members.

In British Columbia, War Bride Associations were formed in the Lower Mainland, the Interior, and on Vancouver Island. According to the few remaining war brides in Powell River, now in their 80s, no War Bride Association was ever formed in Powell River and District. Without an Association, there was no definitive record of war brides in the area, or collection of war bride stories.

By the beginning of the 21st century, the story of the Powell River & District war brides was a "lost chapter" in the town's history.

WWII Powell River & District Service Marriages

The following lists have been researched through the help of old-timers in the community, the *Powell River Digester* (published by the Powell River Company), and the Powell River Company monthly newsletter sent to servicemen and women during WWII. These lists were researched, for the first time, in 2011.

The *Powell River Digester* and Powell River Company monthly newsletter reported, without bias, on service weddings overseas, and in Canada. Thus, the Powell River Company reporting gives a unique opportunity to compare the pattern of marriages overseas, and within Canada.

The national figures for overseas marriages, according to Branch of Service, are 80% Army, 18% Air force and 2% Navy; the Powell River percentages followed, fairly closely, the national trend. The vast majority of war brides were from the UK, with much smaller numbers from Holland, Belgium, France and Italy. The Powell River overseas marriages followed the national trend with 24 from England, 4 from Scotland, 1 from Ireland, and 2 from Holland.

WWII Powell River & District Marriages

War brides	Total = 31	22 CA	07 RCAF	02 RCN
War bride groom (RAF)	Total = 01		01 RCAF WD	
Marriages in Canada (50% in B.C., 50% in other provinces)	Total = 40	14 CA	16 RCAF	10 RCN

The national figures for service marriages within Canada are not available. The Powell River Service List for marriages on the home front, indicate a different branch of service pattern to those of overseas marriages: the Air Force service branch achieving the highest rate of marriages, the Army in second place, and the Navy a close third. These figures indicate that in WWII, with training facilities such as the British Commonwealth Air Training Plan, and the location of naval facilities on the East Coast, many service marriages were taking place in central and eastern Canada.

The Powell River numbers are too small to show a national trend, however they do suggest, in addition to many local servicemen marrying overseas, a higher number of servicemen married within Canada. Of those marrying in Canada, 50% married in B.C., and 50% married in other provinces. In peace time, most young men from the Powell River & District area would have married within the province of B.C.

WWI & II War Bride List
Powell River & District

A war bride is a citizen of another country who married a Canadian serviceman overseas.

Errors and omissions are due to the passage of time (nearly 100 years since the beginning of WWI, and 70+ years since the start of WWII).

*Interviews with brides/families 2011

WWI war brides

*Lee (Gray), Barbara   1919 Stromness, Orkney Is. Scotland
Lee, John CEF

*Sikstrom (Latchford), Alice May   1918 Wales, U.K. – engaged war bride
Sikstrom, Ingve CEF   1920 married Edmonton, Alberta

Barbara and John Lee came to Stillwater (Powell River Regional District) in 1930. Alice and Ingve Sikstrom resided in Hay Lake, Alberta. They frequently visited their daughter, Evelyn, in Westview, Powell River, from the late 1950s to 1970s.

*war bride/or family interviews   CEF = Canadian Expeditionary Force

#1 Section – WWII Powell River "boys" marry overseas

Bell (Mason), Helen   1944 Birmingham, England
Bell, William RCAF

Borden, Mrs. Claude   1944 England
Borden, Claude RCOC (admin.)

*Bortolussi (Baker), Mary ATS   1944 England
Bortolussi, Gino CAO

Campbell, Mrs. Jock   1944 England
Campbell, Jock CAO

Coomber (Holley), Joyce   1944 Ewell, Surrey (England)
Coomber, Harvey CAO

*deWynter (Tymstra), Hanna   1945 Holland
deWynter, Scotty CAO

Drayton (Hough), Doris   1944 Epsom, Surrey (England)
Drayton, George CAO

Dykes, Mrs. Raymond   1944 England
Dykes, Raymond CAO

Gann, Mrs. Harman   1944 England
Gann, Harman CAO

Grundle, Mildred WAAF   1944 England
Grundle, Jack CAO

Hill, Iris   1940 England
Hill, Norman CAO

Jack, Mrs. Dave   1943 Scotland
Jack, Dave CEF CAO (married Scottish sweetheart from WWI)

Jacobs, Mrs. Dick   1945 Nottingham, England
Jacobs, Dick CAO

Leese, Mrs. Dick   1944 England
Leese, Dick RAF/RCAF

*Long (Kemp), Margaret   1941 Scotland
Long, Harold CAO

Maple (Brand), Elizabeth WRNS   1944 London, England
Maple, James RCN

Matheson, Toki   1945 Holland
Matheson, Rod CAO

Menzies, Mrs. Gordon (homesick/returned to England)   1945 England
Menzies, Gordon CAO

*Morrissey (Munro), Margaret   1944 Scotland
Morrissey, Joseph CAO

Naylor (Cadman), Sandra WAAF   1944 England
Naylor, Martin RCAF

O'Neil (Milner), Julie ATS	1945 West Acton, England
O'Neil, Frank RCAF	
*Patrick (Wilson), Joan -Timber Corps	1944 Chichester, England
Patrick, Walter RCAF	
Peebles, Evelyn (divorced 1950s, married Joe Skorey RCN)	1944 England
Peebles, William CAO	
Pelly, Mrs. Jack	1943 England
Pelly, Jack CAO	
Razzo, Mrs. Paul	1944 Scotland
Razzo, Paul CAO (Forestry)	
Richards (Cleaver), Winnifred WAAF	1944 Haywards Heath, England
Richards, Stan RCAF	
*Riley (Wilson), Dorothy	1942 England
Riley, Eddie RCN	
Rowe, Mrs. Howard	1944 Ireland
Rowe, Howard CAO	
Taylor, Mrs. Len	1942 England
Taylor, Len CAO	
Walker, Mrs. Cliff	1943 England
Walker, Cliff CAO	
Young, Mrs. Jack	1944 England
Young, Jack RCAF	

WWII war bride-groom

Clark, Sidney RAF	1944 Newbiggin-by-the-Sea, England
*Clark (Stade), Zella RCAF WD	

Finnish war bride

Taylor (Auto) Ester	1941 Finland
*Taylor, Harry RAF / volunteer Finnish Air Force	Killed 1942 England

#2 Section 1947-1959 Postwar BOOM
Veterans & war brides from other areas of Canada relocate to Powell River

*Adams, Mildred ATS   1945 England
Adams, Lorne CAO

*Brant (Cowen), Dorothy – nurse   1941 Rochdale, England
Brant, Cyril CAO

*Cooper (Abbott), Hilda   1943 Nottingham, England
Cooper, Vernon CAO

*Hindle (Kenny) Elizabeth   1941 Rochdale, England
Hindle, Harry CAO

*Kornyk (Evans), Phyllis ARP   1943 Epsom, England
Kornyk, John CAO

*Longacre (Cave), Ruth WAAF   1945 Bournemouth, England
Longacre, Norman CAO

*Mckenzie, Ann   1946 England
Mckenzie, Jim CAO

*Phelan (Barker), Joan – ammunitions ARP   1944 Enfield, England
Phelan, Paul RCN

WWII Italian war bride – British Army
*Wilma Brown (Italian) translator   1950 Scotland
Brown, William – British Army Military Police, Italy

#3 Section
1980 – 2011 war brides (seniors) – Powell River's retirement community

*Gammer (Vanner), Doris ATS (an "unofficial" war bride)   1945 London
Gammer, George – Canadian *Merchant* Navy

*Mansell (Skilton) Joan – farm worker   1941 Reigate, England
Mansell, John CAO

*Miller (Vesty), Joan Edna – munitions worker   1945 Charlton, England
Miller, Orval CAO

Wedding Bells on the Home Front – Powell River District

Powell River & District Servicemen and women married in Canada, to a Canadian citizen from 1942-46.

Service Marriages in Canada

The following servicemen were Powell River "boys". A total of 12 married local girls, 3 married within the province of B.C. (Victoria, Nanaimo and Prince Rupert), and 19 married in other provinces. 6 inter-service marriages were recorded.

*Aprilis (Hancock), Elva
Aprilis, Dino CA
    1945 Nova Scotia

Baxter, Mrs. George
Baxter, George CAO
    1943 Powell River, B.C.

Bentham, Mrs. Tommy
Bentham, Tommy CAO
    1944 Quebec

*Bird (Banham), Peggy
Bird, Duncan RCN
    1945 Vancouver

Bridge, Mrs. Frank
Bridge, Frank RCN
    1943 Halifax, Nova Scotia

Brown, Eileen
Brown, Stewart RCAF
    1944 Powell River, B.C.

Cadwallader, Mrs. Jack
Cadwallader, Jack CAO
    1944 Nanaimo, B.C.

Calder, Mrs. Bill
Calder, Bill RCAFO
    1944 Alberta

Cattermole (Treleaven), Phyllis
Cattermole, M.R. (Monty) RCAF
    1944 Manitoba

Elly, Mrs. Walter
Elly, Walter RCNH
    1944 Canada

Emerson, Mrs. Bill
Emerson, W.H. (Bill) RCAF
    1943 Quebec

Furnival, Mrs. Evans
Furnvial, Evans RCAF
    1943 Eastern Canada

Green, Mrs. Denny   1942 Victoria, B.C.
Major Green Denny Pacific Coast HQ

Hutchinson, Mrs. Lawrence   1944 Canada
Hutchinson, Lawrence RCNV

Ingram (Johnston), Edith   1943 Powell River, B.C.
Ingram, Doug RCN

Johnston (Reed), Marguerite   1943 Powell River, B.C.
Johnston, Robbie CAO

*Lambert (Bauman) Ruby (divorced 1945 remarried 1945)   1944 Powell River, B.C.
Lambert, Russell CAO

MacDonald, Mrs. Frank   1944 Canada
MacDonald, Frank RCAF

MacGregor, Mrs. James   1945 Winnipeg, Saskatchewan
MacGregor, James DFC RCAFO

Martin, Mrs. Ian   1944 Canada
Martin, Ian RCN

Messmer (Hindle), Margaret   1944 Powell River, B.C.
Messmer Gene RCAFO (eldest son of Mrs. H. Zaccarelli)

Mowbray (Gowdyk), Helen   1945 Powell River, B.C.
Mowbray, Fred RCNVR

Parkin (Pickles) Irene   1944 Powell River, B.C.
Parkin, Bob CAO

Parkin (Taylor), Mollie   1943 Powell River, B.C.
Parkin, Jack CAO

Peck (Manwood), Barbara   1945 Powell River, B.C.
Peck, Eric RCAF

Quinn (Karney) Mrs. Bert   1944 Calgary, Alberta
Quinn, Bert CAO

Quinn, Mrs. Eddie   1944 Prince Rupert, B.C.
Quinn, Eddie CAO

Raimondo, Mrs. R.G.   1944 Canada
Raimondo, Spud RCAFO

Redhead, Mrs. Jack Redhead, Jack RCAFO	1944 Canada
Ross, Mrs. Arthur Ross, Arthur RCAFO	1944 Powell River, B.C.
Stevenson, Mrs. O.J. (formerly Mrs. Ed Davis widow) Stevenson, Ossi RCAF	1943 Powell River, B.C.
*Stutt (Bauman), Freda Stutt, Bob CAO	1946 Winnipeg, Manitoba
Tull, Mrs. Harold Tull, Harold RCAF	1943 Vancouver, B.C.
Woodruff, Mrs. Don Woodruff, Don RCNVR	1944 Canada

Inter-service marriages:

Local "boys" married local "girls"; the exception being Betty Parkin who married James Henry Bryan RCNVR from Toronto.

Bryan (Parkin) Bertyne (Betty) RCAF WD Bryan James Henry RCNVR (from Toronto, Ontario)	1944 Vancouver, B.C.
Dore (Oster), Alice (Sis) RCAF WD Dore, Earl CAO	1943 Powell River, B.C.
Fairgrieves (McPhalen), Marjorie RCAF WD Fairgrieves, Bud RCAF /killed in action	1943 Halifax, Nova Scotia
*Liebich (Rolandi) Violet RCAF WD Liebich, Walt CAO	1943 Powell River, B.C.
McLeod, Mrs. Ernie CWAC McLeod, Ernie RCN	1945 Powell River, B.C.
Nutchey (Taylor), Edith RCAF WD Nutchey, Tom RCAF	1945 Powell River, B.C.

Sgt. Dave Jack CEF CAO and his wife November 1941, Scotland.
Dave went overseas with the Seaforths in 1939 and immediately looked for his old sweetheart
from WWI; she was still single, and waiting for Dave!
Photo: Powell River Digester April 1943

Pilot Officer Stan Richards RCAF married Winnifred Cleaver WAAF,
April 3, 1944 Haywards Heath, Sussex, England.
Photo: Digester Sept. 1944

1945 Vancouver—William (Bill) Peebles CAO.
Inset: Evelyn Peebles WWII war bride.
Photos: Bill Peebles collection

September 1940 Private Norman Hill CAO with his overseas bride Iris Hill.
Photo: Powell River Digester Nov. 1940

WWII Powell River "boys" marry overseas

Bell, Helen
Bell, William (Bill) – attached RAF, RCAF overseas

Newsletter July 1944
"Flying Officer Bill Bell threw the whole Shipping office into an uproar when he sneaked off early in July to marry Miss Helen Mason of Birmingham."
December 1944
"Back home too are ruby-cheeked Flying Officer Bill Bell, with his English bride."

Digester Vol. 21 February 1945
"Flying Officer Bill Bell of the Shipping Department dropped in on us. Bill flew "Wimpies" and Liberators all over the Western Mediterranean and up to the Bay of Biscay, over the North Sea and North Atlantic. He brought back an English bride to share his future in Powell River. Bill is attached to Western Air Command for the present."

Borden, Mrs. C.L.
Borden C.L. (Claude) – Staff Sergeant RCOC (admin.) Overseas

Digester Vol. 20, 1944 March list of marriages: "Have you forgotten --- Claude Borden?"

July 1944 Claude Borden letter: *"Guess all the local swimmers are taking a bit of sun tan at Willingdon beach. Would prefer a nice cool dip in Powell Lake. Thanks a million for the cigarettes and newsletters."*

April 1945 Claude Borden letter. *"--- am in a reasonably peaceful spot in Holland. Would you say hello to the old gang at home and overseas and give my congratulations to Jack Grundle in bringing an English bride safe and sound to Canada."*

Digester Vol. 21, August 1945 "At a recent divisional track and field championship meet held in Holland, Sgt. Claude Borden came through with a victory in the sprints in fast time."

Bortolussi (Baker), Mary - ATS
Bortolussi, Gino – Sergeant CAO

Digester Vol. 18, September 1942
"Bortolussi won the 100 and 200 yard dashes, creating new records in both events, despite the presence of a heavy gale. The Powell River iron man also led his division to victory in the mile relay, nipping 14 seconds off the established record and beating the British Army record by 2 3/5 seconds. Not satisfied with these achievements, Bortolussi went out and ran anchor in the 440 yard dash relay and again led his team to victory in record time."

July 1944 "We understand Gino Bortolussi is out of Italy. Read something in the paper about him running fourth in an Allied meet in Rome."

Campbell, Mrs. Jock
Campbell, Jock – Private CAO

February 1944 "----- the top rumour of the month is a report that Jock Campbell had been finally trapped (married), after dodging some cannily set snares over the past twenty years."

Coomber, Joyce (Holley)
Coomber, Harvey Jr. – Signalman CAO

July 1944 "Harvey Coomber is engaged, but only till October, when wedding bells will ring out ye old chimes."

October 1944 "Harvey Coomber Jr., early in October, took himself and his bride, Miss Joyce Holley of Ewell, Surrey, to the village church, gulped out an "I do" --- and joined the rapidly expanding membership of the PRSFPEW (Powell River Society for the Perpetuation of English Women).

deWynter, Hanna (Tymstra) from Holland
deWynter, Joe (Scotty) – Lance Corporal CAO

July 1944 "Scotty deWynter is out in Italy and run across several of the boys already."

May 1945
Scotty: *"Well, the war with Germany has at last been won. And can't say how happy we are. Guess all you back there in good old P.R. are just as happy too. So we may be seeing you all again in a very few months now. Thanks again for the cigs and my best wishes to you all."*

Drayton, Doris
Drayton, George – Corporal CAC, CMF

May 1944 "George Drayton early this year celebrated his promotion to Lance Corporal by marrying Miss Doris Hough, at Epsom, Surrey."

Dykes, Mrs. Raymond
Dykes, George - CSM, CAO

February 1944 (re: marriages) "And CSM Raymond Dykes is in double harness."

May 1944 "Paul Razzo is out of hospital and back again at the job of depleting Scotland's timber reserves. Paul runs a caterpillar along with his brother George --- and Ray Dykes as CSM looks benevolently on --- we hope!"

October 1944 "Heck, we almost forgot to mention that Sgt. Dykes 9th Coy, CFC, CAO, proudly announces the birth of a son and heir on October 12th."

Bortolussi (Baker), Mary - ATS   WWII War Bride from England
Bortolussi, Gino - CAO

George Baker and family, originally from England, lived in the small village of Wildwood, near the Powell River Townsite in the early '30s. They came out to Canada in 1929, and returned permanently to England in 1936 because Mrs. Baker was homesick for the "old country". George worked for the Powell River Company. Mrs. Baker, on her return to England, corresponded with friends in Wildwood.

Mary had attended Wildwood school. She was 14-and-a-half years old on her return to England. At age 18 she joined the ATS.

When war broke out Gino volunteered to go overseas with the Canadian Army. Before leaving, he had been given the Bakers' address by a neighbour in Wildwood. The neighbour suggested: *"Why don't you visit the Bakers while you are in England?"*

Gino was stationed at the Aldershot army base; on having a weekend pass, he decided to look up the Baker family. The Baker family gave Gino an exceptionally warm welcome. The family were very good to him, inviting him for meals and a place to stay when on leave. Gino and Mary started to go out together, inevitably they fell in love.

The Bortolussi Family

Gino was the son of Marino and Amabile Bortolussi. He had four siblings: Nellie, Aldo, Leah, and Leo. The family grew up in the mainly Italian community of Wildwood village.

Marino Bortolussi came to Canada in 1920 and his first job was building the Canadian railroad. His second job was working in the Alberta coal fields at Brule. When the mine closed down, he came to Powell River and worked in the Shingle Mill with Doc Jameson. He belonged to the Italian Hall Society.

From 1931-32 the Bortolussi family lived in a house at Riverside (known as Little Italy) in the Powell River Townsite. In 1933 Marino bought a one acre lot with a house and three two-roomed rentals in Wildwood, for the cost of $1,000.

The Bortolussi children were exceptional athletes. Prior to WWII, Gino and Aldo were well known lacrosse players. Aldo was killed on a bombing mission over Germany.

During WWII Gino represented the Canadian Armed Forces in the 100-yard sprint. In 1942 and 1943 he was Canadian Army Sprint Champion.

In 1988 Gino Bortolussi was inducted into the Canadian Sports Hall of Fame.

Mary Bortolussi (Baker) age 89 January 2011

"During the war I was in the ATS and worked in an office, filing. We had ration books – no bananas – nothing was available; however, the food at the army base was alright.

I met Gino when he visited our home. We had known the Bortolussi family before the war, when our family lived in Canada. We fell in love. I married Gino in England, October 1943. My sister Gladys was my bridesmaid. We never went to too many pubs, however, we did go to a few dances.

I left England as a war bride in 1946 on a French ship the *Ile de France*. The food was French. It was good. The war brides on board had no children, some were pregnant. The journey took either eight or nine days.

We crossed Canada by train. Lots of wheat fields. Along the way the train stopped to let war brides off. Gino met me at the station in Vancouver. He was wearing his civilian suit, the last time I saw him he was in uniform.

After a few days in Vancouver, we came up to Powell River. First of all we lived on Willow Street in the duplexes built for the ex-servicemen, then we got a company (Powell River Company) house on Maple Street. Gino worked in the sales office for the Powell River Company.

In 1947 my family immigrated to Canada and came to live in Powell River. Dad found work with the Powell River Company. My sister Gladys married Al Roberts, however the marriage did not last. After my mother died, Dad married a widow in Westview, Doreen Watson.

Gino spent two-and-a-half years in hospital in Vancouver for a spinal fusion. I continued to live in Powell River. When Gino came back he continued to work for the Powell River Company in the same department. He was transferred in 1963 to work in the company office in Vancouver but later he was transferred back to Powell River in 1973. Gino continued to work for the Powell River mill until he retired. We then moved to Vancouver to live.

We had three children who were born in Powell River: James, Sandra and David. October 1993, we celebrated our 50th wedding anniversary in Deer Lake Park, Burnaby, with friends and family. Gino died in 1997. **I have no regrets at coming to Canada as a war bride."**

Overseas wedding of Geno Bortolussi CAO and Mary Bortolussi (Baker)
ATS October 1943, England.
The Baker family had originally lived in Wildwood District, Powell River,
however they returned permanently to Britain in 1936 because
Mrs. Baker was homesick for the "old country".
Photo: Powell River Digester

Mary and Geno Bortolussi, Wildwood District, Powell River, July 12, 1991.
(L to R) Sandra Smith (Bortolussi), Jordon Smith, Laura Hunter, Gordon (Dint) Hunter,
Nellie Hunter (Geno's sister), Mary Bortolussi (Baker), Geno Bortolussi
Front: Stephanie Smith
Photo: Leah Merrell

*September 1945 Oosterwolde village, northern Holland: Zus Tymstra
and unknown Canadian soldier with wooden shoes.
Photo: Hanna deWynter (Tymstra) collection*

*December 23, 1946—skating on a lake in northern Holland: Simy,
Hanna and Klassje Tymstra, and a friend.
Photo: Hanna deWynter (Tymstra) collection*

August 1923—the Tymstra family having tea outside their home in
Oosterwolde village, Holland:
Back row (L to R) Hanna, Jantje (mother), Ge and Klassje Tymstra
Front: a friend (on deck chair), sitting Simy Tymstra
Photo: Hanna deWynter (Tymstra) collection

1986 Powell River, B.C. Joe and Hanna deWynter (Tymstra) and children:
Back row (L to R) John, Jean and Norman deWynter
Front row (L to R) Cheryl, Joe and Hanna deWynter, Shirley
Photo: Hanna deWynter collection

deWynter, Hanna - WWII war bride from Holland
deWynter, Joe - CAO

Joe deWynter came to Powell River in 1940, and worked for the maintenance crew of the Powell River Company before he was called up. He was in the Canadian Army with the Westminster Regiment and saw service in Italy, Belgium and Holland. During the liberation of Holland by the Canadians, he ran a canteen for the army out of a hotel in the small village of Oosterwolde in northern Holland.

Hanna (age 88) 2011

"My father Uiltje Tymstra was the principal of the village school of Oosterwolde. My family lived in a house near the school. The house came with my father's position. My parents, Uiltje and Jantje, had five children. I was the fourth child to be born in 1923. My older sisters were: Klassje (born 1914), Zus (1916) and Simy (1918). My youngest sister Ge was born in 1924. My older sisters were engaged to be married before the war, however, they had to wait until the war was over to be married.

When the war started I was a teenager and going to school. I remember, one morning, the German planes going over our house before they bombed Rotterdam.

As a teenager I went hiking, bike riding, swimming, and skating with my friends. One had to take great care with one's bike because, if left unattended, it would be stolen. I continued with my studies, however in 1944, the schools were closed because there was no heat or electricity in the buildings.

Some of the boys worked in the Dutch underground, including my sister Simy's fiancé Lou Somer. Others were taken to work in German factories and lived in terrible conditions in camps. During the occupation the Germans sent young boys (German) to our village. During the war we had two elderly refugees living with us.

Living in a village in a country area, we were a lot better off than those living in the towns. Those on rations in the towns had a difficult time getting enough food to live on. We had to be self-reliant. Most of what we obtained, food and clothing, was through bartering. Money was useless. Mother made butter from cow's milk and cheese from sheep's milk.

We had two spinning wheels and we spun wool into yarn. For our work we were given some of the yarn. We could then trade the yarn for milk and eggs. There was no electricity for light in the dark winter evenings, so my father made electricity by turning the pedals of a bike in our front room. This enabled us to carry on spinning.

On April 13, 1945 our village was freed by the Canadians. What a joyous time it was! *The Germans were finally gone. To celebrate our freedom, our village had a special parade on May 12, 1945. There was no gas to run any vehicles, so the villagers used horses to pull farmers' wagons. I was with my sisters on one of the wagons. We all massed at the village town hall. Lou Sumer, who had been in the Dutch underground, did a "take off" of Hitler. At last we were free.*

Lou and my sister Simy were married after the war. Simy wore a beautiful dress made from curtains. There was no other material available. Henk, my sister Zus' fiancé was still in Indonesia. He had been in a Japanese prisoner of war camp. After they were liberated the married men were sent back first. Eventually he came back, and they were married.

I first met my future Canadian husband, Joe, when he was running a canteen for the army from the hotel near my house. Joe came to the back door, I opened the door, and he asked me if someone could do his laundry. I really wanted nothing to do with those Canadians! We met again at dances, and started seeing one another. We fell in love.

My parents were horrified that I would even think of leaving Holland and making a home with Joe in Canada. They eventually accepted the idea, and later came to see our growing family in Powell River. My mother said, on one occasion, if two of her daughters had married Canadians, she would have moved to Canada. She really liked Powell River, and Canada.

I flew over to Canada from Holland with our youngest son John in 1947. It was a terrible journey to get to Vancouver, there were five changes: Prestwick, Gander, New York, Toronto, and Calgary. At New York there was a tremendous amount of paperwork even though I was in transit, and not leaving the airport. There was no food on the planes, it was included in the airfare but had to be picked up at the airports. I was too air sick to eat or care.

Flying over the Prairies I saw a vast landscape, and what seemed to me, a few small towns.

Poor Joe, when I landed in Vancouver, I looked a mess. I was ill with air sickness. For the first time I saw Joe in civilian clothes. I recognized him, but did he recognize me? After a few days in Vancouver we came by boat to Powell River. For a few months we lived with Joe's family at Mowat Bay in Cranberry. They were very good to me, they made me feel welcome.

I was very busy in the postwar years, looking after our family of five children and helping my husband with his business. I enjoyed skating on Cranberry Lake with Joe, and the children. Of course, I had skated in Holland with my sisters.

I quickly adjusted to living in Canada. I had been taught to speak a number of languages in Holland, including English. I have had a good life in Canada."

Gann, Mrs. Herman
Gann, Herman- CAO

Digester Vol. 20 March 1944
"The presence of Mrs. Herman Gann, wife of Sgt. Gann, was one of the bright spots of the (Beaver Club) reunion. Mrs. Gann clicked with the local contingent."

November 1944 Herman Gann: *"Am pretty lucky. My wife presented me with a baby girl on 28th October."*

April 1945 Herman Gann: *"As I write this I am in quiet German village enjoying the Company's fags (cigarettes). My wife and I hope to see you all in Powell River at the Reunion."*

Grundle, Mildred - WAAF
Grundle, Jack - Corporal RCAF Overseas

Digester Vol. 18 April 1942
"Jack Grundle is at an Air Force camp in the north of Scotland."
September -"Jack Grundle came down from Scotland (for the 1942 London reunion)."

February 1944 "We have official confirmation on Jackie Grundle. His wife is LAW (Leading Air Woman) Mildred Grundle, and the picture we have shows Jack can pick 'em."

Digester Vol. 20, March 1944
(photo caption).
"Mrs. LAW (Leading Air Woman) Mildred Grundle and Jackie Grundle, just married overseas."
"And there is a chubby-faced Jack Grundle, who has beaten brother Bert to the draw and has come out well in the lottery. Jackie is the latest, but not the last of our boys to pick up a bit of old England."

May 1945 "And speaking of British brides. Must say thus far our lads have done some slick picking. All the girls seem to like Powell River and are settling down fine. Jack Grundle and Martin Naylor and families out shopping is quite a sight."

Vol. 21, June 1945 "Two other Powell River brothers, Bert and Jack Grundle, have returned after three years overseas; Jack in France with the RCAF, and Bert in the Mediterranean with the Radar Division of the Air Force."

Hill, Iris - ATS
Hill, Norman - Sergeant CAO

Digester Vol. 16, January 1940
"Norm writes from England, in describing his voyage across the Atlantic, Norm says:
"I can't tell you what boat we were on – but it was a big liner and we were all comfortable. We were escorted by British warships."

Digester Vol. 17, April 1940
"Norm writes he has had extensive instruction in musketry, Bren gun and anti-tank rifles with a good amount of squad drill, PT and bayonet fighting, with the odd fatigue thrown in. In his concluding paragraph he writes:

"Believe me, I am proud to be both a Canadian and to be here to do my share, however small it may be."

Digester Vol. 16, September 1940
"The first "casualty" in the ranks of Powell River's fighting forces is reported from England. Norm Hill, a well-known local athlete with Canadian First Division in England, writes that he has recently taken time off to get married. His bride is an English girl.
Norm states the troops have experienced numerous air raids. He writes: *"I had the good fortune to see the RAF in action against the Hun recently, and these boys are sure on the job. I wouldn't have missed the show for anything. We saw several Huns plummet out of the skies, and it was a grand sight. Put your money on the RAF, and put it on the nose."*

Digester Vol. 17, April 1941
Norm writes: *"For a long time I have billeted with Sir Ernest and Lady Benn. Recently a girl came here to work who had an uncle in Powell River. The uncle is Alfred Sherwood (a member of the electricians' union). Small world, isn't it?"*

April 1943 *"Have just finished the NCO course and am hoping my promotion to corporal may come through shortly. My wife is looking forward to coming out to Canada. The cigarettes arrived out of the blue yesterday, and were a real treat. Please thank the Company on my behalf."*

August 1944 *"Received 600 cigarettes and a copy of the Digester and they were certainly appreciated. My wife and I took part in a recent sports meet. I won the standing broad jump, 9ft. 2 inches, and my wife and I won the three-legged race."*

June 1945 *"About 15 have been discharged in the past month. These include --- Norm Hill."*

Jack marries Scottish Sweetheart from WWI

Jack, Mrs. Dave
Jack, Dave - CEF veteran of WWI, WWII – CSM, CAO

Digester Vol. 17, 1941
"Another former employee, Dave Jack, machine room, has joined the benedicts. Dave, on one of his furloughs, went north to Scotland, and married an old schoolgirl sweetheart."

Digester Vol. 17, November 1941
"And from the old First Division in England comes word that Dave Jack, of the Machine Room, is now a full-fledged Sergeant."

Digester Vol. 19, April 1943 story with photo
"Sgt. Dave Jack was overseas with a Highland regiment in the last war. In those active days he made the acquaintance of and walked out with a charming Scots lassie. After the war, Dave came to Canada – and came alone. For a variety of reasons he decided to seek fame and fortune before sending for the lassie of his choice. Came the depression years and there was not much fame and fortune for anyone. But, Dave remained single. And when the present war broke out he was one of the first to leave Powell River. He went overseas with the Seaforths in 1939, and went on leave to Scotland – and found his old sweetheart like himself, still single and just waiting for Dave."

Digester Vol. 19, October 1943 – Company Sergeant Major Dave Jack of the Seaforths didn't go to Sicily with his outfit.
Dave Jack writes: *"Just before the outfit left for Sicily, they lined us up and hauled all of us old crocks out and told us we were staying behind. Believe me, it was tough seeing that bunch go and not being able to sail with them. Guess it looks like England for us --- until the going gets really tough and the SOS goes out for the "old reliables".*

June 1945
"A pretty fair summer all around. Willingdon beach well crowded in June and July. Nice a lot of the "old" soldiers like Dave Jack --- hanging around the old swimming hole regularly."

Jacobs, Mrs. Dick
Jacobs, R.A. (Dick) - Private CAO

Digester Vol. 17, December 1941
"Two more chips of the same block are "Papa" Jimmie Jacobs, with the Canadian Scottish in Victoria, and son Dick in England with the first battalion of the same regiment."

July 1944
"We heard stout reports of good work by Dicky Jacob with the Scottish in Normandy. Several of the fellows comment on Dicky's skill as a forager and morale builder.
Dick Jacobs is still with us and he has done a grand job ever since D-Day in one of the hardest jobs of all, stretcher bearers. They were magnificent."

January 1945
"Well Dickie Jacobs has finally been hooked. Married a lass from Notts, and quite chirpy about it."

Dickie Jacobs: *"I suppose you are aware of the fact that I finally went off the deep end and got myself hitched to a lass from Nott, and I'm warning all wolves to keep away from my door when I get back to Powell River because I'm bringing a 25lb with me."*

June 1945 letter from Russ Lambert
"Quite a few P.R. boys here, including Dick Jacobs. Dick was on the Scottish team which won top honours in the Third Division."

July 1946 D-Day
"Hitting the beaches in that first unstoppable assault with the Scottish was Dickie Jacobs."

Leese, Mrs. R.V.
Leese, R.V. (Dick) - Sergeant RAF/RCAF Overseas

June 1944
"And Dick Leese, who left us to join the RAF before the war, has married an English girl."

Dick Leese letter from S. Wales: *"Just a few lines in appreciation of the Monthly Newsletter. I surely do enjoy it. Somehow it makes Powell River seem about one of the best places on earth, and many are the times I've wished I could get back. It has been my luck never to be able to get to the*

Reunions ---- there will probably be loud shouts from some of my friends when they learn I was married six months ago. Ran into Jack Carruthers and Walter Patrick about a year ago."

May 1945 Dick Leese letter: *"This is to thank you for the continued steady arrival of the weekly Powell River News. The News is still just as interesting as ever and affords quite a lot of enjoyment. But reading between the lines Powell River seems to have changed greatly in the last eight years. The success of my transfer (to the RCAF) was very gratifying."*

Wrigley's Directory: R.V. Leese lived at 371 Maple Street, Powell River Townsite, from 1946-48; moved to 1010 Westview Rd, Westview in 1949 and lived there until 1956.

Long, Margaret
Long, Harold - CQMS CAO

Digester Vol. 18 - September 1942
"At Dieppe, the Powell River Casualty list was practically nil. Sgt. Long of Stillwater was wounded but arrived safely in England."

Powell River News clipping January 1945
"Another old friend called on us ----- CQMS Harold Long, repatriated as a result of wounds suffered at Dieppe and Falaise. Harold has been discharged."

Digester Vol. 21 – February 1945
"CQMS Harold Long has been recently discharged following severe wounds suffered in action. Harold Long, wounded at Dieppe and again at Falaise, was discharged on Feb. 5. He was with the South Saskatchewan Regiment, of which Col. Merriett, VC, was Officer Commanding."

Digester Vol. 21 – June 1945
"In the months ahead scores, perhaps hundreds, of our lads will be home or on their way. With them will be their brides from all corners of the United Kingdom --- and to them especially we in Powell River extend a hearty welcome. At this time we wish to extend best wishes to Mrs. Harold Long, Mrs. Martin Naylor ...."

November 1941 Margaret Long (Kemp) and Harold Long CAO married 17th November 1941
at St. Mary's Cathedral, Edinburgh. They spent their honeymoon in Stirling, Scotland. Photo:
Margaret Long collection

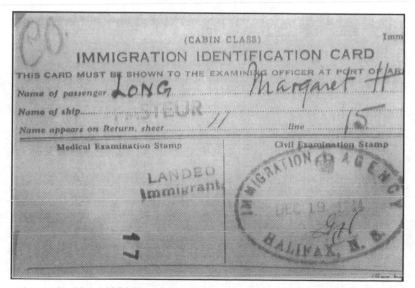

December 19, 1944 WWII war bride Margaret Long's immigration ID card.
Margaret Long sailed on the Pasteur to Canada.
Margaret Long collection

*Margaret Long's invitation to Buckingham Palace for the
Investiture of Canadian soldiers October 27, 1942.
Margaret Long collection*

*WWII Investiture of Canadian soldiers (including Harold Long CAO)
by King George VI and Queen Elizabeth.
Margaret Long collection*

Margaret Long WWII war bride

Lang Bay Lad Marries Scottish Lassie

A reception was held by the Lang Bay, Douglas Bay and Stillwater communities for Mr. and Mrs. Harold Long on April 21st, 1945 at the Lang Bay school (2011 Lang Bay Community Hall). Harold Long was the first veteran to be discharged after being wounded twice.

Harold served with the South Saskatchewan Regiment at Dieppe and in Normandy, France. At Dieppe August 19, 1942 he suffered shrapnel wounds in the left hip, calf and knee when a German hand grenade exploded nearby, also a shoulder injury when clipped by a machine gun bullet. Due to his severe injuries he spent over a year in an English hospital before returning to his regiment.

Two months after the D-Day landings in Normandy (June 6, 1944), Harold was wounded near Caen, on August 19, 1944.

Harold Long: *"We had taken supplies up the line to advance troops, and on the way back to the base the Nazi planes blew up a bridge just ahead of us. As I jumped out of the truck I was hit by bomb shrapnel on my right leg and right arm."*

Harold was one of three brothers who fought in WWII. Harold and Ken were in the Army, while Jack served with the Air Force.

At the reception, Mr. and Mrs. Harold Long were presented with a number of gifts including a Community Plate flatware at the Lang Bay School.

Powell River News 1945
"The school was tastefully decorated with spring flowers, and the honoured couple were seated at the table under a large true lovers' knot.

Hostess duties for the evening were carried out very efficiently by Mrs. David Dickson and Mrs. Gordon Cornell. The bride's cake – a masterpiece of its kind was created and contributed by Mr. Cornell. A thoroughly enjoyable supper was served, thanks to the supplies contributed by other good people of the district.

Dancing to music played by Mr. Dick Dulmage, Eddie McKay and others followed the supper.

Mr. and Mrs. Long have taken up residence in Cranberry."

After living in a house near King's Collision in Cranberry, the couple moved to a Powell River Company house in the Powell River Townsite on Willow Street. They were later able to buy it when the company sold off the Townsite houses in 1955. Harold worked for the Powell River Company until his early death of a sudden heart attack in 1968.

Harold, and his Scottish bride Margaret, loved to dance. They danced at the Square Dancing Club, Round Dancing Club and the Old Time Dancing Club.

Harold and Margaret had two children, Doug and Leslie. Leslie was a surprise child to the couple, she was born 10 years after the birth of Doug, and Margaret initially thought she had the flu! On the birth of Leslie, Margaret remarked,

"See, here is my little flu ----- isn't she beautiful!"

Harold had first met Margaret when he was on leave in Edinburgh, Scotland. They fell in love, and were married on the 17th November 1941 at St. Mary's Cathedral, Edinburgh. They spent their honeymoon at Stirling, Scotland.

Margaret Long (Kemp)

Margaret Kemp was born in Edinburgh, Scotland in 1915, one year after the end of the Great War. She had a happy childhood with foster parents who loved and educated her. Her foster father taught her to read, and gave her a love of the arts which she had all her life.

As a teenager she worked in the family fish & chip & sweet shop. At the age of 16 she was working in the office of a construction company.

During WWII Margaret was living in the London area where she first worked in the offices of the London Transit Authority, and later in the offices at Leavesden Aerodome. In 1939 the Ministry of Defence owned Leavesden Aerodome; it was an important site for the manufacture of Mosquito and Halifax aircraft. The Aerodome was north of Watford and 18 miles northwest of Central London.

Margaret lived through the blitz in London. Her daughter Leslie recalls the story her mother told her on the scary occasion when she was in a beauty shop when the German bombers came over:

"Mother was all wired up with curlers when the air raid sirens went off. Everyone was supposed to head for the shelters, however, Mother told the hair dresser to go and leave her there alone in the parlour. She figured out if the hair dresser spent time removing all the curlers the shop would either have been bombed or the raid would be over. The hair dresser came back after the all clear, fortunately the shop had not been bombed, and Mother was still there with her hair in curlers!"

Margaret fell in love with a Canadian soldier, Howard Long. In 1941 Howard proposed to her on the banks of Loch Lomond. In November of the same year they were married in Edinburgh.

Harold was wounded at Dieppe, and on October 27, 1942 Margaret accompanied Harold to Buckingham Palace for the investiture of the men at Dieppe by King George VI and Queen Elizabeth.

From an old Vancouver newspaper cutting dated December 16, 1942:

City Hero's Wife Attends Investiture in Buckingham

"… some Canadian women were able to be present at Buckingham Palace for the investiture of the men at Dieppe. It was a very moving ceremony, because it was the first in which Canadians were in the majority, and a fine-looking bunch of men they were. Among those lucky enough to have his own kith and kin to see his triumph was Sgt. H. Long, of Vancouver, whose wife accompanied him to the Palace."

On 16th July 1943 Margaret was present at the Presentation of Colours to the Royal Regiment of Canada, and the South Saskatchewan Regiment by the King and Queen.

On the 25th August 1944 Margaret received a telegram c/o National Bank of Scotland, Tollcross, Edinburgh, informing her that her husband Harold Long had been wounded on the 20th August 1944 during the Allied invasion of France. This was the second time Harold had been wounded, the first time at Dieppe. Because of the severity of the wounds, Harold was one of the first Canadian veterans to be discharged from the Canadian Army and sent back to Canada.

In December 1944 Margaret Long started her journey to Canada as a war bride on the *Pasteur*, one of a number of ships used to transport small groups of war brides. Leslie recalls her mother describing the ship as "a rickety old tub". Margaret was not homesick on the voyage because she looked at the trip to Canada as a great adventure; however she was seasick and spent most of the Atlantic voyage in her berth. The seasickness stopped when Margaret was given her first drink of Coca Cola. On arrival in Halifax the war brides were told that a submarine had been following them on the crossing. The Immigration Agency stamped her immigration I.D. card LANDED immigrant on December 19, 1944.

Margaret travelled with her two suitcases on the Canadian National Railway from Halifax to Vancouver with a tourist sleeping car ticket. She had a stopover at Toronto to see the mother of a childhood friend. Margaret recalled her memory of Toronto as "being cold". From Toronto she continued her travel to Vancouver with a change of train at Winnipeg. Her travel ended with a boat ride from Vancouver to Lang Bay, arriving at the home of her mother-in-law Mrs. Jeanne Kennedy.

In April of 1945 Margaret and Harold were feted by family and friends at the Lang Bay school. It was here that the nuptials of a local hero, and his new bride were celebrated.

Margaret enjoyed her new life in Canada. She quickly became involved in community life, a leader of the Cranberry Guides company from 1946-8. Besides dancing, Margaret and Harold were lawn bowlers and alley bowlers at Cranberry bowling alley. Margaret loved to crochet and paint. She enjoyed singing, whistling tunes, and letter writing.

In 1965 Harold gave Margaret a choice, a return ticket to Britain to see family and friends in Scotland or an engagement ring! Margaret chose the trip to Scotland.

In 1968 Margaret lost the love of her life, Harold, after a fatal heart attack. After selling the house on Willow Street, Margaret moved with Leslie to Mooseheart, Illinois. Soon she was homesick for family and friends in Powell River, so moved back to the Powell River Townsite. Margaret found work at the Rodmay Hotel, and later in the Powell River Company offices.

In 1976 Margaret moved to Grief Point, Westview and rented the basement of a house from her friend Dorothy Brant, another war bride.

Memories of Margaret Long:
"She was full of life, curious, very wise, sometimes patient — sometimes not, had a stubborn streak, enjoyed telling stories, loved her garden, watched birds, studied people and nature."

Maple (Brand), Elizabeth - WRNS
Maple, James - PO RCN

Digester Vol. 15 – September 1939
"Jimmy Maple, son of Ernie Maple of the barker mill, has seen plenty of active service with the Canadian navy. Jimmy has been on convoy duty, anti-submarine work, took part in the evacuation of Brest."

Digester Vol. 17 – March 1941 Jimmy Maple letter
"I am glad to be back in Canada to see the folks, but I want to go back to England when my leave is over. When you see what the people are facing over there and how they are facing it, you just want to go back and finish the job. All the fellows feel the same way."

Digester Vol. 18 – September 1942
"He (Jimmy Maple) was at Brest for the evacuation; his ship escorted the *Illustrious* to Gibraltar; he was aboard the *Skeena* when that little ship beat off one of the heaviest wolf pack assaults of the war; he has been dive-bombed and shelled by the enemy."

March 1944
"The first name out of the hat this month is PO Jimmy Maple RCN, in the service since 1938. Jimmy married Miss Elizabeth Brand, WRNS London on March 22nd."

June 1944 Jimmy Maple letter
"Thanks again for the News Letter, which I assure you is most welcome to us all.... Thanks for mention of my marriage to a Scots lassie."

Matheson, Toki - WWII war bride from Holland
Matheson, Rod - Sergeant CAO

Frances Matheson (sister-in-law) 2011
"Yes, my brother-in-law was Rod Matheson. His wife Toki was a war bride from Holland. After the war, Rod worked in the Rodmay Hotel, Powell River, as a bartender. He was a close friend of Bat MacIntyre. Rod and Toki had three children: Judy, Margo and Bruce. The family moved to Kamloops in the '60s. I lost touch with them over the years."

Digester Vol. 17 – May 1941
"Sergeant Bat MacIntyre and Gunner Rod Matheson of the Light Anti-Aircraft unit arrived safely in England after an uneventful voyage."

Digester Vol. 18 – February 1942

"Heading the list (of brother combinations) are the three husky Matheson boys. Overseas, with the 16th Light Anti-Aircraft Battery is Rod Matheson; and somewhere in England in the 9th Armored Regiment is brother C.D. Matheson. The third of the trio, N.P. Matheson, is with the Air Force in an eastern Canadian camp."

Digester Vol. 18 – September 1942

"At Dieppe Sergt. Rod Matheson was in the attacking force…."

July 1944 "Sgt. Rod Matheson is being invalided home."

August 1944 "Latest advices indicate that Sgt. Rod Matheson is coming along fine and will probably remain in England."

April 1945 "Glad to report that Rod Matheson is in the "pink" again and stamping around the English countryside demanding to be sent back to his old unit."

July 1946 (re: Dieppe) "Rod Matheson, with the 16th "Light Acks" faced enemy air attacks and sniper's bullets for over six hours."

Menzies, Mrs. Gordon
Menzies, Gordon - Lance Corporal CAO

August 1943 "Gordon Menzie, with the Tank Transporters, has grabbed his first hook."

Gordon Menzies: *"Please thank the P.R. Company for the 600 cigarettes which I received after a leave in Scotland. … I had a look around Burn's monument. From all account he must have been quite a lad in his day. Also saw the house in which I was born."*

February 1945   "Claude Borden and Gordie Menzies still continue to meet for the odd jam session up in Holland."

May 1945   "And word just through that Gord. Menzies has taken time off to grab an English bride for the journey back home. **Gord joins the almost 100-odd locals that have found their fate (marriage) in the United Kingdom.**

Joseph (Joe) Morrissey enlisted in the Canadian Army on 4th December, 1941.
He was part of the Canadian Forestry Corps in Scotland
where he continued his trade as shoemaker.
Joe met a pretty Scottish lass, Margaret Munro at a local dance.
They fell in love, and married in Scotland.
Photo: John Morrissey collection

The Morrissey family, Powell River, B.C. 1948
Margaret Morrissey holding baby Joseph/Joe Morrissey CAO with
Margaret Morrissey/John Morrissey standing at rear.
Photo: John Morrissey collection

(CABIN CLASS)

IMMIGRATION IDENTIFICATION CARD

ARD MUST BE SHOWN TO THE EXAMINING OFFICER AT PORT OF ARRIVAL

f passenger   MORRISSEY,   Margaret I.S.,

f ship   QUEEN MARY

ppears on Return, sheet   45   line   15

Medical Examination Stamp

LANDED
immigrant.

IMMIGRATION CANADA
JUL 4 1945
HALIFAX, N.S.
WIS

Margaret Morrissey's immigration ID card.
Mrs. Morrissey with her children John and baby Theresa,
travelled on the Queen Mary to Canada, arriving in Halifax July 4, 1946.
John Morrissey collection

1940s postcard of the Queen Mary.
Private collection

Morrissey, Margaret (Munro) - WWII war bride from Scotland
Morrissey, Joe - CAO Canadian Forestry Corps

Digester Vol. 29 – March 1944 List of Marriages: "Have you forgotten … Joe Morrissey?"

Morrissey Family of Wildwood, B.C.

William Francis Morrissey (1889-1978) married Mary Phoebe Lemieux (1884-1927) in Powell River on December 2, 1917. William worked for the Powell River Company. William owned property in Wildwood, from the Lund Highway, back to the Wildwood school.

Joseph (Joe) Richard Morrissey (1918-1976), born in Powell River, was the eldest child of William and Mary Morrissey. He was by trade a shoemaker, and he rented a shop behind Hanson's store (Wildwood pub) where he repaired shoes.

Joe enlisted in the Canadian Army on 4th December 1941; he wrote that his trades were shoe repairer, and logger. Joe went overseas in 1942, and was part of the Canadian Forestry Corps in Scotland, stationed at Bonnerbridge. Joe continued with his trade as a shoemaker, this time repairing shoes for the Canadian Army. Joe encountered three Powell River boys in the Forestry Corps: Archie MacKenzie, Stan Hollingshead and Johnny Aldrich.

Joe Morrissey met a pretty Scottish lass, Margaret Munro at a local dance; they fell in love, and married.

Margaret Munro (Gunn)

Margaret was born in Torachilty, Contin, Ross, Cromarty, Scotland in 1920. Her father Alexander Munro was a woodworker. Margaret grew up in rural hamlet, with just a scattering of houses. There was no pub or shop in the village. For a period of time, Margaret worked in a sawmill, making railroad ties.

Margaret and her Canadian soldier, Joe Morrissey, were married on the 12th July 1944 at Alness in Scotland, according to the Church of Scotland Forms. Joe went AWOL to attend his own wedding! After arriving in Powell River, B.C., Margaret received instruction from the Catholic Church so she could marry Joe in a Catholic ceremony.

Margaret had a son, John Gunn Munro, born in 1938. John was adopted by his step-father Joe Morrissey; the papers could not be found in later years, so John had a change of name registered in Scotland.

Margaret and Joe Morrissey had a daughter, Theresa Margaret Morrissey, born in Ardgay, Ross-shire. The family lived at Rowan Tree Cottage, Church Street, Ardgay.

Five more children were born in Canada: Joseph William, Mary Elisabeth, William Francis, Edward Thomas, and Cindy Marie.

Joe was shipped back to Canada for medical care. He had a serious case of peptic ulcers and was taken from the train on a stretcher, directly to the Veteran's hospital in Shaughnessy, B.C.

Margaret and the two children, John and baby Theresa, sailed to Canada on the *Queen Mary* which was outfitted as a war bride ship. It had been a troop ship during the war. They left their cottage at Ardgay in style, by taxi! They travelled to Southampton by train. According to their immigration ID cards they arrived as landed immigrants at Pier 21, Halifax, Nova Scotia on July 4, 1946. Their journey across the Atlantic took four-and-a-half days while the journey across Canada took five days. The last part of the journey was from Vancouver to Powell River, by the *Princess Mary*.

John Morrissey (age 73) October 2011

"I was just 7 years old when we left Southampton on the Queen Mary. For me going to Canada was an exciting adventure. I had never been on a boat… and certainly not a big boat, and the Queen Mary was big! I was the happiest kid you could have ever met.

There was a huge crowd to see the Queen Mary off on her voyage across the Atlantic. We were told not to go to the side of the deck, where we boarded, and throw anything over — there was some concern it would cause the ship to shift to one side with so many people on board!

It was exciting to explore the Queen Mary. The three of us, my mother and my baby sister Theresa, had our own cabin. It was amazing — there was electricity, and water which came out of a tap! We had lived in a cottage with well water, and oil lamps. The first thing I did was to stick a pair of scissors into an electrical socket — I not only did it once, but twice! Of course I got a shock, both times.

I was in and out of the bathtub two or three times a day, it was great to turn the taps on, and the water just whooshed out. In Scotland we bathed in a metal tub, in the kitchen, once a week.

The food was great – couldn't believe it! Our family was the only one in the dining room, everyone else was seasick.

When the Queen Mary arrived at Southampton, tugs pushed her into place at the dock. I remember leaning over the side of the boat. I was so excited I threw my stamp album over the side of the boat, and spat overboard at the crowd below – after all I was just a kid!

On the train we were in a coach, and the bunks folded out at night. I was in a top bunk. We had a black car attendant, he was gentle with the kids, he became one of the family. Everyone in our coach took up a collection for him at the end of the journey.

There was a special coach attached to our train – it could have been for the Governor General. I remember someone allowed me to use the bathroom in it.

We sailed on the Princess Mary to Powell River.

My mother loved Powell River, as soon as she saw it. She had no difficulty in adjusting. Our hamlet in Scotland was isolated with no shops. Powell River was like heaven with great shops, and a cinema!

My father, after working at his old trade as a shoemaker for a short time, went to work for the Powell River Company. I remember when I first attended school, the other kids made fun of me because of my Scottish accent.

My mother had no regrets at leaving Scotland. She went back a couple of times to the "old country" to see friends and family.

I went back, for the first time, in 2008. I could remember exactly where I lived. Sixty-two years had passed since I left Scotland."

Naylor (Cadman), Sandra - WAAF
Naylor, Martin - Flying Officer RCAF Overseas

Digester Vol. 17 – February 1941
"During the last month several well-known local boys have been called to service or notified to report in the near future. These include Martin Naylor, already in the east (Canada). **All are scheduled for the Air Force, which brings Powell River's contingent in that vital sphere to 60 members.**"

Digester Vol. 17 – August 1941 "Of special interest is a recent letter from Martin Naylor, popular field and track star. Martin is now stationed at the Sea Island School, and states he just finished a flight in the "Spirit of Powell River", the trainer plane donated to the government by Powell River residents last year." I had my fingers crossed when I climbed into that plane. I couldn't let the Powell River gang down and she landed as slick as a whistle".

Digester Vol. 18 – June 1942
"Martin Naylor is flying with regular RCAF fighters in Britain."

Digester Vol. 18 – August 1942
"… another Powell River boy crashed the headlines. Sergeant Pilot Martin Naylor, in a "Beaufighter" had been shot down off the English coast, but Martin and his gunner, with five seconds to escape from the plane before it sank, dived overboard and were picked up within minutes and rushed to hospital. Twenty-four hours later, Martin led his squadron to victory in a RCAF track meet. Forty-eight hours later, he was in London to meet the Powell River boys at the Beaver Club reunion."

Digester Vol. 18 – September 1942 Powell River Reunion, London.
"Sgt. Pilot Martin Naylor arrived late in the afternoon (for the 1942 Powell River reunion), **apologizing because he had spent the night in a hospital after being shot down over the channel the night before**."

November 1944
"And from FO Martin Naylor a flash that he married Miss Sandra Cadman on October 23. Martin picked himself a bride from the WAAF's and we are looking forward to seeing her soon."

January 1945
"Flying Officers Harry Cooper and Martin Naylor arrived in Powell River together around the middle of January. Both are expecting discharges within the next few weeks, and will return to Powell River."

February 1945
"We expect – Martin Naylor back in the plant any day – he is awaiting discharge."

Digester Vol. 21 – February 1945
"In January three more are returning (including) – Flying Officer Martin Naylor, who flew Beaufighters, and Spitfires, for over two years over France, Belgium and Holland and who, like Bill Bell, returns with a bit of Old England in the presence of Mrs. Martin Naylor.

March 1945 "Martin Naylor is now officially discharged… Caught a glimpse of Martin's bride and he can still pick the winners."

"And speaking about British brides. Must say our lads have done some slick picking. All the girls seem to like Powell River. (Jack Grundle and Martin Naylor and families out shopping is quite a sight.)"

"Martin Naylor … back in the office and settling down to the old grind. Martin and his bride are living in the 1000 block, Ocean View (Joe Sweeney's old place) and Martin in the backyard is something worth seeing."

July 1945 "On D-Day, June 6, 1944, Martin Naylor was in that great air armada that protected the landing."

O Neil (Milner), Julie - ATS
O Neil, Frank - LAC RCAF Overseas

April 1943 letter from Frank: *"Both Tom Nutchy, and I received the cigarettes O.K., although mine were weeks after Tom's. Also received the Powell River News which the Company is so kindly sending. The English have me baffled to what goes into their cigarettes. They have one particular brand called Park Avenue, which recalls Hyde Park, and when you think of Hyde Park, you think of Rotten Row.*

The log book of our squadron reads like a Cook's Tour of Germany, Italy and France – but I still don't see how a country like England can be so waterlogged and still float. Harry Freeman and I are holding a reunion here this week. Harry was with Bill Bell before Bill left for the Middle East."

March 1944 Reunion film "We showed them on Sunday, March 5 and over 1,100 people came out – Frank O Neil's mother was there."

July 1944 "And here's one for the dopesters. LAC Frank "Scoop" O Neil has got himself engaged and will be bringing back a little of Old England with him."

December 1944 "And here's BIG NEWS, "SCOOP" had been SCOOPED. On January 1, 1945, that once gay buck around town, that inquiring reporter, LAC Frank O Neil, stood timidly at the alter to await the arrival of his bride, L/Cpl. Julie J. Milner, ATS, of West Acton, England. When the news reached Powell River, a bunch of lads gathered round the Bank of Commerce and sang "*Goodbye Boys*".

*17th November 1944 Wedding of Joan Alice Patrick (Wilson) and Sgt Walter Patrick CAO
at Chichester Registry Office, England. Walter met Joan when she was working
for the Women's Timber Corps.
Photo: Joan Patrick collection*

*1948 Cranberry Village, Powell River, B.C.
Joan Patrick with baby Laura Patrick
Photo: Joan Patrick collection*

Mark and Laura Patrick 1958 studio photo Townsite, Powell River
Left corner: Joan Wilson school photo age 15
Right: Joan Wilson 1944—showing off her first pair of nylons.
Photo: Joan Patrick (Wilson) collection

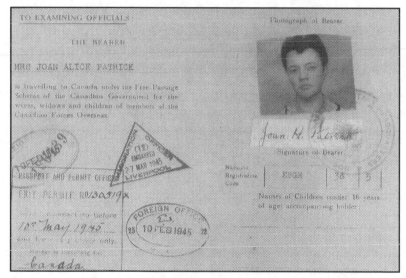

Joan Patrick's exit permit stamped 10th February 1945.
The card states that Joan was travelling to Canada under the
Free Passage Scheme of the Canadian Government for the wives, widows and
children of members of the Canadian Forces Overseas.
Joan Patrick collection

Patrick (Wilson), Joan – Women's Timber Corps
Patrick, Walter Jnr. - Corporal RCAF Overseas

Digester Vol. 16 – October 1940 "Jack Redhead and Walter Patrick are with the Air Force at St. Thomas, Ontario."

April 1943 Walter Patrick letter: *"Thanks again for the cigarettes. They sure are good after some of the English brands we have sampled. Haven't done much in the way of soccer or basketball over here, but now that Harold Foster and George Rennie are here, we might get together."*

December 1944 "… expecting immediate discharge. Corp. Walter Patrick recently returned from overseas."

Joan Alice Patrick (Wilson) 1926-1980   Douglas Bay WWII War Bride

The Patricks of Douglas Bay

The Patricks are a well-known Douglas Bay family. They were originally from Barrow-in-Furness, England, and crossed the Atlantic to Canada in February 1911, docking at Halifax – sailing just two months before the *Titanic* went down.

Walter Patrick Sr., his wife Hannah Patrick (Parks), and their two daughters Madge Patrick (MacGillivray) and Nora Patrick (McQuarrie), came to the Powell River Townsite in March 1911. Their two sons Walter Patrick Jr. and Syd Patrick were born in the Townsite. Walter Jr. was born on December 25, 1912 in Dr. Henderson's tent hospital. The family lived on Cedar Street, Powell River Company Townsite. The Patricks owned recreational property from the 1920s in Douglas Bay; in the early 1940s, they moved there permanently.

Walter Patrick Sr. worked for the Powell River Company; however, he lost his job in the big political purge of the early 1930s. Walter Jr. and Syd Patrick went to work for the Powell River Company in the late 1930s, after the mill was unionized. Walter Patrick Jr. was an apprentice papermaker, and Syd an apprentice electrician.

Joan Wilson - Women's Timber Corps

Joan's father, John McKenzie Wilson (known as Mac), was in the regular British Army before the war. He had a five-year tour of duty in India. During WWII he saw action in Africa and Italy. Later, his unit was under the command of General Montgomery in Germany, liberating concentration camps.

Joan's mother was a bar maid. Joan was mainly brought up by her maternal grandparents, Mr. and Mrs. William Moody. William had been a Royal Navy cook for 22 years before he retired. He served on the HMS *Iron Duke*. This famous battleship was the flagship of the Grand Fleet in WWI, and fought in the Battle of Jutland 31st May 1916, inflicting damage on the German battleship SMS *Konig*.

The family lived in Portsmouth. The city was very badly bombed during WWII. On one bombing raid, Joan was buried with other school children, and had to be dug out. On another bombing raid the house they lived in took a direct hit. They lost everything, and they stood on the street with only the clothes on their back. The authorities sent them to live in the country. All their family photographs were lost in the bombing raid.

The family quickly adapted to country living. The boys, to supplement their rations, poached rabbits and pheasants!

During WWII Joan was one of 4,900 women in Britain who joined the Women's Timber Corps, known as the "Timber Jills" (men were called timber jacks). They attended training camps, and were taught basic forestry practices, such as: how to handle an axe, use a saw, drive a forestry vehicle, and how to handle horses. They were shown how to fell trees for pit props, railway sleepers, telegraph poles, and wooden crosses for graves. The distinctive badge of the Timber Corps women shows a fir tree and a Royal crown.

Corporal Walter Patrick Jr. RCAF Overseas was stationed as a mechanic at Croydon Airport. He met Joan Wilson, sitting outside a pub. He discovered she was in the WTC and was amazed that the young woman he was talking to had a job of cutting down trees! They continued to meet, fell in love, and were married on the 17th November 1944 at the Chichester Registry Office. Walter was 31 years of age, and Joan 18 when they married. Because of her age, Joan had to get a letter of permission from her mother in order to get married (her father was fighting overseas). Clothing for the bride was difficult to obtain in wartime Britain; Madge MacGillivray (Patrick) from Powell River, sent the bride underwear as a wedding present!

On returning to Canada, Walter Jr. worked in the Powell River Company mill garage. Joan came out to Canada with other war brides on a war bride ship in 1946. She was terrified of coming to Canada, as her only knowledge of Canada was obtained through movies showing cowboys and Indians.

Her memories of travelling by train across Canada included diapers (nappies) hung in every coach and Red Cross workers, at every stop along the way, helping the war brides and their children. The Prairies were endless, and some war brides were put off in isolated spots, with only a buggy and horse waiting to take them to their new home.

Walter had rented one of the new Powell River Company duplexes on Willow Avenue (called Stork's Alley) in the Powell River Townsite, later they moved to Westview Village.

On arriving in Canada, Joan was undernourished. During the war, she had given a portion of her rations to her younger brother, John. Every day, when she lived in the Townsite, she went down to the Company store for a very special treat – an ice cream sundae. Ice cream was generally not available in Britain during the war. Joan could never sleep in a bedroom with the door closed, due to her childhood experiences of being bombed.

The Patrick family members were very good to Joan. She quickly jumped wholeheartedly into west coast life. Walter and Joan had three children: Laura, Mark and Lester. They enjoyed wonderful summers in Douglas Bay on the Patrick family property. Joan loved the outdoor life: swimming, fishing and camping.

Walter had promised Joan that within five years of coming to Canada he would pay her fare for a visit to Britain. Joan, with a two-year-old Laura, visited her family in 1950. After this visit Joan was able to settle in Canada.

Joan's daughter Laura lives on the old Patrick property in Douglas Bay.

Peebles, Evelyn (divorced 1950s/remarried Joe Skorey RCN)
Peebles, William (Bill) - A/Corporal CAO

March 1944 "… and W.E. Peebles gets his firsts leg up with a lance corporal hook."

Bill Peebles letter: *"Thanks for the cigarettes you have sent me and have just received word that another 1600 are on the way. Have seen Naples and Pompei and a lot more. Met a fellow by the name of Hank who came from P.R. the same time as us in 1940."*

May 1944   "A/Corp Peebles is among recent arrivals in Italy."
Bill Peebles married Evelyn, an English girl while overseas. They lived in the Veteran's Village, Cranberry, Powell River. They divorced in the 1950s. Later, Evelyn married Joe Skorey, RCN.

Joe Skorey RCN
December 1944 "Discharged too …Joe Skorey back in the Machine Room."

Pelly, Mrs. Jack
Pelly, Jack - Sergeant CAO

April 1943 "Corporal Jack Pelly, Canadian Scottish overseas, has taken an English bride."

July 1944 "Jack Pelly …wounded on the opening day of the assault (D-Day) and is in hospital in England."

Razzo, Mrs. Paul
Razzo, Paul - Private CAO Timber Corps

April 1943 Paul – *"Received your gift of cigarettes OK and they were very much appreciated. All the Powell River boys in this unit are in good health. We haven't a very big outfit, but we cut from 20-25 thousand a day. This is small stuff to the Powell River crowd, but not bad for over here."*

Digester Vol. 29 – March 1944 (from a list of those who have married) "Have you forgotten … Paul Razzo?"

March 1944 "Paul Razzo is out of hospital and back again at the job depleting Scotland's timber reserves. Paul runs a caterpillar along with brother George…"

*Wedding day—Eddie Riley and Dorothy (Dot) Riley Wilson 1942
Wakefield, Yorkshire, England.
Eddie and Dot Wilson were high school sweethearts in Powell River, B.C.
before the Wilson family returned permanently to England in 1933.
Due to WWII Eddie and Dot met again.
Photo: Riley collection*

*1944 Cedar St, Powell River Townsite.
Dot Riley and baby Robert (Bob) Riley age 4 months.
December 1944 Eddie was able to obtain leave from the Canadian Navy
to see his son for the first time.
Photo: Riley collection*

1948 Dot Riley and children with 1938 Chevy car, Powell River, B.C.
Photo: Riley collection

1949 Wedding of Ken Wilson and Joan Christian (granddaughter of Emily Fishleigh,
Westview Village pioneer), Nanaimo, B.C. Back row: Robert Wilson, Ken Wilson,
Joan Wilson. Middle row: Dot Riley (Wilson)
Front row: Bob Riley (child), Agnes Wilson, and Allan Riley (child)
Photo: Joan Wilson collection

Left: The Riley children reading a comic, Powell River, B.C. 1950.
Chevy car in the background.
Right: 1950 Veterans' Village, Cranberry Village, Powell River, B.C.
New home of WWII veteran Eddie Riley RCN and family.
Photos: Riley collection

Informal wedding photo of Eddie Riley RCN and Dorothy Riley 1942,
Wakefield, Yorkshire, England.
Photo: Riley collection

Richards (Cleaver), Winnifred - WAAF
Richards, Stan - Flying Officer RCAF Overseas

May 1943 "Stan Richards came into the money with his promotion to WO."

July 1944 "… and WO Stanley Richards, who did some useful high jumping in his youthful days, leaped easily over another hurdle. Stan married Miss Winifred Clever at Haywards Heath on April 3 last."

September 1944 "And a last minute report that Stanley Richards has emulated Jack Maguire and picked up a well-earned and not before time, Pilot Officer's ring. (A belated, but welcome wedding gift, Stanley?)"

Digester Vol. 20 – September 1944
"Among our recent overseas bridegrooms is Pilot Officer Stan Richards, RCAF, son of Mr. and Mrs. Arthur Richards of Powell River. Stan was married to Miss Winifred Cleaver, WAAF, of Haywards Heath, on April 3 last. It was a service wedding. Both bride and groom are serving their country in uniform.

Riley (Wilson), Dorothy WWII bride from Yorkshire, England
Riley, Eddie – RCN

Robert Wilson Sr. (1868-1950) came directly from England to Powell River in 1922. He worked for the Powell River Company for 15 years, living at #3 Cedar Street. After age 70 his health declined, and he was cared for by his daughter Violet Wilson until she died in 1947. Robert Wilson Jr. and his wife Agnes cared for him prior to his death on January 1, 1950.

Robert Wilson Sr.'s obituary *Powell River News* January 5, 1950:
"Robert Wilson --- a resident of Powell River for more than 27 years, Robert "Dad" Wilson passed away in the Powell River General Hospital on New Year's Day in his 81ˢᵗ year. The late Mr. Wilson was born in Spalding, Lincolnshire, coming directly to Powell River and working some 15 years for the Powell River Company. His daughter Violet predeceased him two years ago. Surviving relatives --- Robert, Powell River."

Robert Wilson (Jr.) came to Canada in 1922, the same year as his father Robert Wilson (Sr.) and sister Vi Wilson. Robert Wilson (Jr.) was accompanied by his wife Agnes Wilson (Pickles) and infant daughter Dorothy (born 1917).

Robert and Agnes had previously lived in Wakefield, Yorkshire. Their son Ken was born in Powell River and was 5 years old when the family returned to Wakefield in 1933. Dorothy was 16 years of age when they returned to the "old country".

Robert Wilson (Jr.) like his father had worked for the Powell River Company; however, he lost his job with the Powell River Company in 1933-34 in a political purge when 350 millworkers were blacklisted. With no hope of getting a job in Canada, Robert Jr. returned with his family to the "old country".

Dorothy (Dot) Wilson had attended Henderson Elementary School, Powell River Townsite. **When she left Powell River, Dot left behind her school sweetheart, Eddie Riley**, who coincidently, shared the same birthdate.

Dorothy was a Powell River Company Paper Queen, and her dress and regalia are in the Powell River Museum. She had a reputation as a good athlete.

In 1939 Britain was at war and the Wilson family, like all British families, was involved in war work. Prior to the war Dorothy (Dot) had been working at Woolworths, however she was now assigned to work in a munitions factory as a "blue cap" girl, overseeing the loading of shells with live explosives. Ken worked at Bradley & Craven, which in peace time made machinery for making bricks; in wartime it was given an additional job, to assemble 135mm guns for small tanks. Robert was a truck driver, a dangerous job in wartime Britain with no street lighting, and the headlights partially covered.

Meanwhile, back in Canada, **with the outbreak of WWII, Dot's sweetheart Eddie Riley joined the RCN. While on leave he looked up his old school sweetheart Dot Wilson in Wakefield, Yorkshire.**

Ken Wilson remembers the first time he saw Eddie coming down the street to the Wilson residence; Eddie was wearing bell bottom trousers and carrying bananas!

Dot Wilson and Eddie Riley were married in Wakefield in 1942. Their wedding photo shows a radiant bride in an attractive dress, carrying a beautiful bouquet of roses. The groom wore his sailor uniform.

A pregnant Dorothy came over to Canada as a war bride in 1943 with a ship bringing English evacuees to Canada. Adult female supervisors were required to look after the children. Especially welcome were those going on a one-way trip to Canada – war brides!

Dot's destination was Powell River, B.C. Her grandfather Robert Wilson Sr. and Aunty Vi Wilson were still living in the Townsite. Also living in Powell River were her mother's sisters Beth Parkin (Pickle) and Frances Olson (Pickle). Both families, the Pickles and the Wilsons, were from Wakefield, Yorkshire.

The Powell River Company had promised Eddie his old job back in the machine room when the war was over. Eddie's family lived at Mowat Bay, Cranberry Village, Powell River. His brother Harry Riley was also in the Royal Canadian Navy.

Eddie was with the navy in the North Atlantic and the Mediterranean.

Powell River Company Newsletter (February 1943), excerpt from Eddie Riley's letter:
"Boy this is some country. Have spent a day around the bazaars (North African ports) and believe me, it was an experience. Things are cheap out here, particularly souvenirs. The Mediterranean is a perfect, beautiful blue and the weather is nice and warm. Have just had a swim in the "Med". The white terraced buildings are also lovely and some of the old Roman ruins are in a remarkable state of preservation. Received 1,000 cigarettes from the Company just before leaving and they are sure worth their weight in gold out here where all we get are Egyptian or Turkish flavors."

Dot boarded with an Italian lady, Mrs. Vaselli, in Cranberry. One month after arriving in Powell River, Robert (Bob) was born. In December 1944 Eddie was able to get leave from the navy to see his young son for the first time.

Eddie participated in the D-Day bombardment at Normandy. His observations are recorded in the Powell River *Digester*:

Digester Volume 21 November 1945:
"The other pictures, showing something of the shambles of Cherbourg after naval shelling and heavy bombing had passed by, were taken by PO Eddie Riley, now back in Powell River. Eddie states that the concrete emplacements, sheltering the Nazi defences of the port were blown sky high by the furious naval bombardment in the early hours of June 6, 1944. The Warspite, Rodney, Ramillies and other British and US battlewagons were on their targets that historic morning."

The Wilson family in Yorkshire decided to return to Canada in 1947 to be with their daughter Dorothy.

Ken Wilson, at age 18, recalls going to the Cunard shipping office in Leeds to make arrangements for the family to travel. They were able to get tickets for the *Aquitania*, a transatlantic liner that had seen better days. She had been converted into a hospital ship in WWI, and a troop ship in WWII. By WWII she was the only four funnel ship left in the world. After the war in 1950, she was scrapped in Scotland.

Ken Wilson (August 2011) describes his journey on the *Aquitania* in 1947:

"The Aquitania had been used as a troop ship during the war. It had not been converted back to a passenger ship. We were travelling "C" class and my father and I were sleeping with 10 other passengers in a canvas petitioned cubicle in the hold. My mother was in a cabin with other female passengers, her cabin was in the bow of the ship and it was pretty rough there, as they were directly hit by the waves.

Because we were in "C" class we were allowed up on "B" deck! The food was excellent, the first non-rationed food we had seen. Every day the same movie, "Cleopatra" was shown.

Apart from seeing the same film every day on the voyage there was no entertainment for the passengers. Some spent their time playing cards and gambling.

While on board the Aquitania we received a message to say that Aunty Vi Wilson had died in Powell River.

We landed in Halifax, and from there we came across Canada by train with a change at Montreal. The train was 18 hours late in arriving at Montreal so we missed our connection. We slept in the railway station; the cleaning staff kept moving us from one bench to another.

From Vancouver we boarded the Gulf Stream to come up to Powell River. I recall a relative buying me a banana ice cream split. Something we had not seen during the war. On returning to Powell River we stayed with my grandfather Robert Wilson Sr., at #3 Cedar Street, because he needed care.

My father reapplied for work with the Powell River Company but he was refused work due to past grievances. He found work with City Transfer. Fortunately, I found work with the Powell River Company.

A couple of weeks after my grandfather Robert Wilson Sr. died on New Year's Day 1950, the Powell River Company gave us notice to leave #3 Cedar Street."

Dot and Eddie had four children, Robert (Bob), Allan, Valerie and Rick. They lived in the "Vet's Vill" (Veteran's Village), Cranberry Village.

In 1949 Ken Wilson married Joan Christian (granddaughter of Emily Fishleigh, Westview pioneer) in Nanaimo, B.C.

Apart from Robert Wilson Sr., who was too sick to attend, the following family members attended: the groom's parents Robert and Agnes Wilson, sister Dot Riley (Wilson), and nephews Bob and Allan Riley.

Rowe, Mrs. Howard
Rowe, Howard - Gunner CAO

Digester Vol. 17 – February 1941
"In the Artillery is Howard Rowe, son of Mr. C.S. Rowe of the beater room, who went overseas with one of the first units."

Digester Vol. 20 – March 1944 (in a list of those who have married)
"Have you forgotten … Howard Rowe?"

December 1944 Howard: *"Many thanks for the 300 cigarettes I received last night. At present, I am in one of our hospitals waiting for my leg to mend. I had it broken about 10 miles north of Rimini when I got into an argument with one of Jerry's 105s. I lost out!"*

March 1945 "Howard Rowe is back home. Still on crutches, but looking remarkably well in spite of a nasty big wound. Howard went to Vancouver last week to meet his bride, just over from Ireland."

Taylor, Mrs. Len
Taylor, Len - Lance Corporal CAO

Digester Vol. 16 – April 1940
"Leonard Taylor … has recently enlisted with the famous Vancouver Seaforths and is now training somewhere in the east."

Digester Vol. 17 – February 1941
"The Seaforths, who will be to the fore of any invasion by Britain is attempted, include Len Taylor, son of Ernie Taylor, Powell River."

Digester Vol. 18 – May 1942
"Norm Hill and Len Taylor have taken English brides."

Digester Vol. 20 – February 1944
"The Vancouver Seaforths, who have been in the thick of the fray since Sicily, included Len Taylor …"

Walker, Mrs. Cliff
Walker, Cliff - Sergeant CAO

Digester Vol. 16 – March 1941
"Word comes of the safe arrival in England of Cliff Walker, former high school student. Cliff is on the artillery and has been promoted to corporal."

June 1943 "Gunner Cliff Walker is now Lance Sergeant."

July 1943 "Sgt. Cliff Walker also took the plunge and was married in England in May last."

Cliff Walker letter: *"Thanks ever so much for the 600 cigs received just as I was heading away for my honeymoon last month. I've been getting the News Letter regularly and it's quite a feature. It's certainly surprising how the lads get around. The letter regarding the reunion came a bit too late. I was back from a 14 days leave and found it waiting for me. As it happened that was the big day for me so it would have been a bit hard for me to show up. Had a lovely time in glorious Devon. Ah! What cider!"*

July 1946 re. D-Day
"The supporting troops included … Gunner Cliff Walker."

Young, Mrs. J. L.
Young, J. L. (Jack) - Sergeant RCAF Overseas

Digester Vol. 20 – March 1944
"Cpl. Jack Young is another who feels the noose slowly tightening. *"Anyway,"* said Jack, *"I was always partial to school teachers, and I know she will like Powell River."*

****

Ester Taylor (Auto)   Finnish war bride
Harry Taylor (1918-1942) - RAF/Finnish Air Force   *1942 died in action

Harry Taylor Jr. left Canada in 1939 to join the RAF and fight in WWII. He was the eldest son of Henry (Harry) Edwin Taylor Sr. (1889-1972), a man well remembered in Powell River as the editor of Powell River's 50-year book which was published in 1960.

Harry Taylor Sr. had immigrated to Canada from England in 1911, and by 1913 had joined the Royal North West Mounted Police in Regina, Saskatchewan. On June 22, 1917 Harry married Marion Hall Muirhead (1897-1935); they had seven children, four boys and three girls.

During the Great War, Harry joined the Canadian Expeditionary Force. After the war he returned to his job with the Mounted Police. In 1928 Harry retired as Sergeant of the Royal Mounted Police detachment at Prince George, B.C. In 1929 Harry was Indian Agent for Williams Lake, B.C. Thirteen years later, in 1942, Harry was promoted to Superintendent of Indian Affairs for the Caribou, North Vancouver and the Sunshine Coast. In the late 1960s Harry moved to Powell River, B.C. where his daughter Mrs. Joyce Macleod, and husband Dr. Jim Macleod lived.

Harry Taylor Jr.

A Secret Mission to Finland

In 1939 the RAF asked for volunteers to fly in the Finnish Air Force in the **1939-40 Winter War between Finland and Russia.** Harry Taylor volunteered. A small group of volunteers were flown to Finland by the RAF on a secret mission.

A second group of RAF volunteers were asked to fly 12 Bristol Blenheim planes to Finland for use by the Finnish Air Force.   On the 23rd February 1940 they left Scotland and, with two short stopovers in Sweden and Norway, arrived safely in Finland on the 26th February 1940. These volunteers returned by the same route to Scotland and arrived safely back on March 13, 1940.

The Finnish Government, on March 12, 1940, signed a peace treaty with Russia. However, the war against Russia continued in what is known as the **Continuation War (a continuation of the Winter War).**

Finland now collaborated with Germany to fight a common enemy, Russia. Germany agreed to send Finland military equipment to fight the Russians.

On December 5, 1941 Britain declared war on Finland due to its alliance with Nazi Germany.

The help the British Government gave Finland in the Winter War was done in secret. No one was to know about the RAF volunteers who were in the Finnish Air Force, and the RAF volunteers who delivered 12 Bristol Blenheim planes to Finland.

The mission was so secret that both groups of volunteers had to travel under false passports, and wear clothing which did not identify them as RAF flyers. If they had been captured by the Russians or the Germans, the British Government would have denied any direct involvement in the missions.

Britain gave covert help to Finland during the Winter War as it wanted to prevent Finnish nickel ore getting into the hands of the Russians, or the Germans.

Other foreign volunteers in the Winter War included 300 men in the Finnish-American Legion.

The planes that were flown to Finland showed the Finnish blue swastika symbol. Harry Taylor, and the first group of RAF volunteers, wore the Finnish Air Force uniform which also showed the blue swastika. The Finnish Air Force had first used this insignia in 1918, just before it was used by the Nazi party of Germany. The swastika is a centuries-old emblem.

****

Harry's adventures were just beginning when he landed in Finland in 1939. It was in Finland that he met a Finnish girl, fell in love, and married; then later escaped with his wife back to Britain.

On arriving in Finland, Harry and the first group of volunteers were given living accommodation in summer chalets. Harry and his friends went to a nearby town to have a coffee at a restaurant. It was here that Harry met Ester Auto.

Ester Chandler (Taylor):
"I was having coffee in a restaurant with some girlfriends when we met this group of young men and got talking, and I ended up with Harry."

Harry and Ester were married in Finland in May 1941. Six months after their marriage Britain declared war on Finland because of Finland's collaboration with the

Germans. It was not safe for Harry to remain in Finland; after the British declaration of war against Finland, he could be imprisoned or shot. For his own safety, Harry was interred by the Finnish authorities and sent to neutral Sweden. With help from the British Embassy in Sweden, Ester was able to join him three months later.

It is unknown what happened to the other RAF volunteer flyers in Finland; however, Harry and Ester, after a harrowing escape from war-torn Europe, eventually arrived safely in Britain on January 15, 1942. Harry immediately rejoined the RAF and went for "ops" training in Lossiemouth, Scotland.

In December 1942 after a bombing raid, Harry tragically died when his Stirling aircraft crashed near its base in Lakenheath, Suffolk. A few weeks before his death his only child, Rita, was born in London, November 1942.

Many years later, Ester recalled their escape across wartime Europe. Through a diplomatic exchange in Lisbon, the couple crossed Europe in a closed compartment. They first travelled by train to Lubeck, Germany, followed by coach to Hamburg, then by rail through Germany and France to Spain. They arrived in Lisbon, Portugal, via Madrid, Spain, on September 16, 1941. They had to wait four months before being transported to Britain. The couple enjoyed a delayed honeymoon.

After the death of Harry in 1942, Ester remained in London with baby Rita, enduring the blitz raids until the V1 rockets started arriving:

Ester Chandler (Taylor):
"Then they started the V1 rocket raid, and I decided to go back to Scotland as the only place I knew anybody."

June 6, 1944 - D-Day landings in Normandy. The tide had turned and it was only a matter of months before the Allies defeated Germany.
September 19, 1944 – Finland made peace with Russia and joined the Allies. The Germans were furious and there was bitter fighting in northern Finland.
May 7, 1945 – Germany signed an unconditional surrender. May 8, 1945 – the war in Europe was over. Finland retained its independence.

After the war was over, Ester and Rita remained in Britain. Ester remarried 14 years after the death of her husband, to a Mr. Chandler, who was serving in the Royal Navy. Rita grew up in Britain and married a Mr. Groves, a farmer; they have four children and live on the Isle of Wight in southern England.

The Finnish Government, to commemorate the 70th anniversary of Finland's independence, issued a special medal for the Winter War in 1988. Ester applied to the Finnish Embassy for Harry's Winter War medal. The records were checked in Helsinki, and Harry Taylor was awarded posthumously the Commemorative Medal of the Winter War 1939-40. This medal was presented to Mrs. Ester Chandler (Taylor) and Mrs. Rita Groves (Taylor) at a champagne reception at the Finnish Ambassador's residence in Kensington, London.

The survivors of the second group of RAF volunteers, who delivered the 12 Bristol Blenheim airplanes to Finland, during the Winter War, were also presented with the same commemorative medal.

Because Canadian Harry Taylor Jr. was tragically killed in WWII, he never had the chance to bring home to Canada his Finnish war bride, Ester and daughter Rita Taylor. In 1990 and 2002 Mrs. Rita Groves (Taylor) visited her cousin Mrs. Janice Orchiston (granddaughter of Harry Taylor Sr. and daughter of Dr. and Mrs. Macleod) in Powell River, B.C.

Harry Stuart Taylor (1918-1942) RAF.
Volunteer in the Finnish Air Force during the Russian invasion of Finland 1939-40.
Photo: Janice Orchiston collection

December 1988 London, England.
Mrs. Ester Chandler (Taylor) receiving a Finnish war medal posthumously
for Harry Stuart Taylor.
(L to R) daughter Mrs. Rita Groves (Taylor) and wife Mrs. Ester Chandler (Taylor)
Photo of Harry Taylor and medal.
Photo: Janice Orchiston collection

Veterans & war brides from other towns relocate in Powell River in the postwar period

Mildred Adams   WWII war bride

Mildred (2011): *"I remember the night the lights went out (street lights) when war was declared on September 3, 1939. I had trained as a legal secretary but immediately joined the ATS.*

I met my husband Lorne Adams at a church supper. Lorne was a paratrooper and trained at Ringway (Manchester) Airport. We fell in love and got married, in uniform, at a registry office. Lorne had a three-day pass. My father liked Lorne, but he was not keen on me marrying a Canadian and living in Canada. My mother was more understanding. No wedding photographs were taken in the registry office.

I travelled as a war bride, with my infant daughter, to Halifax and docked at Pier 21. The boat had been outfitted for war brides and their children. I was given a bottom bunk in "the bowels" of the ship. I shall always remember the food, it was amazing. We had eggs and oranges which were in short supply in England. There was some pilfering on board by war brides; nappies (diapers) went missing. The ship was huge, and I was too scared to go near the railings and look down at the ocean.

As we went across Canada on the train, I felt sorry for brides getting off in isolated areas. The train took an unexpected detour at one point, and we ended up in Vancouver with no one to meet us. I had to explain to a Red Cross worker that my husband was waiting at a different station. Eventually everything was sorted out.

For my first year in Canada I stayed at the Adams' family farm in Turtle Valley, near Shuswap Lake, between Chase and Salmon Arm. The farm was principally a dairy farm, with a few pigs. There was no indoor plumbing and water came from a stream. It was isolated. Once a week the family made a trip into town. Neighbours in the community were very kind and put on a special welcoming party for the war bride. In the summer months I used to take a book with me when I went to the outhouse. My mother-in-law remarked I wouldn't be reading in the outhouse during the winter months. She was right; I only stayed a few minutes there when it was 40 below! I remember the first time I was asked to go out and call the cows home – I just went into a field, sat down, and cried. My new life in Canada was so different from my life in the "old country".

After one year on the family farm we moved to Powell River. My husband had heard from Ann Bradley (a relative) that there were jobs at the mill. I also found work, in the Powell River Company offices. Accommodation was difficult to find.

We had four children: Susan, Kevin, Mark and Craig. My sister Margaret came to Canada after the war with her husband (an Englishman). She lives in Powell River."

<u>Dorothy Annie Brant (Cowen)</u> (1921-2005) **WWII war bride**

Dorothy (Dot) Cowen was born in Broughton, Stockbridge, England in 1921. She was the only child of Dorothy and Jim Cowen. Jim Cowen had served in WWI. The Cowen family later moved to Rochdale where, after leaving school at age 14, Dorothy went to work in the cotton mills. In 1939 Dorothy, at age 18, left home to train as a nurse in one of the London hospitals. The nurses enjoyed going to dances in their time off. With the start of WWII there was a Canadian presence in Britain. The Canadians, when on leave from their barracks, went to dances in order to meet English girls. It was at one of these dances that Sgt. Cyril Brant met a pretty English nurse, Dorothy Cowen.

Cyril Brant was born in Toronto; later the family moved to Nelson, B.C. where Cyril grew up. Sgt. Cyril Brant was in the Princess Patricia's Canadian Light Infantry. He was an anti-aircraft gunner, and trained men under his command. Sgt. Brant saw action in France, and was wounded (shrapnel in the back).

Dorothy Cowen and Cyril Brant fell in love, and were married in 1941. Dorothy Brant lived at home with her parents in Rochdale while Cyril continued to live in the army barracks. Cyril headed for Rochdale on all his leaves.

Two children were born in Britain: Ian in 1942 and Leslie in 1942. The youngest boy, Neil, was born in Vancouver in 1945.

Dorothy and the two boys, Ian and Leslie, left England for Canada in May 1945 on V-E Day on the *Brittannic.* The parting with her parents was difficult, she was an only child, and her parents envisaged they would never see her or the grandchildren again. They were able to visit the family in Powell River in 1963.

On the train crossing Canada the children were handed a banana by the Red Cross. Leslie, having never seen or tasted a banana before, refused it! Poor Dorothy, she was hoping Leslie would take it, and they could have shared it together. Dorothy had not seen a banana in six years, since the war started.

Dorothy and the children were met in Vancouver by Cyril's sister, Ivy Eperson. They went to live with her until Cyril came back from the war in September 1945. Cyril was a plumber by trade. The family lived in Vancouver and Richmond, B.C.

before moving to Powell River in 1956. The family lived in Westview, Powell River and Cyril worked as a self-employed plumber.

Dorothy adjusted well to life in Canada. She enjoyed the outdoor lifestyle. The family went on many boating trips up Toba Inlet. Dorothy and Cyril enjoyed going to dances and attended functions at the Legion. Dorothy was an expert knitter and sewer. Dorothy is remembered as a happy-go-lucky person; she had a great attitude to life and adjusted well to her new life in Canada.

Hilda Cooper (Abbott) WWII war bride

Vernon Cooper was born in Calgary, Alberta and grew up in New Westminster, B.C. In WWII he was a Private in the New Westminster Regiment of the Canadian Army Overseas. He took part in the Italian campaign, and the D Day landings at Normandy. He was in what was known as the Suicide Squad, the first Canadians to land on the beaches.

Hilda Abbott lived in Nottingham, England; however, during the war she was billeted in Manchester where she re-wired Lancaster bombers after they came back from battle.

Hilda Abbott and Vernon Cooper met a dance in Manchester. They immediately fell in love, and married three days later in Nottingham, at a local church, June 21, 1943. The bride borrowed a dress from a relative. Immediately after the wedding, Vernon had to return to his unit. Hilda was extremely worried when her husband went on an "op". On one occasion, she was relieved to see Vernon with the Canadians on a news cast report at the local cinema, looking very much alive and well.

In 1945 Vernon returned to Canada in a troop ship. Back home in B.C., Vernon chose to live in Powell River and work for the Powell River Company. He wanted to live off the land in a rural area, as opposed to life in the city.

In 1946, six months after the war ended, Hilda travelled across the Atlantic in a war bride ship. On the boat many war brides were homesick, missing close family members they had left behind. On the war bride train across Canada Hilda made friends with other war brides. As war brides left the train, in different provinces, there were "Goodbye" parties.

Many war brides, while in England, had the impression from their Canadian husbands that they were wealthy, but the majority were not. They were disillusioned when they arrived at their destination in Canada. Hilda had the impression that she was coming to a big city, but soon found out that Powell River was a small town with "nothing there". She initially had a hard time coping with the isolation and the lack of city amenities.

The first home they lived in was a small four-roomed house with an outhouse at the back! Later a new house was built with an indoor bathroom. The Coopers lived at 5680 Manson Avenue, Powell River. They had two children, Lorraine and Penny, both were born in Canada.

There were many happy memories of fun times at the lake and beach. Hilda's close friend was another English war bride, Joan Patrick. The Coopers and Patricks had a great time boating at Douglas Bay in the Powell River Regional District.

After Vernon retired from the mill, Hilda and Vernon Cooper moved to Vancouver. Their old neighbour Rudi Pearson has fond memories of the Cooper family.

Elizabeth Ellen Hindle (Kenny)   WWII war bride

As soon as war was declared Harry Hindle enlisted in the Seaforth Highlanders. His parents, Mary Ann and Edward Hindle, were originally from Lancashire. Harry decided to look up numerous aunts, uncles and cousins in the Rochdale area when he was stationed in London, England. While staying at Rochdale he attended a dance, and that is where he met an attractive and vivacious young woman, Elizabeth Ellen Kenny.

Elizabeth lived with her parents in a large house in Rochdale. Her father was a landlord and owned a number of residences. Her younger siblings: Kathleen, Stephen and John lived in the family home. Elizabeth worked in the local woollen mill.

Harry and Elizabeth fell in love and decided to marry. Harry was 25 years of age and did not need his parents' permission, however Elizabeth, age 18 did. They had a very quiet wedding in the local registry office, September 1941. The reason for this quiet wedding was that Elizabeth's mother was ill; later that year she died.

When Harry was on leave the young couple resided in the Kenny family home. Elizabeth's father, after the death of his wife, joined the Army. Thus, Elizabeth was left with her father's job of rent collecting.

With her father and husband away in the Forces, Elizabeth had the sole responsibility of looking after her three younger siblings, and baby Georgia who was born in 1943. There was severe rationing in Britain, and Elizabeth found it difficult to feed four hungry children. At times, there was no food in the house.

Harry was away with the Canadians in the long Italian campaign. He lost many of his friends; it was a costly campaign. In 1946, after the war was over, Harry was shipped back to Canada. He went to live with his parents Mary Ann and Edward Hindle in Powell River, B.C., while waiting for his wife and children to join him. Harry and Elizabeth's second child, Kathleen, was born in 1946.

In November 1946 Elizabeth had to say painful goodbyes to her family after she received notification that she would be leaving on one of the last war bride sailings. Elizabeth was especially close to her sister Kathleen; they were both emotionally devastated at the parting.

Suffering from severe malnutrition and home sickness, Elizabeth boarded the T.S.S. *Letitia* in Liverpool, with a four-year-old child and a baby. During the voyage Elizabeth and baby Kathleen were very ill with seasickness. They stayed in their cabin the entire voyage, with four-year-old Georgia bringing them food. Fortunately, Georgia was not seasick.

Other people were kind on the voyage and they wrote good will messages, at the end of the voyage, on the ship's menu:

"Lots of Happiness in you new life. Irene Thurston"

"The best of luck--- happiness. Margaret Moynham"

"A wee gal with Raven Hair,
The mother of two children rare,
Were on my ship as passengers,
The best of ever had to fare,
God Bless You, and I wish you luck
Always.
from your Stewardess, Nurse H.R.M. Jones October 1946"

For those who were able to eat on the voyage, the food, after years of strict rationing, was memorable: roast turkey, fillets of white fish, braised ox tongues, and lamb cold cuts followed by *ice cream* (few had seen this delicious dessert during the war years).

The train journey across Canada proved difficult for Elizabeth, as she continued to be ill. A kindly black steward was very good to the family. Four-year-old Georgia continued to help her sick mother.

Georgia remembers the train ride across Canada and the war brides destined for the Prairie Provinces and Alberta getting off, until the only ones left were those going to British Columbia. Due to her illness, Elizabeth was unable to look after some treasured possessions she had brought with them. Some very nice things were stolen during the train ride. When they arrived in Vancouver, baby Kathleen had only one diaper, the one she was wearing. The other diapers had been stolen by other war brides. Harry met them at the railway station. They stayed a few days in Vancouver before taking the boat up to Powell River. It was late at night when they boarded; the water was pitch black, poor Elizabeth --- another boat ride!

Harry and Elizabeth went to live in one of the small houses behind the Hindle store on Marine Avenue, Westview Village, (Powell River). When Georgia walked into her new home she saw a beautiful doll sitting on an upholstered chair. The doll was a welcome home present from her father.

Georgia felt at home with her Hindle grandparents as they spoke with a Lancashire accent, just like the relatives she had left behind. Georgia remembers that first Christmas in Canada --- delicious food in plentiful servings.

Elizabeth weighed only 100 pounds when she arrived in Powell River due to severe malnutrition during WWII; she was put under doctor's care. By the time her third child Harry was born in the Powell River hospital, she had put weight on. Georgia recalls when her father, for the first time, brought a bunch of bananas home; her mother ate every one of them! Elizabeth had not seen a banana for six years.

Harry gained employment with the Powell River Company and they moved to a rented house in the Townsite. They moved to Westview Village after the Townsite houses were sold off in 1955. Harry became boss of the clothing crew, and worked in the mill until he retired. For Elizabeth, England was always home; she especially missed her sister Kathleen. Her friends in Powell River were English, some were other war brides.

Rochdale, England 1941: wedding day of Cyril Brant CAO and Dorothy Brant (Cowen)
Photo: Brant collection

Rochdale, England 1944.
Dorothy Brant and children Leslie (L) and Ian (R).
They left for Canada on the Brittanic on V-E Day, May 8, 1945.
Photo: Brant collection

Nottingham, England—June 21, 1943 wedding of Hilda Cooper (Abbott)
and Vernon Cooper CAO.
The bride borrowed her wedding dress from a relative.
Bride's family front row (L to R) bridesmaid Lily Abbott (sister)/
Iris Abbott—child (sister)/Vernon Cooper CAO/
Hilda Cooper/male unknown/bridesmaid (friend)/Mary Abbott (mother) with John Abbott (child)
Photo: Lorraine Fisher

April 24, 1946—Epsom, England.
WWII war bride Phyllis Kornyk (Evans) and John Kornyk CAO and wedding party.
Photo: Phyllis Kornyk

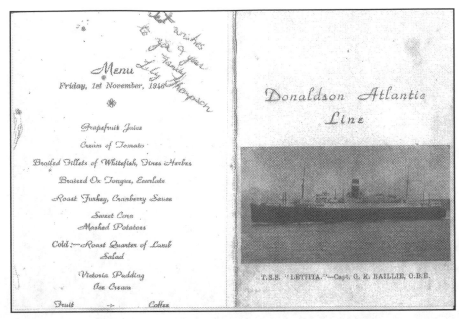

Menu for the Letitia, Friday 1st November 1946.
War bride Elizabeth Hindle sailed on the Letitia
with her daughter Georgia (4 yrs.) and baby Kathleen.
Elizabeth was seasick and homesick: four-year-old Georgia looked after
her mother and baby sister.
Hindle collection

1946 Rochdale, England: Kathleen Kenny and niece Georgia Hindle.
Top left hand corner: passport photo of Elizabeth Hindle 1946 Rochdale, England.
Photo: Hindle collection

Phyllis Kornyk (Evans) WWII War Bride

Phyllis came over to Canada as a war bride after WWII. Her husband came looking for a job at the mill in Powell River in 1958. There was nothing available at that time; however, he found a job delivering parcels. The Kornyks had arrived in Powell River by the new ferry route up the Sechelt Peninsula from Vancouver. It was difficult finding any type of accommodation in Powell River at that time; eventually, they bought a house on Joyce Avenue in Westview. Phyllis' daughter was born in Powell River.

Phyllis immediately liked Powell River as it reminded her of Epsom Downs, England – the area which she had grown up in. Phyllis did not drive at that time and walked everywhere. She recalls shopping at Super Valu.

Early life in England

Phyllis Kornyk's parents were Alfred and Isabelle (Bella) Evans. Alfred was of Welsh descent and he was born in London within the sound of Bow Bells. He was a true Cockney. Bella Evans grew up in Epsom. Alfred and Bella married in Christ Church, Epsom, Surrey, England just after WWI. They went to live with Bella's mother in a two-bedroom house on the Commons property which was owned by Lord and Lady Rosemary.

Phyllis' grandmother made a living by dressmaking. She made clothes for the children of Lord and Lady Rosemary. Phyllis, as a small child, was used as a mannequin to model the clothes for their son Charles.

Phyllis was born in 1923 on the Epsom Commons. She attended a Church of England school at the back of the Rosemary estate. Her siblings, Hilda, William, Margaret and Jay also attended the same school.

William (born 1921) served in Montgomery's 8th Army during WWII.

Phyllis grew up on Epsom Downs with her family. It was a fairly isolated area. During the war Epsom Downs' racetrack was used for the billeting of Canadian soldiers.

Her parents attended church and did not allow Phyllis to go to pubs to socialize. She was age 16 when the war broke out. She had briefly worked in a mental institution before working in a laundry. After work, on nights and weekends, she had to be on fire watch. Phyllis was trained to put out the bombs which caused the fires. The family had an air raid shelter in their backyard.

Her father, Alfred Evans (born 1885), had been a professional soldier in the British Army for 20 years. He served in the army in India in the "Old Contemptibles". He was known as Taffy Evans. Alfred started at age 12 as a drummer boy in the army. He was musical and played the clarinet. He was a wonderful ballroom dancer, winning a gold medal in India. He left the army after WWI and married Bella Evans. Alfred worked as a cook in a mental institution in Epsom.

Phyllis, like her father, loved dancing and attended dances with friends at the local church dances at Epsom Downs. It was here she met John Kornyk and other Canadians. There were no English boys around, as they were overseas fighting in the war.

For about three months Phyllis met John at church dances. Phyllis stood out as she was an exceptional dancer -- sadly John was not a good dancer. Needless to say romance blossomed as the two started dating – meeting for walks in the countryside and going to the movies.

Phyllis and John were married during the war on April 24, 1943 when Phyllis was 20 years of age. They had a beautiful church wedding in Christ Church, Epsom. Phyllis wore a lovely white satin dress "not that fancy with lace and a bit of train". An army friend of John's was his best man, while Phyllis chose Amy the girl next door, and her two sisters, Jay and Margaret, as bridesmaids.

The material for the dress had been provided by a professional seamstress who also designed the bride's and bridesmaids' dresses. The dressmaker sewed for royalty and was able to get material which was not available to the general public, who relied on saving up clothing coupons. Phyllis' father worked for the husband of the dressmaker, so was able to place a special order.

Wedding dresses were difficult to get during wartime. Phyllis' professionally sewn and designed wedding dress was let in and out twelve times for other war brides! Eventually, without her knowledge, the dress was borrowed and dyed for a dance. The dress was never returned.

For their honeymoon Phyllis and John stayed with an aunt and uncle in Goole, Yorkshire.

John was with the Canadians on D-Day. Phyllis, at the weekends was on fire duty. On one occasion she put out a fire bomb.

After the war was over, John went back with the Canadians while Phyllis waited for transportation especially organized for the thousands of war brides in the United Kingdom. Her parents did not want her to leave England.

Phyllis was with other war brides on a troop ship that sailed from Liverpool. Some brides were pregnant. There were no children on board. Pregnant women were allowed the bottom bunks. There were six brides to a room. Phyllis remembers the meals on board – wonderful – especially the bacon and eggs (something not obtainable in England during WWII rationing). She piled her plate up high.

Everyone was excited.

They landed at Halifax. For every war bride a soldier escorted each one to their section of the train. On the journey across Canada, Phyllis recalls a stopover in Montreal. She went downtown to shop with other war brides. They were surprised that none of the shop assistants spoke English. No one had told them that Quebecers were French-speaking.

The journey by train across Canada continues to be etched on Phyllis' mind, even after 65 years.

Phyllis Kornyk (87) January 2011:

'What a massive land. I nearly freaked out. Going, going, going. I kept my fingers crossed and hoped to see a city. It was so different from the City of London. Just kept on going, going, going.

The train stopped at various locations to let small groups of war brides off, sometimes it was only one bride on an isolated track with no houses in sight. Half a dozen relatives waited by the track. Some war brides simply could not get off the train. Many had come from the London area and the isolation just freaked them out. These brides were then put in a special compartment at the end of the train. They returned to Halifax and were put on the next boat to return to England.

My destination was Winnipeg. My husband in his uniform was there to meet me. We stayed a couple of nights at a hotel, then took the bus out to the family farm.

My mother-in-law was Ukrainian and did not speak English. Everyone else spoke Ukrainian and English. They translated for me. They tried to fatten me up on cream and butter as they thought I was too thin after all those years of rationing. I found the meals too rich.

We stayed a month at the farm, then moved to Winnipeg where my husband was employed as a truck driver. After we came to Powell River in 1958, John worked here delivering parcels until he retired. He was known as Speedy John."

Phyllis has no regrets at coming to Canada. To this day, at age 87, she vividly recalls the train journey across the country:

"Going, going, going (the train). No towns. Nothing."

Ruth Longacre (Cave)   WAAF   WWII war bride at Lund

Ruth Cave was in the WAAF and worked as a radar controller during WWII. She met Norman Longacre, a sergeant in the Canadian Scottish, at an afternoon dance at the Pavilion tea room in Bournemouth. They continued to see each other prior to the D-Day landing of June 6, 1944.

Ruth and Norman were married in Bournemouth, October 6, 1945. The bride wore a beautiful designed wedding dress, this was unusual in WWII as material was on coupons and generally not available.

Susan Watson (Longacre) 2011:
    "My mom's sister-in-law was a seamstress; she made mom's dress and those of her attendants. The material was from other wedding gowns and re-fashioned."

Ruth Longacre sailed for Canada on a war bride ship in May of 1946, she was seven months pregnant. Ruth lied about her due date because she did not want to wait in England until the birth of the baby. Ruth told her daughter Susan that the Red Cross informed the brides if their marriages did not work out, the Red Cross would ensure their return to England. On the train trip across Canada some brides refused to get off the train and join their husbands, and waiting relatives. They felt that their spouses had misrepresented themselves.

Shortly after Norman's marriage to Ruth, in the fall of 1945, Norman's regiment was returned to Canada. He came directly to Lund, B.C. to work with his brother who was a logger.

Ruth's daughter Susan was born in the old Powell River hospital in July 1946. A few years later her son David was born in 1955. Norman continued in the logging

Wedding Day October 6, 1945—Bournemouth, England.
Sgt. Norman Longacre CAO and Ruth Longacre (Cave) WAAF.
Norman brought his English bride to the isolated fishing village of Lund, B.C.
Photo: Susan Watson

1946 WWII war bride Ann Mckenzie and her husband Jim Mckenzie
at a wedding reception hosted by his family in Courtenay, B.C.
The couple were married in England at a registry office.
Left hand corner: Jim Mckenzie CAO a tank driver with 71 XI Hussars.
Photo: Ann Mckenzie

1945 Waltham Abbey Church, Essex, England
WWII war bride Joan Phelan (Barker) and Paul Phelan RCN.
Joan worked in a munitions factory at Enfield, near London.
Photo: Phelan photos

1952 Powell River, B.C.
The Phelan family: Paul and Joan Phelan with their two children, Kathleen and baby Michael.
Photo: Phelan photos

industry until 1962. At this time he became a part-time fisherman and part owner of the Lund Hotel until he sold his shares in 1969.

Susan Watson (2011):

"Mom had quite a time adjusting to living in Lund, having come from a city with all the perks that went along with it. She also came from a large family and found it lonely here for quite some time. My grandparents came to Lund in 1948 and spent a full year with us, after that she was much happier and made some life-long friends. We lived in the Lund Hotel until 1953, and then moved to a new house on the point above the breakwater. They sold in 1999 and moved onto our (the Watson) property in a modular home. Dad passed away in 2007, and Mom a year later."

Ann Mckenzie   WWII war bride

Ann Mckenzie (2010):

"I grew up in Liverpool and then the family moved to Bridgewater in Somerset. I worked at Sackville House, London, which was a centre for the repatriation of Canadian soldiers. I was a stenographer.

We had an Irish girl staying at our house. She was going out with my husband before I became his girlfriend. While he was away in Italy, she met an American and married him. Jim came round to our house on his next leave, my mother felt sorry for him, so she asked him to stay. We started going out together, usually to our "local". We'd sit around the fireplace, it was cozy and warm. Jim didn't dance, I loved dancing. Generally, the Americans and Canadians were not good dancers.

We fell in love, and we married at a registry office and didn't tell anyone – including my mother! I just wore an ordinary cotton frock while Jim was in uniform. My mother wasn't very happy that I had married a Canadian. She knew I would be leaving home to go to Canada. I was 21 when I got married in England in 1946. There were no English boys around as they were away fighting in the war. There were loads of American and Canadian boys in England, plus a few Norwegians. After the war was over Jim went back with his regiment. He was a tank driver with the 71 11th Hussars. I came as a war bride to Canada after he had left.

All the war brides, without children, gathered at Hyde Park House. We then travelled by train to Liverpool. We were on a ship with returning soldiers – there were hundreds of them. There were about 200 war brides on board. No children. The food was marvellous compared to the rationing we had in England. I piled my plate up. I could not believe the food, it was just wonderful. Some girls went to two or three sittings but I only went to one. A number of war brides, even though they were married, had romances on board. We docked in Halifax. It was all every exciting.

We came across Canada in a big, long train. It was slower than the trains in England. I spent a lot of time in the observation dome. All I could see was grass to the horizon. Not a house, not a home, not a hut in sight; no people, no towns, no nothing. It was boring. We had a two-hour stop in Winnipeg. We took taxis down to the Hudson Bay Company so we could shop for clothes (only available in war-torn England with clothing coupons). I got off the train in New Westminster and missed all the celebrations in Vancouver. My husband and his sister met me there; he was not wearing his uniform and he looked quite different! I hardly knew him.

We stayed a few nights with his sister in New West then we went to see his folks in Courtenay, on Vancouver Island. First we went to Victoria then took the little train up to Courtenay. We had a very nice wedding reception there. I wore my best dress on this occasion plus a spray of fresh flowers.

My husband had promised me we would stay on Vancouver Island but we ended up in Powell River. He broke his promise! *We came here (Powell River) because my husband got a job in the mill with the Powell River Company. There were no jobs on Vancouver Island. First we lived in the little duplexes (dubbed Storks Avenue) near Henderson School, in the Powell River Townsite.*

I have no regrets at coming to Canada. I have no regrets in living in Powell River all these years, however, I had been promised Vancouver Island!

We have three boys: Ian, Bruce and Andrew."

After becoming pen pals, a sailor in the Canadian Navy and an English girl fall in love.

Joan Phelan (Barker) (1923-2005)

At the beginning of WWII, Joan Barker was just 16 years of age. Joan went to work in the offices of the Enfield Rifle Company, a large munitions factory at Enfield, 14 miles from London. British children completed their state education at age 14. After finishing her education Joan had attended a private business school for two years, taking business and secretarial courses. Like other British women she had to spend her "spare time" on ARP (Air Raid Precaution) duty at the Enfield factory. Enfield was a prime target for German bombers.

A Royal Small Arms factory had been built at Enfield Lock in 1815. It became the main site for the production of weapons for the British Army, especially the "Lee

Enfield" rifle. During WWII a large munitions factory was built at Ponders End, Enfield.

Joan Barker was the eldest daughter of Bill and Lily Rose Barker. Bill Barker worked as a purchaser of meat for 30 butcher shops in the Waltham area. He allowed the customers in his own shop at the local Co-operative to keep their meat in his shop's fridge. Bill opened the shop on Sundays so customers could pick up a fresh Sunday dinner roast. In Britain, few householders owned fridges during the war years; they shopped and queued every weekday for scarce items.

Joan Phelan (78 years) 2001:

"I met my husband Paul during the war years. I went into London with a girlfriend to see a picture show. We stopped a Canadian sailor in a London park to ask directions to the picture house. We got talking, and ended up having tea together in a café. We exchanged addresses. Paul and I became pen pals."

Paul visited Joan and her family when on leave in England. He often brought difficult-to-obtain food items to thank the Barkers for their generosity of hosting a Canadian serviceman. Joan and Paul's pen pal friendship led to love and marriage.

According to Paul Phelan's war-time diary, he first met Joan on July 19, 1942 in St. James Park, London. His 1944 diary details their courtship by mail:

Entries in Paul Phelan's diary (February – September 1944, WWII):

February 29, 1944
I still do not know how to answer Joan's letter of Feb. 29 in which she took the lady's privilege of asking me to marry her — what a step to take! I could not support myself in pre-war time, and can I support myself and Joan when the war is over?

May 8
Tonight I wrote probably the most important letter of my life asking Joan to marry me. A blank picture of Canada I painted so she would not marry me under any illusions. It will be weeks before I receive an answer.

May 26
There is yet no answer from Joan as to whether or not she will marry me. The thought scares me, never having been a brave man; I know God will show his will.

August 1
Requested 28 days leave to be spent in England. That should be long enough for Joan and myself to decide whether or not to marry.

Sept. 6
Joan tonight made me the happiest of happy men. Under Eleanor's Cross at Waltham, she asked me to ask Mr. Barker if we could be married this leave. God grant me the right words of asking.

Sept. 7
Mr. Barker gave his consent.

Sept. 22
The eve of my wedding and my thoughts were varied. Joan returned from work at 12:00 covered with confetti, her bicycle taped with coloured rags, a cardboard ring and the letter "L" learner on rear of bike. I love her dearly.

Sept. 23
My wedding day. Joan looked lovely, and was quite nervous but listened to solemn wedding service read by Mr. Clark in Waltham Abbey. At Barker's home, 20 people sat down to a wedding feast — a huge wedding cake being the pièce de résistance. Stayed night at Strand Hotel. Many cables from mother and other loved ones from home.

Sept. 25
Went to Bath for our honeymoon.

Sept. 29
Both Joan and I were in tears on saying goodbye. It was hard to bid a tender farewell to my loved one.

After the war was over, Joan found it heart wrenching to leave her family in England. She was not to know, it would be the last time she would see her father alive. She left on the *Letitia* with 806 dependents of Canadian servicemen (some were children) in 1946. Joan was one of 76 war brides heading for British Columbia.

The *Letitia* was late in docking, and had to wait in "stream" while her space at Halifax dock was occupied by the *Scythia*. The *Scythia* was being loaded with German POW's for England; later to be returned to Germany. One war bride, Mary Mathews, after the long delay, prior to docking, was heard to say, *"I'll certainly by glad to get off this ship!"*

Joan boarded a war bride train, destination - British Columbia. Along the way some brides were getting off by lonely railroad tracks, not a house or a town in sight.

Joan and the other war wives had a great welcome from their husbands on their arrival in Vancouver. An old newspaper cutting records their arrival:

"The brides and children in their very best bibs and tuckers were immediately engulfed in the arms of anxious husbands, many of whom had waited months for the reunion. Mrs. James Corbett says Canada is "just swell" – particularly the west and the great mountains of British Columbia. Paul Phelan, a five-year veteran of the Navy came from Powell River to meet his bride Joan, who comes from the arsenal town of Enfield, England."

After the war, prior to Joan arriving in Canada, Paul had found work with the Powell River Company in Powell River. They lived in Wildwood village. Joan immediately loved Wildwood; she knew she was "home". For one year they lived in a shack near Peggy Bird's residence. They then moved into their house which was located on King Street, Wildwood, near the Catholic Church. Joan and Paul had three children: Kathleen (born 1948), Michael (1952) and Barbara (1957). The children had a wonderful life growing up in Wildwood. They all attended the Wildwood school.

Kathleen recalls Aunty Peggy Bird with affection, plus the many generous Italian neighbours. Kind neighbours taught Joan basic cooking, canning etc.

A second wave of Italians came to Powell River after WWII, many settled in the district of Wildwood. Some could not speak English. The Wildwood Parent-Teacher Association, headed by Peggy Bird, launched an English for New Canadians program. Joan and Paul participated in the program, teaching English to Italian immigrants.

Paul worked in the steam plant at the Powell River mill until his early death in 1962 from a brain tumor.

Joan Phelan (78) 2001:
"After Paul died I had to find a job as I had three small children to raise. I found work in Wildwood dispatching for the E&H Company. It was a good job because I was able to look after Barbara, who was only five-years-old, in the office."

In 1963 Joan's mother sent her the money to travel to England. It would be the first time Joan visited England, after leaving as a war bride in 1945. Soon after her arrival, she booked her ticket "home" to Canada.

Looking Back: Reflections Joan Phelan (1923-2005)

Joan (2001): *"I never had any reservations about moving to Canada, and was never homesick. I had married a good man."*

Wilma Brown   WWII Italian war bride

In 1958 William Brown brought his wife Wilma, and family to Powell River after finding employment with the Powell River Company. The Browns lived in Westview and their three girls, Christina, Juliana and Carmen attended local schools.

Adjusting to the isolation of Powell River and the wet climate was not easy for Wilma, who came from sunny Italy. On wet, rainy Sunday afternoons Wilma despondently would say, *"I wish the Russians would bomb this place!"* Wilma's mood quickly changed on sunny Sundays, and the family would head for an afternoon of fun on Willingdon Beach.

Wilma and William met at the British Military HQ in Trieste, Italy, in postwar Italy. Trieste had been divided into four sectors: British, American, Russian, and Italian.

—————————————————————————

Towards the end of WWII a very young William Brown, age 18 trained for the Military Police in the British Army.

William had a gift for languages and his talents were put to good use by the army; he was attached to the Special Investigation Unit at Trieste. He worked undercover in the vice squad, tracking down those working in the black market, prostitution etc. in postwar Italy.

Also working at the British HQ was Wilma, a beautiful Italian girl; like William, she had a gift for languages, and could speak Italian, French, German, English, and friulano (an Italian dialect). Wilma helped with interpretation, worked the switchboard, and typed documents. Wilma had returned to Italy after escaping to Austria with a girlfriend during the turbulent years of partisan fighting.

William, attracted to Wilma, made excuses to visit her office: to sharpen a pencil, require help with translation of documents, etc. They started going out together. Wilma was always late for these dates; this resulted in William giving her a present, an alarm clock!

Their romance could have derailed when Wilma became irritated with a British officer who dumped documents for immediate typing on her desk at the end of the working day. In annoyance, Wilma left the British HQ and moved to the American HQ. Needless to say, William and Wilma's romance continued.

Wilma travelled on frequent weekend visits to Santa Maria, la Longa, to attend to her elderly grandfather. This entailed being stopped and questioned at various checkpoints. The questioning annoyed William, he spoke sharply to the soldiers on duty: *"Leave my fiancée alone!"* This put their friendship on a more formal footing, and eventually led to their marriage in Scotland in 1950, at Linlithgow, West Lothian. William's family were present, and Wilma's girlfriend from Italy. They honeymooned in the Lake District – unfortunately it poured down most of the time!

William continued with his tour of duty in the army until 1957. The couple went to Egypt, Cyprus, and then returned to Scotland. In 1957, due to the recession in Scotland, the family moved to Canada. They flew to Vancouver, B.C. with just their suitcases, the rest of their belongings packed in trunks to be shipped later.

After working in security as a watchman for the PGE, William was able to get work with the Powell River Company; the Brown family moved to Powell River in 1958. Wilma put her gift of languages to excellent use in Powell River. She helped as an interpreter on visits to the doctor etc. for Italian, German and French friends.

Wilma and William loved to dance, and attended many dances in Powell River, including those held at the Italian Hall in Wildwood. Often they would hold informal, impromptu dances in their kitchen.

Wilma and William's children: Christina, Juliana and Carmen remember with amusement their mother's early attempts at cooking. On one memorable occasion Wilma made a birthday cake which, instead of being springy was compressed and hard. With a smile, William brought out his drill and made a hole in the middle of the cake for the candle! In time Wilma, finding the right recipes, became an excellent cook. Their father is remembered as an amateur magician. The family had fun watching him doing a number of tricks – one amusing trick was, with slight of hand to change egg shells into a cake!

In retrospect, Wilma had difficulty in adjusting to the climate in the Powell River area after living in beautiful, sunny Italy. She also missed the social life of people interacting on the streets outside her grandfather's shop. After one trip to Italy, Wilma admitted that she enjoyed the freedom of living in a country like Canada, where there are no restrictions for women (such as driving) as they went about their daily lives. The Canadian climate was not the greatest but there were benefits to life in Canada.

Looking back, Wilma and William's children remember the great love their parents had for each other.

1950 Linlithgow, West Lothian, Scotland
Wilma and William Brown (RMP—Royal Military Police).
William met his Italian bride at the British Special Investigation Unit in Trieste, Italy where
Wilma worked as an interpreter.
Photo: William Brown collection

1950 Wilma and William Brown on their honeymoon.
Photo: William Brown collection

(L to R) William Brown RMP with Mrs. Brown (mother)/unknown RMP by the entry to the British Special Investigation Unit, Trieste, Italy, 1950.
Photo: William Brown collection

Royal Military Police ready for inspection at the British Special Investigation Unit, Trieste, Italy, 1950.
Photo: William Brown collection

1980-2011 war brides (seniors) –
Powell River's retirement community

I was an "unofficial" war bride because my Canadian husband was in the Merchant Navy

Doris Gammer (Vanner)

Doris Gammer (88) February 2010 Powell River

"In 1939, at the beginning of the war, I was working in Woolworth's in Luton. I was in the ARP (Air Raid Precaution) service. It was my job, with another employee, to go up on the roof when the siren sounded and be prepared, with a bucket of water, to put out any fires. I was staying with my Aunt Nellie (my parents were deceased). We had an Anderson shelter in the back garden. It was really cold in there at night.

I joined up when I was 18. I was in the ATS from 1940-45. I took my training in Halifax, England. At first I was assigned to a gun site. Radar was used to spot any enemy planes coming over. It was the girls' job to make a fix on the planes, and it was the job of the men (who were in the Army) to fire the guns. Later I worked in the ATS stores, and the post office on the base.

All our clothes, our meals and a bed were provided for. We did not get ration books; only a few clothing coupons (from 1943-45 only 10 coupons a year). If we were going on 48-hour leave we were given a small amount of sugar and tea to take with us. Tea was very hard to get. So anything we were taking home was really appreciated. If we ran out of tea at home, my aunt would take her teapot to a café and ask for a pot of tea. This had to be paid for, of course. The teapot was taken home and after the tea was drunk, the tea leaves were dried out be used again.

There were times when I was in London during an air raid. I rushed to the Underground to take cover. There were all kinds of people sleeping there. The trains kept coming and going all the time while people slept.

After V-E (Victory over Europe) we all had street parties. I threw my ATS uniform in to the flames – it went up in smoke – the war was finally over!

I met my future husband George in a pub. The pub was right across from the ATS camp. Like all the British pubs it was a friendly place, and we would get around the piano and have a sing song. I was with a party of eight when George came in. His ship had just docked. George was in the **Canadian Merchant Navy** and worked with radar on the ship. He made voyages to Canada,

United States and Australia. It was dangerous work because the ship could have been torpedoed at any time.

After our evening at the pub, George started to follow me back to the camp. I was a bottle blonde. I was engaged at that time to a civilian. George was persistent and asked me out for the next evening. So we started to see each other. We fell in love. I broke off my engagement. We decided to get married in England.

I didn't have to get permission from my aunt to get married as I was 21; however, George was 20 and required his parents' permission. His mother did not want him to get married in England. She suggested I come out to Canada for a year, and then if I liked it over there, to get married in Canada. George was the "baby" of nine children. She refused to sign the papers; however, George's sister Christine had the same name as her mother, so she signed the papers! My aunt advised me, if I was going all the way to Canada, it was a good idea to get married first in England. So we did.

The dress was borrowed from a friend of a friend, of a friend. It was a white wedding gown. I remember we had silver cardboard horseshoes for good luck. The wedding was scheduled for noon on a freezing day on January 27, 1945; however, there was an air raid on, so it was postponed to 4pm. Photographs were taken of the wedding but none came out.

The reception was held at my aunt's place at 9, Goldsmith Road, Walthamstow, London. I had bought the cake on the black market. I had no idea when George would be on leave in England for the wedding, so it was in a tin for three months before we were actually married. It turned out to be a flop. English wedding cakes are traditionally fruit cakes with marzipan and icing on; when this one was cut into there was no marzipan and instead of a fruit cake it was a plain white cake – and it was stale!

Our honeymoon was memorable; we were bombed on the second day and injured in an air raid. We were all sitting around having breakfast when the house was hit by a buzz bomb! The roof and chimney came down all around us. The windows shattered and there was glass all around us. We were covered all over with soot. Auntie Nellie was injured and sent to hospital. George and I had head wounds and had to go to a first aid station. We were both bandaged up. All around us were people with serious injuries, some near death. That night we stayed (on the second night of our honeymoon) in a Baptist church basement on bunk beds. We both had separate top bunks. We stretched our arms across the space between us, and held hands. We were glad to be alive.

After our honeymoon George was due to rejoin his ship, however the port of departure had been changed, and George had not been informed of the change. By chance he found out the port of departure and he rejoined his ship as it was leaving – he was taken out in a pilot boat, and all the ships in the shipping lane had to be stopped while he boarded. In the meantime I had a knock on the door and the MPs (military police) wanted to know where George was — they accused him of going AWOL (absent without leave).

Because George was in the Merchant Navy, I was not an "official" war bride. My husband had to pay for my travel arrangements to Vancouver.

I had to do the same paperwork as other war brides and have a medical in London. After that I was on my own. I was notified of my sailing from Liverpool, and then had to find my own way.

We were limited to the amount of money we could take with us. We were only allowed five pounds. I used newspapers to line my suitcase, so I put some pound notes between the sheets. I went through customs, and no one discovered them.

I sailed on the Mauritania with "official" war brides on March 20, 1946 from Liverpool. George had bought me a 1st class ticket but the accommodation was 3rd class. Yes, I was in a state room but I was sharing it with five "official" war brides, and their babies. The beds were bunk beds. Some had cribs at the side for babies. Because I was an "unofficial" war bride, I was directed to have my meals with a small group of English businessmen who were sailing to Canada, then on to the U.S.A. They were kind to me and gave me advice on where to stay in Halifax. I cried when I said "Goodbye" to them. They had been very kind.

A band was playing when the Mauritania landed. There was no Red Cross to greet me. I was all on my own. It was too late to get a train that day, so I had to overnight it until the next day. I got off in Montreal. I remember shopping, and buying a white pair of shoes, and matching hand bag. I felt all alone travelling by myself across Canada. The journey seemed to last forever, day after day. I kept thinking, when the heck am I going to get to Vancouver?

George met me in Vancouver. He was now in civilian clothes. **At first, he did not recognize me! In England I had been a bottle blond, I was now a natural brunette!**

At first, we lived in a summer cottage at Horseshoe Bay. The toilet was at the top of the garden. We then moved to the (British Columbia) Lower Mainland. My husband worked as a printer. Our daughter Sandra was born in Vancouver. A few years after I had been in Canada, I applied for Canadian citizenship.

In the 1980s we came to live in Powell River. Our daughter Sandra also lives in Powell River. I am now a widow. I have no regrets at coming to Canada as an "unofficial" war bride. It took a long time, but eventually the Merchant Navy received recognition for their contribution in WWII.

1941 Reigate, Surrey, England.
Registry office marriage of Joan Mansell and Sergeant Major John Mansell CAO.
After the ceremony the happy couple and bride's family headed to a pub for a meal.
Photo: Joan Mansell

(Left) 1939 Luton, England: Doris Vanner ARP age 17,
top of Woolworth's building demonstrating firefighting equipment.
(Right) Doris Vanner ATS 1942
Photos: Doris Gammer collection

George Gammer of the Canadian Merchant Navy and his "unofficial" WWII war bride
Doris Gammer (Vanner) ATS, September 1946 Vancouver, B.C.
George and Doris were married in London on January 27, 1945, however Doris
*was denied official war bride status because George was in the **Merchant** navy.*
(Right hand corner) First Class ticket purchased for the Mauritania by Doris Gammer.
Photo: Doris Gammer collection

Vancouver, B.C. 1944
(Left) George Gammer of the Canadian Merchant Navy and friends.
Photo: Doris Gammer collection

Note: In 2001, the Canadian Parliament recognized the contribution of Merchant Seamen in WWII by making September 3rd Merchant Navy Remembrance Day.

A Voyage on the *Queen Mary*

Joan Mansell   WWII war bride

Joan was born in England in 1922. When war broke out in 1939 she was just 17 years of age and was living with her parents and sister. Her father was in the British Army, and when he could, came home on leave. Joan worked on the land at a nearby farm, four miles away. She rode there, each day, on her bicycle; her job was digging and planting on a large vegetable plot. Her sister Gladys worked in a factory making parts for planes.

Canadian soldiers were stationed nearby, and walked by their house to the base. Joan's future husband John was a sergeant major at the base, and he was introduced to Joan by a friend of a friend. They met at a local pub where it was always cheerful with a fire in the hearth, and someone playing war-time songs on the piano.

Joan Mansell (89) 2011 Powell River

"We fell in love, and were married in 1941 at a registry office in Rygate. My mum and sister Gladys were present. I wore a nice blue suit and my husband was in uniform. Afterwards we went for a meal and a drink in a nearby pub. No wedding cake!

John lived on the base and he stayed with my family whenever he was on leave. My two boys, Art and Norville, were born during the war. My mother looked after them while I continued to work on the farm as part of the war effort.

Mum did all the cooking. Our vegetables came out of the back garden. We mainly lived on potatoes. We were registered at a local butcher. Once a week we clubbed our coupons together and purchased a small roast. When your name came up (at the butchers) we could get something extra, like a rabbit, and Mum made a rabbit stew. Occasionally we could get sausages (90% bread, 10% meat), and Mum made bangers and mash. Sometimes Yorkshire pudding was on the menu, often made with dried egg. Occasionally, we had a fresh egg — one egg per person per week, (if available). It was impossible to get fresh fruit, unless one knew someone with an apple tree! Sometimes Mum made a cake, there was no butter for baking, so she saved the cream which came at the top of the milk bottle. We had to queue for everything. Mum did all the queuing for our food because Gladys and I were working.

My mother and I sewed all the clothes for the two boys who were fast growing out of everything. It was very difficult to get materials, everything needed coupons. I had the opportunity to buy an army blanket which had been nicked from the army base by a private in the army. I used the material to make two outfits for my boys. First I dyed the material! The outfits looked really smart with leggings, jackets and hoods which were trimmed with velvet. I was often stopped on the street and the outfits admired. I was asked, "How many coupons did it take to buy the outfits?!" Obviously, I could not say that they were made out of an army blanket!

I shall always remember crossing the Atlantic on the Queen Mary with the other war brides and their children in 1945. *My mother and sister came to see me off at Liverpool.*

I had my boys, Art and Norville, with me. Thank goodness, they were out of nappies (diapers)! The three of us shared a cabin with one war bride, and her child. I think we had good accommodation because of our husbands' rank (sergeant major). The other bride was snooty, and did not speak to me throughout the voyage.

I was sick the whole way across, the children were just fine. I once went to the dining area but did not go in. Two sailors were near the door, ready to grab any of the girls who were about to throw up! My two boys had a good time on board, there was a special play area for the children; they were playing with toys they had never seen before. The Red Cross and Salvation Army helped with the children.

We were on the Queen Mary for four days before landing in Halifax, and we waited a further two days on the ship before going through Pier 21. ***It was the Queen Mary's first war bride voyage*** *and we were told to go on the upper deck, on arriving in Halifax, for a special reception. We were instructed to wave to the dignitaries on the pier — there would also be a brass band playing. Well, it was foggy and no one could see us waving! We couldn't see anyone on the pier; however, we did hear the band playing. Bags of candies and oranges were thrown on the deck as welcoming gifts.*

After we landed, it was a four-day journey across the country by a special train for war brides. We had two bunks on the train, an upper and a lower bunk. Both my boys tried the upper bunk, but after a short time up there, they called out they wanted to come down because the bed kept moving! So we all slept together on one bunk, with one of the boys at the bottom end with a pillow.

The war bride train stopped at one station so the engine could pick up fuel and water. We were allowed off the train for three hours. We were met by local people who volunteered to look after us, and show us around while the train was refueling. A nice couple met us and took us around the town in their car. They asked if I needed anything, and I said, "Yes, the boys need new comics, as the ones they have are falling apart." They stopped and bought some for them. They said it was a gift and refused to let me pay.

Looking out of the window we saw endless wheat fields, acres and acres of them. They just never stopped. Chug, chug, chug we went across the country. Some war brides got out along the way but we finally made it to Winnipeg where my husband was waiting. He looked different being out of uniform, and in his civvies. We met his parents, and they were very nice. After that we drove out to the section which John had purchased for us to farm.

There was a farmhouse but no electricity or running water. We had coal oil lamps and a woodstove. There was an outhouse at the back. I learned to cook on a woodstove — it took only two logs of wood, slowly burning, to bake the bread. Our drinking water came from the village well. We had a phone which was on a party line. I learned to milk cows, so did the boys when they were old enough. Our daughter Joanne was born in 1953. It was a good life on the farm for the children. We eventually sold it when John was offered a good job as a bookkeeper for Manitoba Pool seed depot in Winnipeg.

Looking back, I have no regrets at coming to Canada. I was able to visit my family in England a number of times. John died in 1993 at age 73. I now live with my son in Powell River."

Joan Edna Miller (Vesty)   WWII war bride

Joan lived with her parents, Lillian and Frank Vesty, in Charlton, London's East End. During WWII she worked in a munitions factory in Woolwich.

Joan first met her future husband, Orval Miller, a sergeant in the Canadian Army, on the doorstep of her parents' house. Orval, with two other soldiers, knocked on houses in their neighbourhood looking for billets. They had no success until they came to the Vesty home. Previously, Orval had been asked his name and, finding it unfamiliar, had been received with some hesitation by the English residents. Orval decided, on this occasion, to say his name was John! It must have worked, because the three soldiers were invited to billet with the Vesty family. Orval was always known as "John" to the entire Vesty family.

Joan and Orval started to go out together to dances and pubs. Joan, like many English girls, was a good dancer. They fell in love, married after the war was over, at a church in Church Lane, Charlton. Joan and the bridesmaids wore beautifully designed dresses by a dress designer, who was an old school friend. Because her father had died a few months before her marriage, a talented male school friend was asked to lead the bride down the aisle. Orval's best man was a fellow soldier who was Canadian First Nation.

Orval was in the 2nd Canadian Armoured Brigade; he drove fuel trucks, motorcycles etc. **Orval landed, with his unit in France on D-Day plus six, June 12, 1944. Orval saw action in France, Belgium, Holland and France. Orval stayed with the Canadian Army, from 1945-6, in Occupied Germany.**

Sergeant Orval Miller participated in the Scheldt operation which lasted from October to November 1944. Desperately-needed supplies were coming in through Normandy, however, the Allies needed access to a major port further north. Antwerp was captured as a working port; however, access to the port was from the Scheldt River to the North Sea. The liberation of the Scheldt from German occupation was a hard and bitter fight. Keith Miller recalls his father telling him how the dyke causeways were surrounded by water and the Germans' fire power was aimed directly at any moving vehicles or men on the causeway.

In 1947, Joan's first child was born in Hitchin, Herefordshire in a hospital for unwed mothers. Due to the bomb damage to London hospitals, and overcrowding in the few that remained open with wounded soldiers, expectant mothers were sent out of London. After the birth of her baby at Hitchin, Joan made a point of showing her left hand with the wedding band! Her second child Phil was born in Canada.

Orval liked the English people, their manners and way of life. He would have been prepared to stay in England with his wife and baby after he was demobbed from the army in 1946; however, job prospects were poor, rationing continued and housing was impossible to obtain with so many bombed buildings. Orval, his war bride Joan, baby Keith and Joan's widowed mother Lillian, sailed for Canada for a better life, in 1947.

The Miller family stayed in the mining town of Flin Flon, Manitoba for six years before returning to England in 1953. Joan and Lillian were homesick for the "old country". Lillian missed her other daughter, and a close sister. By this time the economy in Britain had picked up, rationing was over (1954), and Britain was rebuilding. Orval found work at a coal mine in Dover, which mined under the English Channel, and later at a Ford motor factory.

In 1958 the Miller family and Lillian Vesty made a second and permanent move back to Canada. Keith, age 11, recalls they sailed on the *Empress of France*.

Orval found work as a station engineer for the Saskatchewan Power Corp. for just over a year, then worked at Flin Flon in the mines for one year before moving to Snow Lake, a satellite community of Flin Flon. Orval and Joan retired in the Snow Lake area.

In 1980 Keith (a graduate of the University of Winnipeg), came to live in Powell River, B.C. His parents, Orval and Joan Miller, were frequent visitors to the area.

Wedding Bells in Canada

Bride from Nova Scotia learns to speak Italian

Aprilis (Hancock) Elva Irene (1924-2011)
Aprilis, Dino - CA

Elva Irene Hancock, born in White Rock, N.S. 1924, was one of ten children born to John Wesley and Mildred Dean Hancock. Wes Hancock owned a small lumber mill in White Rock, N.S.

Dino Aprilis, born in Italy 1923, was the son of Angelo and Rosaria Aprilis. Angelo was hired by the Powell River Company in 1924 as a stone mason. Angelo, seeing the prospect of long term employment in Powell River, sent for his wife Rosaria and their 6-year-old son Dino. They arrived in Powell River, March 1929. His brother Bruno and sister Ida were born in Powell River. Dino attended Henderson and Cranberry Elementary schools; he graduated from Brooks High School.

Dino Aprilis – Sergeant Canadian Army

Powell River Company Newsletter January 1945:
"----- and recent advices indicate Sgt. Dino Aprilis has picked himself an Eastern bride."

After graduating, Dino went to work in the wood room at the Powell River Company mill. In 1941, at age 18, he volunteered for service with the Canadian Army. Dino was stationed at Halifax, Nova Scotia after initial training in Camrose, Alberta.

Off duty one time, Dino was walking through the Public Gardens in Halifax with two army buddies, when they saw three pretty young women sitting on a bench. The men eyed the girls, and the girls eyed the boys!

Hoping to see the girls again, the three Canadian soldiers walked through the Gardens again the next day. The girls had the same idea, and were sitting on the same bench! Dino and Elva struck up a conversation; soon they were dating, fell in love, and were married December 1944.

Elva continued to live with her parents while Dino lived in the army barracks.

In 1945, after the war was over, Dino and his Nova Scotian bride headed for Powell River where Dino had a job waiting for him. The Powell River Company had promised all their former employees their jobs back, after the war.

Elva, although looking forward to a new life on the West Coast with her husband, was sad at leaving her parents and nine siblings behind on the East Coast. In many ways Powell River, B.C. and White Rock, N.S. were similar, they were both coastal towns, and had lumber mills.

Accommodation was difficult to find in Powell River in the postwar era. At first Dino and his bride lived with his parents in Cranberry. After a few months they found a vacancy in a fourplex nearby. Dino bought a lot in Edgehill and started building a house on it. In 1951 they moved into 5415 Manson Avenue.

Elva learned Italian in order to communicate with her in-laws. She was welcomed into the Italian community and the activities of the Italian Community Club. Picnics, dances and masquerades were all part of the family entertainment.

Dino and Elva had four children: Carole, Lorraine, Cindy and Kathy.

The Aprilis family had memorable summer holidays at Palm Beach.

When the opportunity arose in the late 1960s, Dino and Elva leased waterfront property on the Indian reserve near Scuttle Bay. It was their dream come true. Leslie Adams, from Sliammon, was working at the mill and gave Dino the "thumbs up" when the leases first came available.

Before the road was put through to the leased section, it meant a hike over rough terrain before reaching their lot. First Dino built a cabin at the back of the property, and then in 1974 he built their permanent home nearer to the water.

Dino and his Nova Scotian bride had many happy years living on the beach at Klahanie Drive. Here they hosted many family picnics, Legion of the Moose beach parties, Klahanie Fire Department fishing derbies and their front lawn was the setting for several family weddings. Most evenings, after dinner, they would get in their boat and try their luck at fishing. Many a good salmon dinner was had by family and friends.

WWII brought Dino and Elva together. Dino travelled across the entire country to his army post in Halifax. Under peacetime conditions, Dino would have married a local girl in Powell River, and Elva would have married her former fiancé in White Rock, Nova Scotia.

Elva was often homesick for her Nova Scotian family. Being one of ten siblings she missed regular family events: birthdays, weddings, summer BBQs and Christmas celebrations. About every five years, Elva made the trip back to White Rock, N.S. taking one or all her children with her.

Lorraine Franzen (Aprilis) 2011

"Elva was a wonderful mother, and homemaker. Dad, being Italian, put in a large garden each year and Mother canned all the vegetables, fruit and made many types of pickles. Mom was an excellent cook as well as her ability to knit crochet, bake, sew (costumes for those masquerade parties) and decorate cakes. She was also known for waking up in the morning to find a couple of large salmon in the kitchen sink ready for her to can. She was very proud of the crocheted tablecloths she painstakingly made for each of her daughters and granddaughters. Her ability to do ceramics was also enjoyed by many. She was always there for us when we came home from school and even when we were married, her advice was always available.

She was a long-time member of the Ladies of the Moose and an honorary member of the Powell River Health-Care Auxiliary. She enjoyed volunteering for the community she called home."

Carole Thulin (Aprilis) 2011

"Dad passed away in 2006, Mom then had to give up her waterfront home as it became too much for her to look after. She moved to Duncan Street and kept active in the Senior's Club. With failing health, Mom spent the last three months in the Powell River General Hospital. Sadly she passed on January 2nd, 2011. Her final wishes were that her daughters would return her ashes to her family plot in White Rock, Nova Scotia. We took her home at her favourite time of year which was Apple Blossom Time. She was laid to rest May 28th, 2011. May she rest in peace."

MacGregor (Mikklesen), Florence Marion from Winnipeg, Manitoba
MacGregor James - Distinguished Flying Cross, Pilot Officer RCAF Overseas

Digester Vol. 18 1942 Sept. *"Jimmie MacGregor, son of Lt.-Col. John MacGregor, VC, MC, DCM, has joined the Air Force as an observer."*

Winter Nova Scotia 1943: Elva Hancock and Dino Aprilis CA
Dino firsts met Elva in the Public Gardens in Halifax.
Photo: Aprilis collection

Spring Powell River, B.C. 1945: Dino and Elva Aprilis outside
Dino's parents' house in Cranberry Village.
Elva learned to speak Italian in order to communicate with her in-laws.
Left hand corner: Elva Aprilis and baby Carole (2 weeks) Cranberry Village 1945
Photo: Aprilis collection

*December 1944 Nova Scotia: wedding photo centre: Dino and Elva Aprilis.
After WWII was over, Elva left Nova Scotia to make a new life
in British Columbia—leaving behind her nine siblings.
Photo: Aprilis collection*

*December 1945 Vancouver, B.C.
Wedding day: Peggy and Duncan Bird RCN
Photo: Bird collection*

1948 Wildwood village, Powell River, B.C.
Peggy Bird and baby Bill on his first birthday. For Peggy it was a big
adjustment moving from city to country life.
Photo: Bird collection

1978 Wildwood village, Powell River, B.C.
Bird family (back row) Richard, Tom, Duncan, Peter and Bill
(front row) Linda, Marnie, Bryant, Peggy, Helen and baby David, Nancy
Photo: Bird collection

(Left photo) Lt. Earl Bonner Matheson CAO and wife Elsie Matheson, Brockville, Ontario.
Earl had recently received his commission before a second overseas tour in 1942.
(Right photo) 1945 Vancouver, B.C. Lt. Earl Matheson CAO holding baby Earl, Elsie Matheson.
Photo: Matheson collection

1945 England
Lt. Earl Matheson in hospital attended by Red Cross nurse Miss Westwood.
Earl recuperated on Lady Astor's estate.
Photo: Matheson collection

May 9, 1945 Marriage of James MacGregor DFC RCAFO to Florence Marion Mikklesen
(of Winnipeg) at St. Paul's Anglican church, Powell River.
The next day the couple visited Lt Colonel John MacGregor VC MC DCM on duty in Victoria.
Photo: Digester June 1945

(Left) Rosie of the North, Freda Stutt (Bauman) on her wedding day,
January 1946 Winnipeg, with Bob Stutt CAO.
(Right) 1944 Freda Bauman in Red Cross uniform, Powell River, B.C.
Photo: Freda Stutt collection

Powell River Company Newsletter

May 1944 *"Glad to say that Sgt. Jimmie MacGregor is convalescing well and keeping the nurses up to scratch in an English hospital."*

March 1945 *"Just received word that PO Jimmie MacGregor, who has just arrived home, has picked up a DFC on his travels over the continent."*

April 1945 *"Pilot Officer Jimmie MacGregor DFC and all, dropped in to say hello – got married on Tuesday May 8. Brought his girlfriend back from Winnipeg with him. Taking a honeymoon down on Vancouver Island – and to drop in to see "Pop" in the person of Lt.-Col. John MacGregor."*

Digester Vol. 21 1945 May *"Jimmy has had around 50 operational flights and the award (DFC) was made for "outstanding qualities of courage and initiative."*

Note: Lieutenant Colonel John MacGregor VC, MC, DMC was Canada's most decorated soldier in WWI.

WWII pen pals fall in love

Bird (Banham) Peggy
Bird, Duncan RCN

During WWII, Peggy Bird (from Edmonton, Alberta) became a pen pal to Douglas Bird RCN. Peggy had picked Duncan for a pen pal from a girlfriend's photo of her brother and crew on a Canadian warship.

They met for the first time, after the war was over, at an Edmonton railway station. They continued to meet each other; fell in love, and married. Peggy left her comfortable, modern home in Edmonton to live in the quiet country village of Wildwood (today part of the Municipality of Powell River). The first house they lived in was a shack, without running water; quite a shock for a city girl.

Meeting Duncan for the first time

Going on leave from his ship, Duncan corresponded with Peggy to meet up at Edmonton station. They had never met before. Peggy was on the platform with her two friends, Edna and Chris. There were hundreds of servicemen at the railway station – looking for one person you had never met before, was like looking for a needle in a haystack.

Then Chris had a bright idea; check the names on the duffel bags of the soldiers as they went by. One sailor went by, and they thought it was him. Duncan passed the girls, thought he recognized Peggy, turned back, and called out *"Are you Peggy?"* Peggy called out, *"Are you Duncan?"* And that was the start of the romance.

They all walked in the direction of Peggy's home, dropping off Chris and Edna on the way. Duncan was invited in, however did not stay the night, instead bunked down at the YMCA. After their first meeting, Peggy and Duncan continued to write to each other.

Duncan was demobbed in Vancouver, and travelled up the coast to his home in Wildwood village, near the company town of Powell River. Meanwhile, Peggy had left Edmonton to take up a job at the Bank of Nova Scotia (Scotiabank) in Vancouver.

The phone bills kept mounting up as Duncan in Wildwood, and Peggy in Vancouver kept in touch. Eventually, Duncan thought it was a good idea to get married and save on the phone bills and ferry fares to Vancouver.

Duncan proposed, with words to the effect:

"It is too expensive to keep on meeting and phoning!"

December 1945, Peggy and Duncan married in Vancouver. Peggy wore a smart green suit and Duncan wore his navy uniform.

First Impressions

They honeymooned in Victoria, and came back to Powell River via Vancouver Island. Duncan, philosophically said, on the boat from Comox to Powell River:

"Well, the honeymoon is over!"

It was. Peggy was horrified to see the small house, without any modern conveniences, at the rear of the Bird property. The house had no toilet, no bathroom, no hot water, and chickens running all over the back garden. In the house was one big sink, and a woodstove. It was quite an adjustment for Peggy, moving from city to country life.

Peggy Bird (2011) *"I felt I had come to the land which God had completely forgotten."*

212

Duncan's mother subdivided the Bird property and gave one lot to her son. Peggy was thankful to move into their new home.

The 1946 earthquake was memorable. The newlyweds were still in bed. Peggy recalls the perfume bottles rattling on the dressing table. Later, the neighbours told them they had missed all the excitement with the road rolling in waves, and some chimneys turning around.

Peggy gradually adjusted to, and eventually loved the country living in Wildwood. Duncan and Peggy belonged to the Goat Club. One time the club made a float and won $100! They kept chinchillas, promoted as a quick rich scheme; however, they never made any cash. Besides goats and chinchillas, they kept chickens in the backyard.

Looking Back 2011

Peggy: *"Wildwood village was a wonderful place to bring up a family."*

WWII Dear John Letter

Lambert (Bauman), Ruby **- married 1944/divorced 1945/remarried 1945**
Lambert, Russell (Russ)- CAO

Stuart Lambert (1914-2001)
1970 – *"My brother Russell married Ruby Bauman in Powell River while on leave in 1944. In 1945, while overseas, he received a Dear John letter breaking off the marriage. After the divorce, Ruby immediately married another local boy. Russell said he would never get married again."*

Life in the Canadian Army

Russ Lambert letter to his grandfather John Lambert, Sidney Army training camp, Vancouver Island 1942:
"…The Columbia Movie Picture Company is here in Victoria from Hollywood and is making a picture called "Commandos at Dawn". So we take the part of the commandos, sometimes in different scenes so if you see the picture, when it comes up to Powell River way, you might happen to see me in it. Sometimes we are dressed as Germans. Well how are things in P.R. and on the farm? I suppose you are busy at the potatoes now."

Powell River Company newsletter July 1944

"*Fusilier T.R. Lambert is with a Canadian Unit in Kingston, Jamaica (guarding German POWs).*"

Russ Lambert letter:

"*Haven't heard or run across any P.R. boys here in Jamaica. Fruit is plentiful, and do we boys ever go for the bananas, pineapples, coconuts, etc. The native come through the camp every day selling them. There's quite a lot of sports and it looks like we'll have a good ball league, there being several American and Cuban teams.*"

October 1944   "*Fusilier Russ Lambert, after nearly two years about in West Indian sunshine and seriously depleting rum reserves on the islands, is back at Dundurn, Saskatchewan, along with Cy Zilnic.*"

February 1945   Russ Lambert letter from England:

"*Brick houses everywhere. Haven't really been warm since I arrived. Guess you know I was married to Ruby Bauman on my last leave. The newsletters look better than ever now that we are over here.*"

June 1945   Russ Lambert letter:

"*I'm back with the Canadian Scots again. Have been stationed in Belgium, Holland and Germany since my last letter, and am now back in Uden, Holland. Quite a few P.R. boys here including the Poole boys --. Things were very quiet in this area on V-E Day – and the civilians, for the most part, kept out of sight.*"

<u>Wounded Canadian soldier at Lady Astor's Estate, England</u>
Memories by Elsie Matheson

Earl Bonner Matheson enlisted with the Canadian Army January 1940. In March 1940 he went overseas as an artillery gunner.

In 1941 Earl came back to Canada to get his commission. When he was home on leave in Vancouver, he asked Elsie Aileen Grant to marry him. They had a Christmas wedding. The minister came to perform the ceremony, after first enjoying his Christmas dinner!

The couple moved to Ontario in 1942 where Earl took his commission at Brockville. Lt. Earl Matheson returned overseas a year later. Serving in Germany with the Canadian Scottish, on February 18, 1945, Lt. Matheson received a bullet wound in the chest, and a fractured right shoulder blade. Initially he was sent to a hospital in Belgium, later transferred to England where he recuperated on Lady Astor's estate.

Elsie Matheson (92 years) 2011 Powell River

"My husband went missing in action. I was living in Vancouver and sharing a place with a girlfriend. Our first son, Earl Grant Matheson, was born while Earl was overseas, and he had not seen him. Our hearts were in our mouths when the telegram boy, on his bicycle, stopped at our house. We had no idea which one of us would get the telegram – well it was me!

I was so relieved, to hear later, that he had been found. He was sent to Lady Astor's estate in England to recuperate. The "boys" enjoyed going to the local pub. On one occasion they were stopped by Lady Astor. She spoke to the wounded servicemen with authority, and conviction.

Lady Astor:

'You fellows, I'm trying to be kind to you and get you well,
yet you are destroying yourselves by going to the pub and drinking!'

Lady Astor organized entertainment for the wounded men.

Earl came home to Canada on a hospital ship. When he arrived in Vancouver, kind grandparents were thrusting baby Earl in his arms – the first time he held his son. Elsie and Earl Matheson had two more children, Sandra and George."

Rosie of the North marries Canadian soldier

Stutt (Bauman), Freda (January 8 1921 – March 14 2011)
Stutt, Robert (Bob) - **CAO**

Digester Volume 18 February 1942
"The 9th Armored Regiment recently arrived in the Mediterranean area – including R.J. Stutt."

Company Newsletter January 1945
"Out in Italy, Bob Stutt is now eating the rich and nourishing grub furnished in the Sgts' Mess."

Bob Stutt came out to B.C. from the Prairies in 1939. In 1940 he was able to get a job with the Powell River Company. In 1941 he volunteered to join the Canadian Forces and go overseas. Bob met, and fell in love with a local girl, Freda Bauman, during his stay in Powell River. During the war, Freda worked in the Powell River Company mill plant and on the Boeing project. She was a Rosie of the North.

Freda Stutt January 8, 2011 (Freda's 90th birthday):

"I met Bob when he came to work for the Powell River Company in 1940. He left for the Army in 1941. We wrote to each other during the war. Bob served in Sicily and Italy. While he was

away in the war, I was working in the mill. I worked from 1943-44 on the Boeing subcontract for patrol and rescue planes. When the Boeing contract expired on November 1, 1944, I was transferred to the main mill plant in the shipping department, preparing rolls of paper for shipment.

I married Bob on January 19, 1946 in Winnipeg. It was a surprise wedding — a surprise for me! Bob had invited me to Winnipeg to meet his family. He was waiting there to be demobbed. I knew nothing about any wedding plans until I arrived.

We had to get permission from his CO to get married. It was difficult to get a wedding dress, the war was just over, and the dresses had been picked over just before Christmas. I did find a lovely blue dress which suited me. Bob wore his army uniform. I sent a telegram to my folks in Paradise Valley, Powell River, announcing our marriage.

We returned to Powell River because Bob had a job with the Powell River Company waiting for him."

6

WWII Child Evacuees

The London Blitz

War Child: Memories, 1939-1945

Rosemary Entwisle M. Ed.

WWII Canada's Guest program: British Evacuees (CORB)

Margaret's story — a child evacuee from Britain

Our Evacuee Cousins

Bev Falconer

Germany: child evacuee and refugee

Childhood Memories: Evacuee and Refugee

Elisabeth von Holst

The London Blitz

Excerpts from:
War Child: Memories, 1939-1945

Rosemary Entwisle M.Ed.

Crash! Crumpp! Whine of descending bombs, in the dark, in the middle of the night, family crouching in the shelter of the steel table, our kitchen table and thump means a bomb fallen nearby. "Thank God it is not us!" we think or exclaim.

So many nights in 1940, 1941, 1942 and 1943 passed with this scenario forming a part of our night's rest. We went to bed not knowing whether we would be intact or damaged, wounded or homeless, mangled in the ruins of our lovely Georgian house in Dulwich, London. The fear was suppressed, no one talked of it. It was the elephant in the room. We replaced it with humour that helped to ease tension with laughter. I do not know how my mother, abandoned by my father, coped alone with all of the responsibility of such a context and a family of four children of whom I was the youngest by five years. Nonetheless, she did, and did not lose her mind but stayed sane and looked after us all.

It all began in late summer 1939; we were on holiday in Blue Anchor, Somerset, beside the sea. Mother, my brother Gordon and I were there in the last few days of our stay.

It was a lovely warm sunny day, somewhere about midday, when Mother and I had walked the few yards from our cabin on the beach to the water tap. I was wearing my fairly new knitted yellow two-piece swimsuit. I recall feeling a lazy, pleasantly relaxed sense within me as I watched the water running clear and sparkly in the sunlight. We walked back to the hut and there within a few moments was a complete change of mood, a sudden falling, a dank chill on us as the radio proclaimed that war was now declared: *"England is at war with Germany"*. Everyone recalled those dramatic moments in later years, just as people recall what they were doing when John Kennedy was assassinated.

Next scene – during the "false war" period at the end of 1939 and the beginning of active hostilities. I am walking down the stairs to the basement, am halfway down descending into the empty dimly lit areas below where my elder brother Edward had his workshop and lathes. Just below the bend in the stairs I was frozen to a stop by a wailing banshee sound that went on and on and wavered up and down. Never before had I heard anything like it. It was an air-raid siren.

During 1940, I recall heavy duty guilt burdening me, in case while I drew the curtains at night I left some cracks between them that would allow light to get out and signal the enemy that "here is a target" or perhaps get my mother into trouble with the authorities for the light showing; she might be charged as an enemy spy signaling something to the planes in the sky. Closing out the dark became a responsibility indeed.

Walking anywhere became an adventure; you never knew what you might find. On the pavement or sidewalks and in the roads, lumps of shrapnel would lie in your path, remembrances from the battles of the night before, or bits of bomb, glass fragments from bombed houses, or sometimes houses that had been whole the day before had become ruins overnight. All the railings from the stately houses in Dulwich disappeared early on in the war to add to the supplies of metal for the war effort. The wall of our front garden was denuded in this way and presented its face to the world like a mouth with only stumps of teeth remaining, as the remains of the railings stood in the stone like amputated stumps of what had been graceful arms of wrought iron.

During the days there were constant bouts of dogfights in the sky between British and German fighter planes and sometimes flights of heavy bombers came over; mostly however, bombings were at night and the sky lit up with searchlights criss-crossing, and illuminating the many barrage balloons that appeared very early in the war as swiftly as measles spots only they were huge – over-inflated elephants of things that looked eerily beautiful, silver grey, in the lights in the sky at night, moving gracefully if clumsily in the winds.

One lovely summer's day, in the morning as I recall it, about midmorning, I remember looking up at the sky for hours from our garden watching fighter planes wheeling, dodging and diving, sometimes fatally, down towards the earth in the Battle of Britain, a decisive encounter that the British planes won, fortunately for us all. It was horrible for me to see smoke trailing from some of the planes, thick, black and corrugated, as they caught fire or were fatally damaged. Falling downwards, planes and small figures in parachutes also tumbled from the sky.

At night I went to bed not knowing what to expect, something dreadful might happen or it might not, and I guess we all fell asleep with our ears subconsciously primed to waken at the first sound of the air-raid siren as it was vital to be quick as possible to run down the stairs, through the hall and three rooms to take shelter underneath the kitchen table, a steel Morrison shelter. It was a far more convenient shelter method than the outdoors Anderson shelter dug into the earth with narrow benches on each side and a corrugated tin roof. In our shelter we had the warmth of the house for comfort and soft bedding to sit or lie on, complete with a sturdy wire mesh all around the sides, plus being able to nip out quick and grab a snack from the surrounding shelves and cupboards. No shivering out in the cold for us! We would be in there sometimes for a long time, others not so long, and listen to the very loud gunfire from the heavy artillery unit just behind our house, and wait for the whine of bombs, trying to locate where they might be falling, close to us or far away.

In the daytime going to school, we would have to take little boxes on a strap round our necks containing our gas masks and sometimes, unexpectedly, an alarm would sound and we would all have to trek from our classrooms to the Anderson shelters at the school and put them on in a gas mask drill. It felt pretty crowded in the shelters then. We would also have to carry iron rations with us in case of need in a disaster and these would be required and inspected by the teachers.

Air raids continued steadily throughout the war but gradually the form of assault from the air changed. Raids were no longer formalized, as I recall, possibly inaccurately or not, when early in 1944 manned raiders disappeared and were replaced with pilotless missiles, known as buzz bombs because you could hear them overhead and know they were about to fall as the sound of their engines cut out. This was the first wave. They were known as V1s. Life at my home continued as ever, except that early in 1944, I think, my dearly loved elder brother Edward, left us to train as a pilot in the Royal Air Force (RAF). I missed him a lot. Later in the early part of the year he left England to train in South Africa, in Pretoria I believe and also in Bloemfontein. I was proud of him doing his part in defending our country. That left my middle brother, Douglas, to be the man of the family.

Now there came another change in death from the sky. In the early summer of 1944 the buzz bombs no longer buzzed, if they ever had; I recall a sound of engines droning and then a silence as they cut out lethally descending to earth. The missiles (V2s) had changed to simply falling without any sound; now there was no prior warning of their presence, they simply happened, with their varied consequences.

Mother and I were walking in the garden on a late afternoon, I think, when she told me that we two children were to go and stay with our Aunt Rita in Manchester for a while. My acquaintance with Aunt Rita was thin; I had not seen her for a long time, although I think that when I was small and we lived in Manchester before moving to London in 1938, I had seen her quite a bit. Anyway, though, I knew who she was I felt I was being sent off to a stranger and to an unknown place, an alien land. My inner self was full of resistance, though as usual for a child, it did no good.

Though in reality, my brother and I were to become evacuees, it did not strike me that way. I never thought of us as evacuees.

To me, evacuees were children who several years ago at the beginning of hostilities stood in long lineups with labels around their necks stating their names and next-of kin's names and getting on ships for America, or going on trains to the country, to faraway parts like Devon and Cornwall where there were few to no bombs and they did not know anyone in their new homes. These to me were unfortunate ones. I suppose now that these were publicly and ubiquitously organized evacuees while my brother and I were privately and individually organized evacuees, privileged if you like, to be moving out of vulnerable territory to a rather less vulnerable environment and to live in a nice home with a caring relative. We were lucky ones. And my mother was right.

Off we went on a late July day leaving my mother, who was all-the-world to me, especially in view of my father's dereliction. Parting was so awful that I had to keep on trying to impress on myself to keep myself stiff-upper-lipped, and not crying, that "it is not forever" as her dearly loved figure receded from my view down Dulwich Avenue, waving goodbye. Smaller and smaller – soon to leave my life forever in spite of my affirmations.

After a numbness of a journey, we were greeted by Aunt Rita and her housekeeper, Annie, who was grey and somewhat creepy I felt. Auntie was a good-looking woman with auburn hair, a good slightly full figure and an elegant carriage. She was unmarried and had no children, but she was kind to us and looked after us well.

It turned out to be interesting exploring Auntie's house which she had designed and had built herself during the 1930s. She was a medical doctor and included in the house design was her office and in an adjacent area, her pharmacy where a pharmacist operated. I enjoyed looking around the shelves here, all kinds of varied drugs and liquid and bottles of pills. The house was beautifully furnished throughout in the thirties style.

One Saturday morning I was picking out the notes of the Irish song "Danny Boy" on Aunt Rita's piano. I was about 11 o'clock. We had been expecting Mother to come for a visit on the day before, the Friday of the English Bank Holiday weekend August 4th. I was very much looking forward to seeing her again; she was really the centre of my world, literally because she looked after us all alone because Father was absent. However, she had not arrived on Friday and I was exhausted with the excitement of expecting her and expecting till hope gradually dwindled and I was sent to bed, still hoping she would arrive.

On the Friday evening there was a strange atmosphere in the house and a low energy. Moving around I thought I heard odd snuffling sounds here and there. I could not understand and indeed did not find out the cause. Mother will turn up tomorrow, of course. So strangely enough, I was picking out one note at a time on the Saturday, a really sad Irish song of loss, unaware of the news of my own major loss about to break on me.

Strangely, again, my father arrived in the afternoon. Huh? No one was expecting him, surely. And there was still no Mother. Very odd. He brought with him two pretty dresses and terrible news. Mother had died the day before when a V2 landed in the garden of our home. She was found, what remained of her, in the garden by my unfortunate brother Douglas when he returned from a shopping expedition in London. No one mentioned to me these facts at the time; I learned them later from Aunt Marion. Our home was totally destroyed along with her.

So time passed and the day came when we had to return to London. We went to live with my father, towards whom I had great hostility because of his abandonment. He had acquired the flat beside his medical practice flat and had this flat, #12, 140 Park Lane furnished and refurbished to accommodate the remains of his family, my brothers Douglas and Gordon and myself, along with my beloved ginger cat Perry (named after a squirrel in one of my Bambi books that Mother had given me) who had survived the bombing. Perry was beautiful, a marmalade with long hair. I loved him wholeheartedly. Douglas had given him to me as birthday present. He was a happy reminder of happier times.

I was delighted when Father showed me to my new bedroom; it looked attractive, had a superb view over Hyde Park and the complex of roads around Marble Arch and the Arch itself, at that time a free-standing piece in the centre of the roads circling around it. I reunited with some pieces of furniture salvaged from my bedroom in Dulwich Wood Avenue, and the wall lights from our old living room there, elegant seashell-shaped lights of a warm off-white shade delighted me so much that I can see them now in my imagination. I was the lucky one; my brothers were given bedrooms at the back and Douglas' room backed onto scaffolding from previous bombings earlier. You stepped out the back door onto a cement floor and a section of the building that was propped up with wooden scaffolding. A narrow escape for his room indeed!

The end of our private evacuation had come and I had a new home for September 1944.

Life puttered slowly on and the war had now by the late months of 1944 turned in the Allies' favour. Bombings were almost forgotten. Life overlooking Marble Arch was calm and watching the people in the streets and the mobs attending Speaker's Corner were always interesting.

Until one early morning in May 1945; this was when my history as a war child came to an end. It was a Sunday and I was shocked awake by a very loud blast and shattering glass. A bomb had fallen on Speaker's Corner, just across the road from us. Fortunately, the Park was empty at the time and I believe no one was hurt but really I do not know as there were always people strolling in the Park. We were okay apart from frazzled nerves for a while.

After we picked ourselves up and cleaned up there was no more destructive furor until the noisy celebrations of V-E (Victory in Europe) Day, which felt very happy and joyous to mark the end of destructiveness.

WWII Canada's Guest program: British Evacuees (CORB)

Thousands of British children were privately evacuated to Canada during WWII. They were sent by well-off British parents: the aristocracy, the upper classes and professional people. Some came with their mothers, often accompanied by the children's nanny. Entire private schools came to Canada with their own teachers who taught the British curriculum.

There was great resentment from the general population that the wealthy were able to send their children to a safe country, away from the expected bombing of Britain's major cities. Evacuating all children abroad became a major class issue. Under great pressure by the general public and the press, the British Government conceived a plan known as CORB (Children's Overseas Reception Board), whereby the Government sponsored children to go abroad to participating Dominion countries. Anyone could apply, and CORB would select from the applicants.

The Canadian Government was at first unwilling to take the evacuees from Britain, mainly due to the shortfalls seen in a previous British program, the Home Children scheme where poor and orphaned children were sent from Britain to Canada to work on farms as free labour.

Home children had been sent to Canada for decades. In 1833, Canada had received its first shipment of 230 children by "The Society for the Suppression of Juvenile Vagrancy through reformation and emigration of children". Dr. Barnardo's Homes sent 30,000 children to Canada. A total of 80-100 thousand Home Children were sent to Canada from 1833 to the 1930s, when the Great Depression and WWII brought the project to an end. The Home Children were left for life in Canada. After their servitude ended at age 18, the scheme envisaged them living productive lives within the British Empire.

The Canadian Government changed its mind regarding taking in British evacuees, due to the enthusiasm of the Canadian public to help the children of the "mother country" during a time of war. The Canadian Department of External Affairs made it clear that British children were welcome; however, children who were European refugees were not. The CORB children would be called the Guest Children in Canada.

There were major differences between the Home Children scheme and the British evacuation program. Guest children were coming over to Canada as guests of the country, not as free labour to work on farms. Host families had to have sufficient income to look after the children like guests. Children could be sent to farms; however, they were not to be used as cheap labour. The guest children were in Canada for the duration of the war, and when it was over, they would receive a return ticket home. In contrast, Home Children were given a one-way ticket to Canada, never to return home, to the country of their birth.

In the fall of 1939 a questionnaire was sent out to the Canadian public, asking those who wished to host Guest Children to respond. The response was overwhelming and 100,000 British children were offered homes by the Canadian public.

Powell River News July 11, 1940 – front page

BRITISH CHILDREN EXPECTED SOON

"Preparations are being made to this district for the reception of several children from Great Britain. The first arrivals are expected shortly, but the exact date of their arrival must be kept a secret as a protection during their journey across the Atlantic. One little girl in Westview has already divided her treasures to share with the strange little girl when she arrives.

The evacuation of children from a war zone is undoubtedly a good move. With modern methods of warfare the civilian population are often victims and the less non-combatants there are in the danger zone the better. It is a pity that all the women and children in Britain cannot be brought over here, or to some part of the Empire."

The enthusiasm for the CORB (Guest) program was just as great in Britain as in Canada. Two hundred thousand applications were received during a two-week period before applications were cut off. It was impossible for the British Government to fulfill the great expectations of the British public for a mass exodus of the nation's children to Dominion countries, such as Canada, in the British Empire. There was not enough available shipping for a mass evacuation and no one, apart from the British Admiralty, seemed to have calculated the risk of German submarines hunting in wolf packs in the killing zone of the North Atlantic.

The inevitable happened; on August 30, 1940 the Dutch ship *Volendam* with 321 CORB children aboard was torpedoed by a German submarine. The *Volendam* was one of 34 merchant ships in a convoy with one destroyer as an escort. It was "an act of God," according to Geoffrey Shakespeare, MP Chairman of CORB that all the children were safely rescued by lifeboats. The British press enthusiastically treated the rescue as a mini Dunkirk.

CORB continued to send children to the Dominion countries. Surely, the attack by submarine on the *Volendam* was a wake-up call for CORB? If so, no one was listening. The enthusiasm for the program seemed to override concerns of real danger to life in the North Atlantic. Sending more children by sea to Canada was a gamble. The odds of all vessels carrying CORB children making the journey safely across were low.

It should have been no surprise to CORB that two weeks after the *Volendam* was torpedoed that another ship carrying CORB children was torpedoed, and this time there was serious loss of life. The *City of Benares* sunk, on the 18th September 1940, within half an hour of being struck by a torpedo in the North Atlantic. There were 406 persons on board, including 90 CORB children. In total, 248 people were lost at sea; this number included 77 CORB children.

For political reasons the British Government announced a *temporary* suspension of the CORB program. In reality the program was cancelled. Due to a lack of communication, there would be one more sailing across the Atlantic by a ship carrying CORB children (29) on the 21st September 1940. Although the convoy was torpedoed and some ships sank, the *Nova Scotia* made it safely to Canada. This was the last CORB sailing. Private evacuation of children from wealthy families continued.

Just under 3,000 CORB children were evacuated to the Dominion countries of Canada, Australia, New Zealand and South Africa. Canada received 1,500+ CORB children, a number far short of the thousands expected. After the war was over CORB children were given a few years in which they could return to Britain with their fare paid for by the government. There were a number of reasons for this grace period: conditions in Britain were so bad with many families without homes (due to the bombing), and food continued to be in short supply; some CORB children were either finishing their high school education or waiting to be demobbed from the Canadian Forces, and others were waiting for their parents to make arrangements to join them in Canada. For CORB children who married in Canada, the decision to stay had already been made.

Some children never recovered from the trauma of leaving two homes, first the one in Britain, and the second in Canada. The readjustment to a Spartan life in bombed-out Britain was difficult: continued rationing, a different educational system, cold houses with no central heating, walking instead of car riding, new younger siblings, and a lack of personal freedom in a more restrictive society. Looking back, many CORB evacuees remember the good food, the kindness of strangers, outdoor activities, the opportunity of a high school education, and the freedom of living in Canadian society.

In 1990 a CORB reunion was held in York, England for overseas evacuees. Many attended, including three of four sisters (Margaret, Joan and Ivy Aldham), who were abandoned by their parents in Canada.

The emotional cost of children leaving their parents and moving to another country was not foreseen by the CORB committee. The question lingers – was it worth it, considering the risks, to transport children thousands of miles away from their families during a time of war?

Guest (CORB) children memories – Powell River, B.C.

The total number of Guest Children who came to Powell River during WWII is unknown.

Bev Falconer, a child during WWII, recalls her Scottish cousins Blythe (13) and Velma (9) Farmer arriving in Vancouver in 1940, to stay with their grandparents and Aunt Pauline. Blythe and Velma had a glorious time enjoying summer vacations at Willingdon Beach, Powell Lake, Haywire Bay and Lost Lake. Blythe and Velma Farmer came to Canada under the CORB program.

Margaret Aldham (Powell River resident):

"I was an evacuee with the CORB program. I never returned home to my parents after the war was over."

In 1940 Margaret left Norwich, England, at the age of 6 with her sisters Ivy (13), Joan (11) and Brenda (8) for Vancouver, British Columbia, Canada. After the war was over, the four sisters never made the return journey home. Their mother Ivy came out for a brief visit in 1952; by this time Margaret was 18, Brenda 20, Joan 23, and Ivy at 25 was married. The four sisters never saw their father alive again after he waved to them goodbye at the Norwich railway station in 1940. An older brother, George, and three younger sisters: Shirley, Doris and Yvonne had been left behind in England. Margaret's sister Ivy felt that the entire CORB experience had led to the total fracture of the family.

Margaret's story (2011):

"I came to Canada under the CORB program in 1940. I was just 6 years of age at that time, with me were my sisters Ivy, Joan and Brenda. After the war was over, our parents decided to leave us in Canada. We wanted to go home but it never happened. I never saw my father again.

Our family lived in the town of Norwich, England. My father worked on the railways as a plate-layer. There were eight children in our family, seven girls and my brother George.

My father had been previously married, and after his wife had died in childbirth, he hired my mother Ivy to look after his two girls Isobel (Izzy) and May. I have no idea what happened to them after my parents married – possibly they went to live with other relatives. My parents (Fred and Ivy) had seven girls. My younger sisters were Shirley, Doris and Yvonne; they stayed in England.

I do remember the blackout in England. I was frightened when the air raid siren sounded. We had a shelter in our back garden. I was told if there was an air raid, and I was walking down the road, to jump into a hedge. I remember the little brown gasmasks.

I had no idea I was leaving my parents and going to live in Canada. No one told me anything. I do remember the four of us getting new socks.

My sister Joan remembers our parents coming to see us off. Dad was wearing his best suit. They waved to us and we waved back. Joan received letters from our father after she came to Canada.

We sailed on the Duchess of York. I have no memories of the journey by sea to Canada. Joan went on the deck, and she remembers seeing torpedoes in the water. A German submarine attacked our convoy.

227

My papers show that we landed in the Port of Quebec on August 20, 1940. I did not realize at that time that I was only a landed immigrant. Years later, I applied for my Canadian passport to go to Germany and, it was then I found out I was not a Canadian citizen. I applied for citizenship and it was granted.

I do remember going across Canada by train to Vancouver. We were on a troop train – it was quite Spartan; the train had been used to transport troops from Quebec. My sisters tried to hide me as we didn't want to be separated. Ivy had her birthday on the train on August 22nd; she was 13 years of age.

Officials of the Children's Aid Society were at the station to welcome the CORB children. We arrived in Vancouver at 10 p.m. on August 26, 1940.

I had my photograph taken, with another evacuee, at the station and it appeared in the newspaper the next day.

I was placed with Aunt Ellie, my mother's half-sister. Even though she had given prior permission for the four of us to stay with her, she seemed surprised to see four girls arriving at her house. Aunt Ellie quickly made a decision that she would only keep two of us. She asked my oldest sister Ivy to decide which two would stay. This was a difficult decision for a 13-year-old teenager to make. Ivy promised our mother that she would take special care of me, so I was chosen to stay with my sister Ivy at Aunt Ellie's.

My sisters Joan and Brenda went to stay with Edna Davidson in White Rock, B.C. Edna then moved to Greenwood, B.C. to teach the interred Japanese. Due to this move, I lost contact with these two sisters. After the war they moved back to the coast; however, I did not see them.

I only stayed a year with Aunt Ellie. She didn't want me. I guess I was a brat. She often threatened me when I was naughty, that she would send me to an orphanage. I kept thinking – please send me!

Edna Davidson's niece Esther offered to take us in. She was a teacher. Esther was married, she had no children and her husband was away in the Canadian Forces. Esther's mother, Eunice lived in the same house. I called her Grandma. I never called Esther "mother". I called her Esther.

I never called anyone Mother after leaving England.

Esther and Grandma were very good to me. I had my teeth straightened out. I had dancing lessons. They took me to Brownies and Guides. We spent happy days at the beach at White Rock, looking for crabs and oysters.

Iris went to high school but our mother in England was insistent that she leave school at age 16 and send some money to England. Iris resented this. When she was old enough, she moved out on her own. Later, she finished high school and took some university courses. She visited me. Ivy married sometime after the war was over.

It hit me in my teens that we had been abandoned, and that our parents did not want us back.

In 1952 I was adopted by Esther and Ashley Shatford when I was 18 years of age. My mother made a brief visit to see me because she had to sign the adoption papers. Ivy was also adopted by the Shatfords when she was an adult. She wanted to belong to a family. She said, "We belong nowhere."

At age 18 I joined the Women's Division of the Royal Canadian Air Force. I trained in Borden, Ontario. I was trained to work in radar: reading instruments with incoming information on the position of aircraft; also to locate flight positions on a map. I was sent on a tour of duty at Beaver Bank near Halifax.

I met my future husband Wally at the Canadian National Exhibition in Toronto. I was working in a recruitment booth for the Canadian Air Force and he was doing the same, nearby, for the army. We had a few dates and later we wrote to each other.

I had signed up for three years; after I had completed the tour of engagement I left the air force. I moved back to the west coast and trained to be a telephone operator. I continued to keep in touch with Wally. He came out to visit me when he was on leave; it was then he asked me to marry him. We were married in 1957. He came out of the army for a time and then, later, signed up for another tour. During this tour we went to Germany in 1960.

I met my brother George when we were over in Germany. He was living there because he had married a German girl. She was not in good health and after her death he came out to Alberta, because Ivy lived there. In the 1950s Ivy sponsored our sister Shirley (now in her teens) to come out to Canada. Later she sponsored Doris, and finally she sponsored Ivy (our mother) and Yvonne who came out together in 1956. My father stayed in England; he died in the late 1950s.

In 1990 I attended the CORB reunion in York, England. My sisters Joan and Ivy also attended. *(Brenda died at age 50).*

On a later visit I went to Norwich to see the house I had lived in as a small child.

I rarely saw Ivy (mother) after she came to live in Alberta because I was living in British Columbia.

Ivy (mother) celebrated her 100th birthday in a nursing home in Edmonton, Alberta in 2004. I was there with my sisters Joan, Shirley, Doris and brother George. Brenda had died in 1982; Yvonne in 1993; and Ivy (sister) in 1995.

I presently keep in touch with my remaining sisters Joan, Doris and Shirley.

Looking back now, although I was deeply upset as a teenager at being abandoned by our parents, I am happy now at having lived my life in Canada.

My sister Ivy felt that the CORB experience led to the total fracture of our family.

Growing up we were out of touch with our sisters, especially the three in England. Our father died alone in the late 1950s, and he never saw his four girls again, after waving goodbye to them at the Norwich railway station in 1940."

Our Evacuee Cousins

By Bev Falconer (2011)

When my brother, Doug, and I heard that our two cousins were coming from Glasgow, Scotland to stay with Nana and Papa while the war was on, we were very excited and curious to meet them. We had never met any of our cousins before because two lived in Australia and five in Halifax. Doug was 8 years old at the time and I was 10, and our cousins Blythe and Velma were about 13 and 9. At those ages it must have been frightening to be separated from their parents. Our cousins had come so far from home into the unknown to live with "strangers" and didn't know when they would ever see their parents again.

Blythe and Velma said that before they left, their dad told them to keep a lookout for the Eskimos selling ice cream cones on the icebergs! He adored his daughters and would have been trying to make them laugh before they faced the wrenching goodbyes. After our cousins arrived in Canada their parents were able to send broadcast messages to them on the radio.

It was the summer of 1940 when we first met Blythe and Velma at our grandparents' home in the pleasant, quiet neighbourhood of West 35th Avenue in

Vancouver. The first thing we noticed was how pale they looked. We had just come from a holiday at Qualicum Beach (Vancouver Island) where we almost lived on the beach – swimming, collecting shells, bowling rocks on the sands and just running around – so we were tanned in contrast.

I was fascinated by some of their belongings. They wore sandals – we wore running shoes. In those days we never saw sandals here. They had some lovely Fair Isle sweaters which were also new to me. But the biggest shock I got was when I saw their hairbrushes! They looked like instruments of torture – they had wire bristles. It was many, many years before I saw them in this country.

Our Aunt Pauline, who lived with her parents and brother, vacated her room for Blythe and Velma, and moved up into the unfinished attic. This would have been quite a sacrifice for her, though she never for a minute gave that impression. We girls liked to visit her upstairs. She always gave us strict instructions not to step off the planks which were on top of the ceiling joints on only part of the attic. If we did, we would go right through the ceiling! Aunt Pauline hade her hope chest up there and we loved it when she showed us all the treasures inside, especially her collection of gorgeous handkerchiefs, special gifts with fine lace and embroidery trim.

Aunt Pauline was about 35 at this time and the private secretary of the head of B.C. Electric. As a top businesswoman, she dressed the part. There was one bathroom in the house, and although this was the norm in those years, for Aunt Pauline having to share the bathroom with two more girls would have taken some organization. She spent a lot of time on her grooming; she had a bath every day, which is the accepted thing now but not common in the 1940s. She plucked her eyebrows, kept her hands and nails in perfect condition, put her hair in curlers every night (and had her hair set at the hairdressers once a week), and always washed her underwear and stockings before she went to bed. And she had quite a few beauty products – especially *Evening in Paris* talcum powder and perfume in their dark blue and silver packaging.

Blythe and Velma had a great time with Aunt Pauline. She and her many close single friends would often go on outings, and once the girls arrived they were included. All these women enjoyed this contact with the girls – lots of surrogate aunts. Aunt Pauline was fun to be with and she was constantly searching for new places to go and new things to do. They took a boat trip up Indian Arm to Wigwam Inn, visited the farm of a family friend at Lulu Island (Richmond, B.C.), took an overnight trip to Victoria, and attended a B.C. Electric picnic on Bowen Island. They also went over to North Vancouver across the new Lion's Gate Bridge which was officially opened on May 29, 1939 by King George VI and Queen Elizabeth on their Royal Visit to Canada. Of course all these trips would be on public transportation so would take a bit of planning – some great little adventures. Blythe and Velma loved Aunt Pauline – we all did.

In the summers our cousins would come up to Powell River where we had a great time. Doug and I had twin beds in the back bedroom. Dad set up a cot in the breakfast nook for Doug to sleep on and pushed the twin beds together so the three of us girls could sleep across the mattresses. Blythe was a real comic and kept us all laughing when she rolled her eyes back and made funny faces. One night there was a mosquito in the room – a very loud mosquito. Blythe declared she wasn't going to open her mouth and let it fly into her mouth. She didn't stop talking though, no, no, no. She just talked through sealed lips!

Often on Sundays, Dad took us up on Powell Lake in our boat. Sometimes we went up to the Washout. There was a natural pool there where the water got nice and warm and there was a little waterfall nearby where we could get a shower. As we wandered around we found lots of "Shell Oil" – shaped shells which we took home to paint. Driftwood was plentiful and there were also a few planks on the beach so we made a sort of table and had our picnic lunch there.

One time we went up to B & K Bay (Haywire Bay) where the B & K Company was logging. We hiked up the hill to get to Lost Lake. There were lots of wild raspberries on the sides of this old logging road, so we ate them along the way. When we got to the lake we made a great discovery – there was a raft there! Dad took us out for a ride on the lake, moving us with a long pole. Beautiful dragonflies were flying all around the lake. It was a real Huckleberry Finn adventure.

At the end of these outings, after we had tied up the boat we still had over a mile to walk home, each carrying some of the gear we had taken – haversacks, worm can, gas can, fishing rods and nets, the fish we caught, picnic hamper, bathing suits, towels, etc. We slept well those nights.

During the week we took our lunches and walked along the trail to Willingdon Beach on two days for our swimming lessons. On other weekdays we swam at Second Beach which was a shorter walk. There were no change rooms like there were at Willingdon – the boys changed in the bush on one side of the stream and the girls on the other side.

One summer Mom, Doug and I went to spend a couple of weeks in West Sechelt with Nana, Blythe and Velma in a rented cabin. Aunt Pauline came up for a weekend. We went by boat and got off on the wharf at Sechelt. It was a very popular summer resort. Several of Mom and Aunt Pauline's friends were also holidaying in

Sechelt with their families so there were lots of kids around – one day we all went roller skating at the local rink. There were blackberry bushes everywhere and we spent many happy hours chattering away as we picked pots of berries – and sampled more than a few. Mom and Nana had saved up sugar coupons so we were able to make jam with our pickings.

Our grandparents lived in Glasgow until Aunt Pauline (their youngest child) was about 18. So Nana was always basically a city person. She went shopping almost every day except Sunday. Of course before the advent of fridges, frequent shopping was necessary. To save time, most women would deal at neighbourhood shops or phone in orders to be delivered. Our city grandma, however, thrived on the hustle and bustle of the downtown. Before each trip she dressed carefully, starting with corset, slip, good dress, polished shoes, hat and gloves.

On Saturdays Nana took Blythe and Velma shopping with her (all wearing hats, of course). They got transfers when they got on the streetcar so they could first get off on Granville Street (Vancouver) to pick up meat at the shop of James Inglis Reid – the well-known Scottish butcher. The floor and counters were marble and the floor was covered with sawdust. On Robbie Burn's Day Nana would get some haggis and black pudding there. Nana and the girls got back on a streetcar and continued on to Woodward's store to do the shopping. Aunt Pauline worked half a day on Saturdays. The B.C. Electric Company where she worked was just across the street from Woodward's so she met Nana and the girls for lunch there in the restaurant upstairs.

On Sundays Nana took Blythe and Velma to church while Aunt Pauline made lunch for the family, and then played records from her extensive collection of classical and semi-classical music.

Our grandmother was the faithful family communicator. She and my mom wrote to each other once a week – always on the same day. She wrote regularly to Blythe and Velma's parents and as well sent them a Vancouver newspaper once a week. She kept in close contact with her eldest son and family in Halifax and other family members. It's amazing she had the energy to keep up this correspondence after a full day of preparing meals, cleaning house, shopping and doing laundry for a family of six. Nana would have been in her sixties when the girls were there, so this would have been quite an undertaking for her. I imagine she was exhausted when she dropped into bed at night. Aunt Pauline kept a close eye on Nana and did everything she could to lighten her load.

We were no longer able to go down to Vancouver every summer and Christmas to stay with our grandparents. Nana, Aunt Pauline and Mom were very close, so they really missed those times together. Fortunately, they were great letter writers. Nana and Aunt Pauline brought Blythe and Velma up to Powell River on the Union Steamship at the beginning of the summer holidays and picked them up again at the end of summer.

It must have made it somewhat easier that Blythe and Velma's home in Canada was of the same Glasgow background as their own. Culture shock wouldn't have been such a problem. They had an example of meticulous grooming from both Nana and Aunt Pauline. Also of importance to the Scots are education and work habits and Aunt Pauline saw that those were installed. She had a huge dictionary – the kind you see in libraries – it was open on top of a bookcase. Whenever any of us asked about the meaning of a word she always told us, *"Go look it up in the dictionary."* And she made sure we did. Aunt Pauline helped Blythe with her shorthand and business courses, and because she was such a stickler for perfection in her own work, she was an excellent role model. This extra coaching stood Blythe in good stead because she became a top secretary at the University of Glasgow – a job she loved.

Blythe had two very good friends in Vancouver, Pat and Pen, who were twin sisters. They kept in contact every year and Blythe visited them when she returned to B.C. for a visit about 25 years after the end of the war. I don't know if Velma had any special girlfriends but she was interested in boys. She met one during our holiday in Sechelt and spent all her time with him and when she went back to Vancouver she had a steady boyfriend there. She would have been about 12 at the time. She clung to adults too – Nana, Aunt Pauline, my mom and dad. I think she craved being taken care of. I don't know what Velma's work was but she married fairly young to a naval officer, and they had one son. Velma and her husband also came out to visit her B.C. family within a few years of Blythe's visit. The sisters were very close – their dependence on each other during the war years was probably one reason for that.

At the end of the war our cousins felt as torn from their new home and family as they had when they left their parents. Back home there were difficulties with their mother which were not entirely caused by the separation, although new attachments are bound to aggravate an existing jealousy. They missed Vancouver and their family and friends dreadfully. However, after a few years when they settled into their life-to-be, things seemed to work out well for them.

My mom and dad visited their nieces in Glasgow in the 1970s and we visited them in 1983. They were both happy with their lives. Blythe took us on a wonderful extensive tour of the city – she thoroughly enjoyed showing us the city she loved.

Four sisters (L to R) Brenda, Ivy, Joan and Margaret Aldham who came to Canada from Britain under the CORB program in 1940. The program split the seven Aldham sisters with four residing in Canada, and three remaining in England.
Photo: Margaret Aldham collection

Mr. and Mrs. Aldham with their three youngest girls: Doris, Shirley and Yvonne: Norwich, England 1943.
Photo: Margaret Aldham collection

White Rock, B.C. 1943
(L to R) Margaret and Ivy Aldham.
The four CORB sisters were split up when placed in Canadian guest homes, two placed with
one family, and two another. The sisters rarely saw each other.
Photo: Margaret Aldham collection

1940 Vancouver: CORB children Velma and Blythe Farmer.
They were guests in Canada, staying with grandparents, for the duration of the war.
Photo: Bev Falconer collection

Powell River Townsite 1942
Back (L to R) Blythe Farmer, Aunt Pauline Farmer, and Grandma Farmer. Front: Velma Farmer
WWII—for the summer months the CORB cousins Blythe and
Velma Farmer stayed with their Canadian cousins,
Bev and Doug Carrick in Powell River, B.C.
Photo: Bev Falconer collection

Lost Lake, B.C. 1943
(L to R) Velma and Blythe Farmer/Lily, Bev and Doug Carrick.
The cousins enjoyed a fishing trip in the Canadian wilderness.
Photo: Bev Falconer collection

1951 Westview, Powell River, B.C.
(L to R) Glen Roscovich (infant), Ronnie and David—private English evacuees
who stayed with neighbours of Frank and Ruby Roscovich. After the war some British
children stayed in Canada, waiting either for parents to join them or for new accommodation
in the U.K. (thousands of houses were bombed during the war).
Photo: Ruby Roscovich

The Ochs family visiting Maple Valley, Renton, Washington, USA 1956
Elisabeth Ochs and Dieter von Holst were newly engaged.
Top row: Murray Bartels, Hilde Bartels, Gudrun Ochs, Elisabeth Ochs
Middle row: Fred Bartels, Eberhard Ochs, Dieter von Holst
Seated: Peter Ochs Photo: Elisabeth von Holst collection

The Ochs family left Germany for Canada on the Beaverbrae June 3, 1953.
(L to R) Inge, Elisabeth (born 1903), Gisela, Gudrun, Eberhard (born 1895),
Elisabeth (daughter), and Marianne.
The Beaverbrae was launched as the Huascaran 15th December 1938.
From 1948-54 the Beaverbrae carried cargo east bound to Bremen, Germany
and refugees west bound to Canada: monthly sailings with 500-700 immigrants.
Photo: Elisabeth von Holst collection

The Ochs family on the deck of the Beaverbrae June 3, 1953:
Ingve Ochs, Gudrun (Dudel), Gisela (Gisi), Elisabeth (mother), Marianne, Elisabeth (daughter).
Photo: Elisabeth von Holst collection

Childhood Memories: Evacuee and Refugee

Elisabeth von Holst

Excerpts from Childhood Memories:

March 1945

Life was getting more tense – My Aunt, Tante Lotte even announced everyone is allowed to pick two jars of preserves and eat as and when you like. One of my chosen fruit was a jar of mouth-watering pears. In the distance the tanks with their roaring thunder-like sounds of the sometimes high-pitched whistling were heard as they came closer in our direction. We children were helping (we felt or thought) by digging trenches to hide in, but the ground-water came in faster than we could shovel. We had such imagination of moving in there and sort-of 'play house'. Refugees were coming from the train station and collecting on our relatives' farm property. A Cossack-couple were galloping towards us on pony-size, wild-looking horses, the woman holding a baby wrapped in a rough blanket. Everything seemed very exciting. We weren't even aware of the danger.

We had helped pack for the trek with almost all our belongings, because we had planned to flee with our relatives. BUT order from above: all who are refugees (not originally from here) have to be on the train tomorrow morning!!

Mutti sick with strep throat, sisters older than Gudrun and I were getting ready, Marianne stirring blood from the slaughtered (900 pound bear) and I was fighting with the village boys. Brother Peter was wise not to get involved; I remember the breath-taking blow across my back which made me disappear from the fighting scene at this place...

Now there were barely any clothes as luggage... I heard our Mother say: "We'd better take a loaf of bread and some lard, just in case..."

Now on the train we had to fight for the doors to get closed... some people took bicycles that hardly fit... On the way west – nobody knew where we were going, Alarm!! The well-remembered sharp warning sound of those air raids we were used to in our home city, Koenigsberg. Flashes of Father who stayed behind in Koenigsberg... The train stopped near the city of Magdeburg; order: only very important belongings, one per person. We had these shoulder bags with a change of underwear, a gasmask that was tied on individually, a package of Leibniz-Keks (German brand of biscuit), toothbrush, etc. I liked that bag which served as my security blanket and it still amazes me that I never touched the cookies... With very insecure, tense feeling we were almost pushed to hurry and enter the underground bunker. We were used to just going into the basement at home. Miraculously our family with our great aunt, Tante Martha and Tante Lotte's maid, Anneliese and the seven of us stayed pretty close to each other ... My great aunt was 89 – someone offered her a chair, but gave it up to an expectant mother. That impressed me.

Police very active all around us; electricity had gone out … ordered to be totally still, in case of an impacting bomb or such … (Much later we heard that bunker was destroyed with all 3,000 who sought refuge.) The all-clear siren allowed us to find our way back onto the train … It was cold, many windows missing. Our mother asked Anneliese to try to get some heat from the locomotive into the train … and we could soon feel how warmth penetrated very slowly, into the railroad car we occupied… Our preprogrammed destiny was in Nienburg on the Weser River. We stayed that night in a school gym on straw (poor Tante Martha!) We each received a small container with soup. I heard Mutti remark several times in later years: "…there has never again tasted soup as deliciously as in Nienburg on our flight west." It was cream of leek soup.

Next day all of us refugees were helped onto military vehicles and driven to nearby villages. Our names were called first, because Frau Sieling's house was situated at the entrance of Holtorf …Our new land lady was chosen to take all eight of us in, although she lived in a one-family home with her five-year-old son, her husband still being in the war. She was already giving refuge to Frau Schnell, mother with four children from Hamburg who were evacuees because of the many air raids on their city.

Frau Sieling had prepared a delicious dinner for us — we remember that we each had a chair to sit on. White tablecloths were covering the long table set up in the hall, decorated with beautiful flowers in fancy vases. The yellow potatoes gave off such scrumptious scent, that it still brings forth that nostalgic, memory-inducing experience. We were also served meat and gravy, some vegetables and fruit, home-canned, for dessert. That was a special feast, never to be forgotten.

At this time we also got permission to pick the fallen apples off the ground. Food was getting less and less plentiful; I was desperate not to eat any more of those hard-to-digest carrots, only to take another one, less than 10 minutes later. My poor, pain-stricken stomach was revolting in rhythmic spasms. Hunger was domineering and there was this 50kg sack with carrots!

The time in Holtorf was filled with music. Inge joined a church choir and came home filled with music which she passed on down "the organ-pipes" which we were referred to because of our sizes. Lack of paper didn't provide sheet music, so Inge memorized the three parts of the songs they practiced and wrote down the notes for each voice's part as soon as she arrived home. These became family favourites which we used throughout our lives from after the war in West Germany and later on in Canada at all sorts of celebrative occasions.

A type of hop-scotch was played on the sidewalk in front of Holtorf 131. We had to maneuver a round, flat glass object, hopping on one foot, pushing it from one drawn box into the next, never leaving it on the line. How frightened we were when we heard a plane ascending lower and lower between the houses, aiming at us as we were playing! Marianne yelling: "Come on, let's run inside!" Our hearts beating violently of course.

Mutti came home with a real loot when she had two foreign soldiers walk in front of her, carrying a rolled-up blue and white checkered comforter-cover. She was always thinking how to be able to dress us all. As she caught up to them, she pointed to the rolls under their arm, got out her wallet, pointed to that and had them understand what she meant. They reacted promptly, shook their heads when mother insisted on paying for it and passed over the material that turned into two beautiful dresses for the two oldest girls.

September 14th, 1945 Papa's Homecoming

It was an ordinary day during the fall holidays in Holtorf near Nienburg on the River Weser in Lower Saxony where we had lived since March '45. There was an understanding between my parents, that whenever there is a change in our whereabouts, the Red Cross would be notified.

Mutti went with Frau Schnell, the evacuee from Hamburg, a mother of four children, who lived in the same one-family house we did. These two young women (42 and the other younger) had to stand in line for the ration cards everyone was given at a particular store.

Marianne was inside working on making tinsel for Christmas to decorate the tree we were anticipating to have on December 24th. The silver strips were thrown from the airplanes to interfere with the radar; nothing was unused in those days. My brother Peter, Gudrun and I were busy in the harvested potato field, looking for any little potatoes that could be salvaged to cook in the fire. Peter was gladly in charge of this duty. Unfortunately they burnt quickly because of their size and didn't even taste good. It was food, though.

While in the lineup for the ration cards Mutti unexpectedly spotted Papa crawling down the street. "Frau Schnell, I think that's my husband coming." She met up with him and offered him her arm at once.

Poking around in the fire that held the potatoes, I happened to look up the driveway; I saw Mutti walking very cautiously and slowly with someone holding on to one of her arms. I soon realized it was Papa! Being a well-structured, healthy-looking, handsome man only about a year ago, I was shocked that this was the same person. At that moment my legs felt weak, shaky, almost paralyzed.

The sight was heart-wrenching! Father looked like a man who shouldn't be walking; like someone you might see in pictures, being close to death. He weighed under 100 pounds and used to be more than double that. His height was 1.87 metres. I think he had shrunk too. His head was shaved; he wore an old ugly uniform, had one foot wrapped with a piece of sack, the other had a rubber shoe on it. On his back a paper sack was held by some old rope.

The greeting was very carefully done with no tight hugging, just with kisses on the cheek. I was afraid we would knock him over. Mutti had great difficulty getting him into the tight quarters we were occupying in the fine one-family home.

Papa sort of apologized for not having anything to bring us, which he had always done coming from his business trips back home in Koenigsberg. He had gone into a bakery in our new village and asked if he could have just something for his children, because he was coming 'home' from being a prisoner-of-war. That turn-away was a letdown he didn't easily get over.

Mutti had the difficult job of doing what was necessary; to restrict the food and drink intake. There wasn't much to eat anyway, but Papa was not thinking rationally and accused Mutti of letting him starve.

Our great aunt, Tante Martha, who was 90 years old and blind, had to move to another house on the same street, to make room in the bedroom.

Gisela was working on a farm where she received ½ a liter of milk a day for the family. When Papa joined the ranks she asked politely for another ½ liter but the farmer's wife replied, "Why do you devour so much like pigs?" How little did they know why we were even on their doorsteps?

These villagers were just ordered to open their homes to a certain number of evacuees and then also refugees; and we were ordered to board a train which took us west. That's how we ended up where we did. Many people couldn't understand what it meant to have to flee as the front was nearing. (We could hear the roaring cannon-thunder.) It didn't make sense as this one villager commented: "You must have felt guilty to just up and leave your homes!?" I always thought it was like a miracle that Papa found us.

Timeline:

Elisabeth Ochs was born in Ostpreussen prior to WWII. As they were living in the capital city, Koenigsberg which was bombarded by enemy planes, their uncle took the children to a safer place, once in 1941 and then again in August of 1944. (They were Evacuees twice.) As the Russian front became closer and their father sent them to a safer place with their aunt in Leubsdorf, near Cottbus; they became Refugees. When this was not safe here anymore they were ordered to leave immediately by train, just going west. That's when they ended up in Holtorf and witnessed here the end of the war, April 9, 1945. Now Germany was divided in to four sectors by the Allies. They were under English control in Holtorf.

After staying in Holtorf from March of 1945 to the spring of 1946 the Ochs family moved to Niederbieber, near Neuwied, in the Rhine Valley, to be with relatives. They were in the French-controlled zone here. In 1961 the 'Berlin Wall' was constructed and everything east was under Russian control. That was East Germany and all the other three sectors belonged to West Germany.

In the early 1950s, the Ochs family: parents Eberhard and Elisabeth Ochs, and their six adult children: Inge, Gisela, Peter, Marianne, Elisabeth and Gudrun made a decision to come to Canada as a family. Relatives in Agassiz, British Columbia sponsored them. Peter was the first one to arrive in Canada in 1952. Elisabeth (age almost 18) and family members sailed on June 3, 1953 from Bremen to Quebec City on the *Beaverbrae*. In 1954 the family moved from Agassiz to Vancouver.

Elisabeth trained as a teacher. In 1956 her first teaching position was in Van Anda, Texada Island. Her fiancé found a job with the Powell River Company and moved into the staff quarters. In 1957 Elisabeth married Dieter von Holst in Vancouver. Their first home was one of the little cabins (previously an old motel, 'Turnbull Cabins') at Powell Lake. Dieter worked for what later became MacMillan Bloedel; his first job was cleaning the floors and janitorial jobs. He worked up to getting his papers as Millwright to being Supervisor of the Mechanical Department in the Kraft Mill. Elisabeth and Dieter became long-stay residents in Powell River, B.C. (Dieter died in 2002).

7

Stillwater, Kelly Creek & Douglas Bay (Brew Bay)

- For thousands of years **First Nations,** the Cokqueneets (Sechelt Band), lived in the Stillwater area. This was part of their traditional lands. Part of the Sechelt Indian Band Lands #23 is a 60-acre Indian Reserve adjacent to Palm Beach Park. The last of the Cokqueneets to live on the reserve were Chief Tom, his wife Mary, and his son Skookum Tom and families. They left the reserve in 1918 after their numbers were decimated by the Spanish Flu epidemic. Chief Tom's son, Angus and wife, moved to Sliammon, and his youngest son Skookum Tom moved to Sechelt. First Nations artifacts have been found in McRae Cove. In the 1960s a small midden was opened at Canoe Bay.

1929 *Powell River Company Digester* November edition:

"The Stillwater tract encompassed what was undoubtedly the finest strands of Douglas fir ever located in British Columbia. The quality and magnitude of the trees logged along the shores of the Gordon Pasha Lakes have never been surpassed in the history of logging in our province."

- 1793 Exploratory survey of the coast by Captain Vancouver.

- 1860 Captain Richards in HMS *Plumper* surveyed Lang Bay and Stillwater area.

- 1880 Leonard Frolander opened a trading post at Frolander Bay. *Etta White*, a wood-burning side-wheeler, called with mail and supplies.

- Jim Palmer and his son Will Palmer, who came from Oregon, trapped in the Gordon Pasha Lakes in 1898 and they sold furs at Frolander Bay. The Palmer family homesteaded in Theodosia Inlet in the early 1900s.

- 1898 the first Union Steamship Company boat, the *Comox* called at Stillwater. Service continued until 1948.

- Large salmon runs at the turn of the 20th Century.

- Large herring runs – caught in pits on the sandbars by the Japanese shingle bolt workers. Deer and grouse plentiful.

- 1890s Logging started by Farquhar McRae. He logged the shoreline around Scow Bay (Stillwater) using oxen, until the turn of the 20th Century.

- 1900 Land at Scow Bay owned by a Mr. Simpson. He sold it to John O'Brien.

- 1907 Bob Simpkins pre-empted a section of land at Wolfsohn Bay.

- 1908 Brooks & Scanlon bought the O'Brien logging company (which included a railroad). O'Brien became a partner in the new company: **Brooks, Scanlon & O'Brien**. They logged the area south of Powell River on a grand scale. Millions of feet of timber were logged.

- Rumour! A small hotel (1908-1909) was built on speculation at Thunder Bay, by a Mr. Bowes. He gambled that the Powell River Company would locate a mill in the Stillwater area. He lost the gamble! His hotel was abandoned, and later burned down.

- **Scow Bay renamed Stillwater by Brooks & Scanlon in 1908.**

- The **Gordon Pasha Hotel**, Stillwater was built about 1910 in Stillwater Bay at the Brooks, Scanlon & O'Brien's base camp. The hotel had a store, pool hall, restaurant and post office. The postmaster in 1914 was Johnny Brownrig.

- 1890s – The Hastings Mill Company was the first company to log the Lang Bay District. Their camp, the first in Brew Bay, was located by the mouth of Wolfsohn (Wolfson) River. It was the first railroad camp in the area, and the men and their families lived around the shore of Brew Bay (Douglas Bay). They logged the "J" claim.

- 1911 Elder Brothers took over the claim and extended the railroad (Kelly Creek Road).

- 1911 Bob Simpkins married a widow, Elizabeth Lang with four children: Edith (Flinn), Tom, Harry and Fred. The family lived at Wolfsohn Bay.

- 1911-1920 Over 1,000 men worked as loggers between Myrtle Rocks and Stillwater, and far back in the bush to Haslam and Nanton Lakes.

- 1912-13 Lang Bay wharf built.

- 1918 Post office service at Lang Bay store. Postmasters: John (Jack) Young, Mr. and Mrs. George Barrett (Jack's daughter). 1946 Almer McNair, 1948 Norman Fiander. Post office permanently closed 1950s.

- **Wolfsohn (Wolfson) Bay School** 1911-1920 built adjacent to Wolfsohn Bay by the loggers of the Lamb & Pendleton Companies. During WWI it was renamed Lang Bay School in honour of the three Lang brothers who were overseas in the CEF. 1920-1937 a new larger **Lang Bay School** was built in a more central position. After the school amalgamation of 1937 the building became the Lang Bay Community Hall.

- 1913 Robert M. Maitland purchased land at Wolfsohn Bay.

- 1914 Lambs bought the Elder Brothers rolling stock. Lambs extended the railroad to connect with Foley, Stuart & Welch (later Bloedel, Stuart & Welch) at Myrtle Point.

- **1914-1918 The Great War (WWI)**

  The three Lang brothers (Wolfsohn Bay 1911), and Don Dunwoodie, a logger from Stillwater (1913), joined the CEF and went overseas. Wolfsohn Bay was renamed Lang Bay in honour of the Lang Brothers. John Lee and James Lloyd, veterans of the Great War, relocated to Stillwater in the 1930s.

- 1920s Truck logging introduced in the Lang Bay area by Gordon Cornell, Art and Jim Kennedy.

- 1921, January 29th – huge windstorm with gusts of 100 miles-per-hour caused devastation from Thunder Bay to Powell River.

- July 1922 - After an exceptionally dry June, a huge fire, aided by strong winds, swept from Myrtle Point through to Lang Bay. Miraculously, Stillwater was spared. Mrs. Fletcher and Mrs. Finn kept draft horses in the ocean for many hours while the fire went through. The settlers lived in tents, with wooden shiplap floors (courtesy of the Powell River Company). The Lang Bay School survived the fire.

- 1923 Large hall built at Stillwater. Four hundred couples from up and down the coast attended. The Capitol Theatre orchestra from Vancouver was hired to play. Hall burned down Christmas 1925. 1932-47 community hall in a donated bunkhouse from the Powell River Company. 1947 new hall built on School Road, Stillwater. Demolished in 2000.

- 1925 A second disastrous fire. A spark from a Brooks & Scanlon steam donkey started the fire. Settlers in Horseshoe Valley had to flee their homes, many left on railroad flatcars, others found safety in Spring Lake. Millions of feet of felled timber went up in smoke.

- 1926-37 **Annie Bay School** was built on land donated by Mrs. Annie Westerlund (Frolander) in Frolander Bay.

- 1924 **Robert McNair Shingle Bolt Company.** Nat McNair superintendent. The shingle bolt company kept men employed during the Depression years of the 1930s. The Caucasians, Chinese and Japanese workers had their own separate camps.

- 1925-37 First **Kelly Creek School**. Settlement came to Kelly Creek in 1924 when a group of Austrian families came to the West Coast, via Saskatchewan, to find sunshine! They bought land for $2.50 an acre. Some left but a few stayed on: Zilnics, Martinuks, Nassichuks, and Gurlics. The second Kelly Creek School was built in 1958.

- 1928 Brooks, Scanlon & O'Brien purchased by CRT of Campbell River.

- **1930 Powell River Company constructed the dam and power house at Stillwater. 400+ construction workers employed.**

- **1930 Barbara Lee, WWI war bride, moved to Stillwater.**

- 1930s John McRae horse logged at Stillwater.

- 1937 truck logging by George O'Brien, west side of Second Lake. Later logged by Alice Lake Logging Company (owned by Powell River Company).

- 1937-1980s **Stillwater United School.** Three one-room schools (Annie Bay, Lang Bay and Kelly Creek) were united to form a new two-room school enrolling Grades 1-12. The school was built on land donated by the Powell River Company and had electricity and running water. Many christenings in the school by various churches: United Church, Salvation Army, and mission churches.

- **1939-45 World War II**

Thirty plus men and women from Stillwater, Lang Bay, Kelly Creek and Douglas Bay volunteered to join the Canadian Forces. This number included two veterans from WWI, John Lee and James Lloyd.

- 1941-43 CO (Conscientious Objectors) camp between Nanton Lake and Lewis Lakes.

- After Japanese attack on Pearl Harbour December 7, 1941 all Japanese "enemy aliens" removed from B.C. coast (including Stillwater). About 250 Japanese men, women and children were escorted from the McNair shingle bolt camp by the RCMP to Vancouver.

- Six of "our boys" died in WWII: W.R. Dickson (Lang Bay), Harry Donkersley DFC (Douglas Bay/Powell River), James Lloyd (Stillwater), John Maitland (Lang Bay/Vancouver), J.W. Mullen (Lang Bay), and Serge Zilnic (Kelly Creek).

- **WWII War Brides: Margaret Long (Lang Bay) and Joan Patrick (Douglas Bay).**

- Mid 1940s the old "J" claim logged by Roy Brett. This was later taken over by Mahood Logging.

- 1941 Russell M. Cooper general superintendent Powell River Company purchased a beach lot in Douglas Bay and built a summer home.

- **1945 Stillwater became a log site and the population declined.** A number of houses were torn down. The McNairs, Lees and Forrest families built their own homes out of the recycled materials on Scotch Fir Road.

- **1946 – June 23rd Earthquake.** Ina Lloyd recalls running out of her house at Stillwater with her two children. The ground was moving in waves. No damage to the area.

- 1948 Union Steamship Company's last service to coastal communities.

- **All the McNair shingle bolt camps closed by 1950.**

- 1954 Ferry connection via Saltery Bay and Sechelt Peninsula to Vancouver.

- **1954 The last train of logs hauled out of Stillwater. For over 45 years the railroad had operated in the Stillwater area. It was a sad day.**

The information for the history of Stillwater and area is derived from the following sources: "Stillwater" by Marion McRae in *Powell River's 50 Year Book; Bucksaws and Blisters* by Bill Thompson; *Chalkdust & Outhouses* by Barbara Ann Lambert; *Rusty Nails and Ration Books* by Barbara Ann Lambert, and information from Ina Lloyd (McNair), Muriel Fee, Rob Maitland, Bill Thompson and Ted Lloyd.

1930 Hotel Gordon Pasha, Stillwater, B.C.
The hotel was built about 1910 in Stillwater Bay at the Brooks, Scanlon & O Brien's base
camp. The hotel had a store, pool hall, restaurant and post office. Saturday nights were lively
with loggers enjoying music, dancing, card playing, and drinking.
Photo: John Lee Jr. collection

1932 Stillwater dryland sort of the McNair Shinglebolt operations.
(L to R) Hanley (brakeman), Woodrow Runnells (fireman) and Alf Edwards (engineer).
Photo: Almer McNair

1920 Marion and Nat McNair at Hillside, Howe Sound.
In 1924 Nat was Superintendant of the Robert McNair Shingle Company Stillwater Division.
Photo: Ina Lloyd (McNair) collection

1934 Stillwater, B.C.—Nat McNair's Willys Knight car.
(L to R) Ina McNair, June McNair and Almer McNair
Photo: Ina Lloyd (McNair) collection

1930s—Engineer shop at the Stillwater round house: Baldwin engine getting up steam.
Photo: John Lee Jr. collection

1928 Number 4 O'Brien logging engine, Stillwater, B.C.
Photo: John Lee Jr. collection

1924 Brooks, Scanlon & O'Brien logging camp at Tin Hat Mountain:
cook house in the centre: rail tracks to the right.
Photo: John Lee Jr. collection

1928 Brooks, Scanlon & O'Brien logging train going over the Copenhagen Canyon
trestle (100ft), east side of the Lois River. The canyon's name derived from Copenhagen
snuff tins being tossed into the canyon by engine drivers and loggers.
Photo: John Lee Jr. collection

The Great War (WWI) 1914-18

WWI trench song:

Jack Lee having his tea,
Over in France today.
Keep fit, doing his bit,
Up to his knees in clay.
Each night, after a fight,
He sang this tune:

Hi diddle 'ity
Carry me back to Blighty,
Blighty is the place for me.

Take me over there,
Drop me anywhere.

I just want to see my best gal,
Cuddling up so close to me.

Hi diddle 'ity,
Take me back to Blighty,
Blighty is the place for me.

Note: This was a well-known trench song sung during WWI. The name was changed as the song went around the men in the trenches. After the war, and a few drinks, John (Jack) Lee Sr. sang it for his wife and children, in memory of life at the front. In 2011 John Lee Jr. recalled the song he had heard as a child, and sang it from memory.

Volunteers of the Great War 1914-1918
CEF   Canadian Expeditionary Force
Dunwoodie, Don CEF
Stillwater 1913

Lang, Tom CEF
Wolfsohn Bay 1911

Lang, Harry CEF
Wolfsohn Bay 1911

Lang, Fred CEF
Wolfsohn Bay 1911

Lee, John CEF   **Lee Barbara   WWI war bride**
Stillwater 1930

Lloyd, James   British Royal Navy
Stillwater 1939

John Lee and James Lloyd volunteered for service in WWI & WWII.

The Lang Brothers

The Lang Brothers, Frederick (Fred), Henry (Harry) and Thomas (Tom) first came to Wolfsohn Bay (Wolfson/Wulfsohn) Bay as children in 1911. Wolfsohn Bay was named after Johann Wulffsohn, a German consul in Vancouver. It was later changed to Lang Bay, during WWI, in honour of the Lang Brothers who were fighting overseas in France.

The Lang Brothers were born in London, England. In 1901, their father Thomas Lang Sr., a house painter, tragically died. Their mother Elizabeth (Bess) Lang, a nurse, was left with four young children to support.

Elizabeth decided to keep her only daughter Edith (7 years old) and place the boys in an orphanage until plans could be made to start a new life in Canada. Edith

Young (Elizabeth's sister) was living in Canada; she encouraged Elizabeth to leave England and bring her children to British Columbia, Canada.

Tom (6), Harry (5) and Fred (3) were placed in "The New Orphan House," administered by George Müller, in Bristol. The orphanage had an excellent educational record. The money to support the orphanage came from "faith" offerings. Boys were kept and trained in a trade until age 14; girls were kept to 17 years of age and trained as nurses, teachers and domestic servants. On placing her boys in the Müller orphanage, Elizabeth discussed with the officials her intention of taking them to Canada. Thus, the Lang boys were not trained in any specific trade; however, they were given an excellent education.

In 1909 Elizabeth sailed to Canada with her daughter Edith. They travelled by train to New Westminster where Elizabeth found employment as a nurse, and a place in which to live. Elizabeth contacted the authorities at the Orphanage and arrangements were made to send Tom (14), Harry (13) and Fred (11) to Canada. The boys sailed in 1909 by the *Empress of Britain* to St. John, New Brunswick. They were then placed on a train to travel across Canada, on their own, to New Westminster. At Regina (Saskatchewan), Harry was missing after a brief stopover! Tom and Fred hurriedly got off the train to search for him on the station. All three boys missed their train departure. Their mother was frantic when the train arrived in New Westminster with their luggage, but no boys! The boys safely arrived at their destination the next day.

Elizabeth and her children moved to Wolfsohn Bay after her marriage to Bob Simpkins, a retired British Army officer who had served in India. Bob Simpkins came to Canada in 1897, and in 1907 pre-empted land at Wolfsohn Bay. He advertised for a wife in 1911, and chose Elizabeth. After a fire in 1922 the Simpkins moved to Cranberry.

In 1916 all three Lang Brothers: Tom, Harry and Fred volunteered to join the CEF (Canadian Expeditionary Force). The three "boys" enlisted with the 158 DCOR Vancouver, B.C. Tom served with the 29th Battalion, Harry and Fred served with the 54th Battalion. After training in Vernon, B.C. they were shipped overseas to Britain, and from there to France. All three saw action. Tom and Fred were wounded at Vimy Ridge on April 9, 1917. Harry saw action at Passchendaele July 30, 1917. All three brothers returned safely home to Lang Bay.

Lance Corporal John Lee CEF

John Lee Jr. (79) 2011:   *"My Lee grandparents Charles and Helen (Ellen) Lee and their children emigrated from Scotland in 1907 to Canada. My father John Findlay Lee Sr. was born in 1890 on the Orkney Islands at Deepdale Hobbister, Orphir. He was one of ten children. There were five boys: Charles, James, William, Henry and John, and five girls: Susan, Margaret, Robina, Elizabeth and Lillian. Apart from the two youngest children, William and Lily, all the other children were adults when they left Scotland.*

*As soon as the First World War broke out **John Sr. and his three brothers Henry, James and Charles all volunteered to join the Canadian Expeditionary Force.***

My father went overseas with the 29th (Vancouver) Battalion, Canadian Expeditionary Force, the Irish Fusiliers of Canada. The battalion was formed in 1914 and was commanded by Lt. Col. Henry Tobin. It became known as Tobin's Tigers.

As the soldiers travelled across Canada they were met, along the way, by cheering crowds. Some smart Alec wrote on the train, "Berlin or Bust!"

My father suffered from a gas attack during the war.

Sports events were arranged for the soldiers while they were waiting to be demobbed. My father participated in a winning tug-of-war team for Tobin's Tigers.

Tobin's Tigers returned, via Belgium, to England where the men were all given leave.

*My father revisited the Orkney Islands when he was overseas. It was here he met my mother **Barbara Gray (Gunn)**. They fell in love and married in Scotland. **My mother came to Canada as a war bride after WWI.** The Canadian Government paid for dependents to travel 3rd class, free of charge, by sea and railway to destinations in Canada.*

All four Lee brothers saw action. What is truly remarkable that all four brothers survived the bloody trench war in France and came home safely to Canada.

Tragically my uncle Charles, unscathed by war, was killed in a car crash in Vancouver while going to a Remembrance Day service on November 11th, 1944."

Note: It is remarkable that all four Lee brothers, and three Lang brothers survived the Great War. Of the 400,000 Canadians who fought for "King & Empire" 60,000 Canadians lost their lives.

For memories of Barbara Lee (Gray) (1889-1961) – see WWI War Brides in Western Canada.

James Lloyd
WWI British Royal Navy
WWII Canadian Army

James Lloyd was born in an army barracks in England. He served with the British Royal Navy in the Great War. His father, Charles Lloyd pre-empted a section of land in Dropmore, Manitoba, Canada. James took over the farm after his father died.

James and Kate Lloyd had eight children: Albert (b. 1919), Archie (b. 1921), Billie (b. 1922), Andy (b. 1924), Ted (b. 1926), Belle (b. 1928), Roy (1931) and Jean (b. 1934). The Lloyd family left the Prairies and came west to Stillwater in the 1930s.

Archie and Albert Lloyd were the first Prairie boys to arrive in Stillwater in the early 1930s. They "rode the rods" to Vancouver and with their last couple of dollars bought tickets on the Union Steamship to Stillwater. They obtained a job cutting shingle bolts for the McNair shingle bolt company. After the boys were established they sent for the rest of the family. After James Lloyd sold his farm in Dropmore in 1939, he came out west to Stillwater and found a job with the O'Brien logging camp. James only worked there for a few months before WWII broke out. He lied about his age and immediately joined the Canadian Army. He knew if he joined the Navy they would telegraph to see his old records and find out his true age. Five of his children joined up in WWII: Archie and Billy in the Army; Andy and Belle in the Air Force; and Ted in the Navy. The five siblings survived the war. James Lloyd died of natural causes, while in training. Jean joined the Air Force after the war.

Ted Lloyd RCN WWII (2011):

"My father, James Lloyd, was in the British Navy during WWI. As soon as war broke out in 1939 he wanted to join up immediately and fight for the old country. He knew if he joined the Canadian Navy they would check his old records and find out his true age.

During WWII Bill Thompson Sr. was Air Raid Officer and taught us how to put fires out. A few guys at the Stillwater Power House had rifles and just about shot each other. After Pearl Harbour the Japanese (employed by McNair Shingle Bolt Company) were gone. Other workers left for the ship building industry in Vancouver. Labour was at a real premium. As kids we got work in the summer months working on the boom, assistant to the timber cruiser. At the end of the summer we were fired!"

Private Donald Miller Dunwoodie (1894-1990) CEF Reg. # 629869

Prior to WWI **Don Dunwoodie** worked as a surveyor for Brooks, Scanlon & O'Brien. The company base camp was located at Stillwater, B.C.

Don was a logger, however, he was asked by the company to survey between Second and Third Lake because he could read, write and compute.

Don enjoyed living at Stillwater base camp – compared to other base camps along the coast it was paradise. There was the Gordon Pasha hotel, built about 1910, by the Brooks, Scanlon Company, with a pool hall, post office, store, and restaurant. Saturday nights were lively, as loggers in the area gathered at the hotel for a night of music, dancing and drinking. Don enjoyed a drink.

In 1914, when the Great War broke out, Don's friends joined up. Don decided to go with them. He served on the supply line with the CEF in France; secretly he stole supplies and sold them to the French and Belgium farmers. The authorities had their suspicions but could never prove anything.

After breaking an ankle in an accident, Don was sent to a hospital in England. He had a relationship with a redheaded nurse and she became pregnant; not wanting a commitment, he swopped ID's with another patient who was due back at the front. Back at the front, Don continued to steal supplies, this time it was walnut ties which he sold to a French furniture manufacturer.

At the end of the Great War, Don Dunwoodie returned safely home to Canada. Many years later, he wrote about his life on the Western Front. Don spoke frankly to his nephew Harold Hardman, about the stealing, drinking and womanizing. He was a likeable rogue.

Note: If Private Don Dunwoodie had been caught stealing supplies at the front he would have been shot. His WWI story is unusual, and rare. It sheds light on a previously suspected, but unrecorded, area of activity at the front.

My Life at the Western Front WWI

Don Dunwoodie (CEF)
Published for the first time in *War Brides & Rosies* 2012
with the kind permission of Don Dunwoodie's nephew Harold Hardman

I was born in Irvington, Iowa in April, 1894. My Dad ran a general store, the grain elevator and the coal and lumber yards. He gave his brother-in-law a job and two years later Dad was bankrupt. The brother (in-law) was lining his own pockets. We then moved to Algoma, Iowa.

When I was 9 we moved to Enderby, B.C. and Dad worked as a carpenter. As a teenager, I came to Vancouver and worked at many jobs until I became a logger and went to camps in Harrison Lake, Cortes Island, **Stillwater** and Kingcome Inlet. Finally, I became a time-keeper, earning $90 a month plus room and board.

When the First World War started, I found that most of my friends had joined up so I did too. I was sent to Vernon for training. We were then sent across Canada by train to Montreal and boarded ships that took us to Plymouth, England.

Ypres Front:
France 1916 – Hauling Rations with Horses, Mules and Wagons

We left for France near the end of August 1916, and saw our first war on Ypres front, which was quiet then. The first trip for us up the line was to haul rations in for the two companies, A and B, who were in the line. I was swamper on the B company limber wagon. While waiting at the barrier (past which we couldn't go in daylight) for darkness, we heard a big shell go over. I guess it was funny how fast we got under cover. At least the guards on the barrier thought so. They said the shell was a 10-inch howitzer shell and would probably land 10 miles back. Anyway, we finally passed the barrier and half-a-mile farther on had to turn left and go along a road just behind the support lines. We heard several bullets from machine guns go past just over our heads, and saw a few shrapnel shells explode off to our right. But we got our loads to where they were to go and got out with no casualties.

Riot between the Aussies and the Canucks

We were about six weeks on that front and then started out for a rest. We had only marched a few miles when we were turned around and marched back as our relief hadn't been able to get up in time to take over. On the outward march we had passed a division of Australians going in to take over some part of the line. They knew that we were green troops and apparently knew that we were headed for the **Somme**. They had things to say about us wishing we were back with our mothers, accompanied by profanities. When we were turned around and back in **St. Marguerite**, the Aussies were there, too. At first a bunch of them came in to a café where four of us were having a drink. They threw us out and we went back to our quarters and rounded up a bunch big enough to throw them out. We did, and they headed for their quarters, yelling "Coo-ee". Some of our fellows went back and aroused the battalion, and there was quite a fight. Rifles and bayonets, rocks, clubs, and anything that would knock a man down. Quite a few men went to hospital and an Australian colonel was knocked off his horse as he rode into the riot, trying to stop the fighting.

Battle of the Somme

Our relief arrived a day or two later, and we were on our way again. We were rested at a camp (tents) several miles from any town, and no passes were issued. When we left there we marched for several days, then were loaded on French railway cars marked 8 Horses: 40 Men. On these trains we could often get off and walk as they never went faster than a man could run. I think it took 10 days from the rest camp to **Albert**, a town on the **Somme**. It had been occupied by the Germans who were driven out by French troops, I believe, but when we arrived in October they were far enough away that only a 12-inch naval gun mounted on a railcar could reach them. Two companies from each battalion moved up next morning to take over their share of the line. Our section was sent up that night to haul ammunition up to a heavy machine gun outfit behind the support lines.

Our sergeant was in charge. We had a guide for each wagon and the dump was only large enough for two wagons to load at a time. I was with the second wagon, and the sergeant came with us until there was a burst of shrapnel just ahead. He then began to wonder why the other two wagons hadn't caught up with us. We made three round trips that night and were just behind the camouflage nets that hid traffic from Jerry, when daylight caught us. I was riding to spell the driver called Salty, and the mules were tired and taking their own time. By the time we got to the ruins of the sugar refinery, which had only one brick wall standing, the team was a couple of hundred yards behind the others.

Our sergeant appeared from behind the wall and came galloping out to me telling me to whip up those damn mules and catch up with the others. He added, *"You know you are in dangerous country."* I told him that we were a lot safer here than he was hiding behind that wall if Jerry had tried target practice on it. I asked him why he wasn't with his men when we had been on dangerous ground, and suggested that he should shoot himself as being the first of the section to show a white feather. He was going to have me court martialled for using obscene language to a superior officer, and called to Salty that he was to be a witness. Salty told him, with more obscene language, that the only thing he could swear to was that the sergeant had left us when the first shrapnel came over and hadn't been seen or heard until just now. That shut him up, and he rode off to lead the teams into camp.

We took care of our teams, had breakfast, and went to our tents to sleep. At noon we were wakened, and I and one other man, Mac, were told to take our equipment and rations for us and our horses for four days and report to division headquarters at once. There we found about 40 men and horses and met an officer who was to be in charge of the divisional pack train. We were issued pack saddles and told that as soon as more saddles arrived the train would be increased to 90 men. We were shown how to load a pack saddle and put our kits on them and were taken several miles out of **Albert** where we were to camp. All of our rations were turned over to a Negro cook who made the best hash I've ever eaten from canned corned beef, hard tack and onions. Where we stopped had been the site of a three-inch field gun position, and there were lots of empty cases the shells had come in, and corrugated iron sheets that had roofed their shelters. We built ourselves huts of the cases, usually for four men. One end was built with three tiers of boxes, end to end, and high enough to sit up in or even stand in a bent over position. The other end had only two tiers and the place of the third formed the door. The other men arrived a week or two later with three raw replacements and a farrier from the 47th. Also the first rations we had received since we left the section. We had existed by stealing several cases of rations from an officer's club about two miles away, and by searching abandoned dugouts for forgotten cans of bully beef or any canned goods. I found two cans of butter and a four-pound tin of strawberry jam in one, which helped my hut a lot. We also became expert at salvaging rations at the Q.M. store. Our cavalry cloaks could cover quite a lot. Some of the fellows even sewed canvas pockets inside to carry more. We packed everything from ammunition grenades and Stokes gun shells, to rations and barbed wire and stakes. Our officer was deaf as a post and a kleptomaniac. He would steal anything that wasn't nailed down or guarded, whether he had any use for it or not. He even took four of us with packs down to the rum dump with a forged order for 32 gallons of rum and got it. After that our ration increased to whatever you could drink without stopping for a breath. I got so that I could drink over a pint and never missed an issue. We needed that rum as we were on the go 20 hours of each 24 for seven weeks. **The battalion went into the Somme with nearly 1,150 men, and there were about 170 who marched out.** Of course a lot of them returned after a few days, weeks, or a month or two, depending on the wound. The pack train lost no men through wounds, though a couple got sick and went to hospital. They were from other battalions and I never saw them again. When the division left, the packers were returned to their own outfits and there was no more divisional pack train until after I got a blighty just before the Vimy Ridge scrap.

Vimy Ridge

We only marched a few miles out of Albert before we camped for two or three days. Then I think, but am not sure, that we were put on a train and taken to **Brieux**, a coal mine town in **Belgium**, or near that country. There we got our first bath since we hit Albert. The companies had baths in a portable shower bath system that rigged up a pipeline in a canvas shrouded alley where you stripped at one end and got so-called clean clothes at the other end. In November it wasn't exactly a lovely experience. At Brieux we had the use of a mine bathhouse, and had new clothes from the skin out. We had 10 days or more there and got reinforcements to build us up to strength. When they moved us up to take over there, the 47th was quartered in a little place behind **Vimy**. The section took over some stables left there by a British battalion.

The four Canadian divisions were now an army under a Canadian General. Can't remember who he was, but he used to sit in his car not far from our lines and anyone who failed to salute when he passed could expect to be charged and usually got a couple of days of #1 field punishment. This meant, being spread-eagled on a wagon wheel for an hour, twice a day, and so many days' pay stopped.

The French had tried to take the **Ridge**, but had been driven back by the Jerries when they herded a big bunch of French citizens in front of them as they advanced. The French didn't want to fire on their own people, but the civilians yelled at them to stop the Boche, even if they were killed. The French artillery opened up with shells that were filled with a new explosive that developed a deadly gas. The advance was stopped, but most of the civilians, as well as the Jerries, were killed. Then the British tried it and failed. That was when the Canadians were given the job. They mined the Ridge with hundreds of tons of explosive and had more artillery in support than had even been concentrated in a single front that size before. I had to take a pack load of socks up to the line and had to pass batteries of guns from the 9.2s down to the 3-inch field guns. The bigger ones were not bad except that the concussion would nearly knock you down if you were within a 100 yards of them. But the field guns were the worst; there were three rows of them, placed just far enough apart to allow a wagon to go between. The row behind covered the spaces left in the front row. When I came up behind the first row I was stopped by an officer. He told me to wait until the first gun on the right had fired and then start for the gap between it and #2 which would fire before I got there. Then past the row had to angle across in front of #2 to the gap between 2 and 3 in the next row. Wait there until it fired and go through, then angle right to the gap in the front row and repeat. Coming back would be the same after #2 had fired. There were five guns in each battery and they fired at about two or three second intervals. By the time #5 had fired, #1 was ready again. Coming back, I stopped well back to watch the firing so as to be sure which was #1 of one battery and #5 of another. The shells only seemed to be a foot or so above my head, but must have been 10 feet or more. Anyway, I finally got enough courage to try it. I remember thinking that if I made a mistake, I'd never know it. The officer had given me a pair of earplugs before I started through, as he said the sharp report of the guns could break an ear drum.

A Ticket Back to Blighty (England)

A few days later I was given leave with pay, and was delivering the last of the supplies to the railway. I was standing in a limber (a four-foot square box on two wheels) and lost my balance and fell out, then the limber following ran over me. I had a broken ankle. The big push for Vimy Ridge was supposed to start, but anyone that was going to be hospitalized for more than two weeks would be sent back to the hospital in Dover, England and that's where I was sent. Visitors to the hospital all heard that there was a real live Canadian and wanted to see him.

One visitor I'll never forget was a Duchess. She came to the door where Sister Stewart met her and I heard her say, *"I say, I understand you have a Canadian in here. Could I see him?"* Sister led her over to the foot of my bed and said, *"This is Private Dunwoodie."* The Duchess was about 50 years old and was wearing jewels worth a fortune. The old girl looked at me with her mouth wide open and after a minute said, *"Why, I thought you'd be red!"* She wanted to know if we wore blankets and still used bows and arrows. I assured her that even the Indians wore modern clothes and used modern weapons. She invited me to visit her estate and later sent cars to pick up about 25 of us for an afternoon there. It was the biggest private house I had ever seen and we had a good time. We were shown through the estate and then served tea, sandwiches and cakes on the lawn under a big oak tree.

Kew Gardens: A Flagpole from Stillwater

I was sent to a temporary place for Canadians until their leave came through. The house had been owned by Dr. Crippen who killed his wife to run off to Canada with his girlfriend. They didn't get there, and were returned to England where he was convicted. I had been visited by my cousin, Leonard, while in hospital. He had visited at home several years before, and had somehow found out that I was in hospital. He got me a special pass from the OC and took me to **Kew Gardens**, a big London park. There we must have walked for a mile or more, and **we saw a big flagpole, one of two I had helped get out of the bush at Stillwater**. It was, I believe, the tallest flagpole of wood ever erected, although at that time it was still lying on blocks and was not raised until after the war. It was 221 feet long. The other was erected in front of the courthouse in Vancouver. It was 9 feet shorter.

Forestry Camps

We were put in the next draft to go to the 47th, but an order from headquarters directed all men with logging experience to report to the orderly room. Another fellow and I didn't as we wanted to go back to our outfit. Two or three weeks later while we were on the range firing our last practice before the draft was to leave, the two of us were pulled out of our firing positions by a corporal and taken before the adjutant. He bawled us out for not reporting as ordered, and sent us with the corporal to camp HQ. There we joined about 50 others and a few minutes later were formed into a single line at the approach of two officers. One was **General White**, the head of all **Canadian Forestry districts**. He asked each of us what we knew of logging and where we had worked. I told him that I was from B.C. and had only worked in Coast camps and knew nothing about short logs. He said something to his aide who put a checkmark after my name, while two or three others before me had just a straight line after their names. I congratulated myself that I would be staying on the draft.

Back at camp we were marched back to the range to complete our firing course. That was to fire 10 rounds at each of the 500 and 1000 yard ranges. I made eight bull's-eyes and two inners on the first, and nine bulls and one inner on the last. The range master asked me if I would take the sniper's course (six months). He could get me off the draft, but I told him that I wanted to go back to my own outfit.

The next day both of us were ordered to turn in all our equipment except our personal stuff and report to the orderly room. From there 10 of us went to camp HQ where we joined about 30 others from Alberta, Ontario and Quebec. We were marched to the station and put on a train which took us to Sunningdale on the edge of Windsor Park. **The camp was in the park about five miles from Windsor Castle and town. It was a base camp for the Forestry Corps from which drafts were sent to camps in England, Scotland and France.** You could volunteer for anywhere but when I said I wanted to go to France, I was told that being a casualty from France I could only be what they called a "waiting man". That was an extra man in case someone didn't turn out when the draft was called.

Return to the Western Front

I was there two months before a French draft was formed and I was put on as a waiting man. One of the fellows had a girl in Sunningdale he wanted to marry, and he was easily persuaded with £10 (pounds) to be absent the day the draft was called. The £10 would more than cover the loss of pay for being absent. Our draft went to **Conches, HQ** for #2 District commanded by Col. White, a son or nephew of the General. They were loggers for the Eddy Match Company in Ontario and several of the officers were shareholders or foremen for the logging company headed by the Whites. The draft was broken up at Conches and sent to various camps in the district which was south and a little west of Paris.

Stealing Barrels of Whiskey

For two or three weeks I was put in a company that logged just across the railway tracks from the station and warehouses. They had a little steam donkey engine to yard out the trees after they were felled and limbed. The trees were cut into logs on the landing. These were loaded on railway cars and taken to the sawmill. Several of the crew were men I had known in camps on the Coast, all good loggers. The donkey had two wine or whiskey barrels at the back for water, which was piped to them. One day we noticed that a train crew was unloading a carload of barrels into one of the warehouses. Our donkey was being repaired and we wondered if one of those barrels wouldn't give us something better to drink than water. That night six of us, including the engineer, went to the warehouse which wasn't locked and rolled out two barrels. One we set up in place of one water barrel on the donkey; the other we buried under a pile of bush quite a distance away.

Next day everyone was thirsty. By afternoon our lieutenant became aware that we were getting liquor somewhere and he tried the water barrel himself. As we were careful to put the tin cup back on its hook in the real water barrel, he dipped in there and found just water. The pipe which connected the two barrels had been plugged and the cognac barrel placed tight against the end. He spent the rest of the afternoon walking around the setting trying to find where the boys had their cache. We had to go out that night and fill jugs and bottles from the barrel and put the old water barrel back in place.

Bush Sergeant

I never heard what happened to the second barrel as I was sent with Capt. Klock and a crew out to **Chateau Chambray**, about 20 miles from Conches. Here we were to log a private park belonging to the **Chateau**. It was about one square kilometre and had been planted years before with trees from different places in the world. Most of it was hard wood: oak, maple, beech, some pines and some B.C. fir. French foresters had been through and marked trees that were to be saved. All hardwoods had to be cut as close to the ground as possible. I was the only axman in the bunch. There were a few mill men, several teamsters, and the rest were mostly from the cities. Very few of them had ever seen an ax or crosscut saw. I had to show them everything – how and where to put in the undercut, and how to use their axes so as not to cut their feet. Then I took one pair and had them fall four tall slim firs which I had to hew for timbers for the mill. I had no broad ax, but did have an adz. As it happened, I got the timbers smooth enough so that the mill men could use the adz themselves where they needed. I wasn't long as bush sergeant. The fallers had enough logs cut by the time the mill was set up to keep it going and a French Canadian logger was sent to take over the woods.

Shipping Sergeant

I was shipping sergeant and had two trucks and drivers to haul the cut lumber to the station, about two miles from the mill. For the first few weeks we just stockpiled various sizes of railway ties along a siding where they could be loaded easily. At first, I had 8 or 10 Russians who had been out of the line at the time of the Russian revolution. We shipped only a car or two at a time although the stocks were building up at the station. We were making seven trips a day with each truck.

Our camp started in January, 1918, and the mill had cut all the timber early in October. Most of the ties were shipped or at the station, but all the slabs were piled along the wall from one end to the other. My Russians had been taken away and prisoner-of-war substituted. Also my Canadian trucks had been sent to some other camp and seven British Army trucks sent out to take their places. I had trouble with that bunch from the start, especially their sergeant. Of the seven trucks, I seldom had more than three or four actually hauling timber. It all came to a head one day when I had 80 cars to load. All seven trucks had gone for the prisoners and had been late getting back, and the prisoners decided that they wouldn't work hard. There were only 30 cars loaded at noon. I had them lined up, and through the interpreter told them that they had to finish the train before they could go back to the stockade. They would get nothing to eat until they got there. Then I had four men build fires at each corner of the loading zone and gave orders for the guards to shoot anyone going outside the line of fires. It was nearly midnight before that train was loaded and the trucks could take off with the prisoners. Next morning I was making out the waybills for the train when the sergeant came to the door and called me to attention. I saw no officer, and asked in language he could understand just who he thought he was, told him to state his business and then get the hell out of sight.

A little English 2nd Lieutenant stepped up and told his sergeant that he could return to their quarters. I gave him a salute and asked what he wanted. I also told him that I was busy with these waybills which had to be at the station before noon. He told me that the sergeant had come to their HQ last night with a complaint about the hours I had forced them to put in, and a few other things. He told me that wasn't done in the British Army Motor Transport. I told him that was probably why the Canadians had to take over lines that the British Army couldn't. I also told him that two Canadian trucks had hauled more timber in the same length of time than his seven trucks had. He didn't call me a liar in so many words, but might as well have. I had said the above in soldier language, expressing the contempt I felt for that particular unit of trucks, and when he hinted that I lied, I gave him my opinion of him.

Court Martial

The court martial was held the following week. My escorts brought me in where I was turned over to the Provost SM to be marched into court where the charges were read to me. The major consulted me and then told the court, which consisted of a British major and two Canadian captains that I didn't know, that I pleaded not guilty to all of the charges. The lieutenant had already given his testimony before I was brought in. He wasn't in the court when I gave mine. I told how I had had trouble with the British sergeant because they were unable to haul as much timber as the two Canadian trucks. I was asked if I could prove that and replied that our HQ here had my reports of timber hauled in similar periods of time for both outfits which would show that I was right. They were sent for, and I think only the monthly reports were studied. I denied the charges of insulting an officer and using obscenities, but admitted that I had said to the lieutenant, *"Those damn drivers of yours are useless to me because they are either lazy or incompetent."* The president (the major) asked why I had said that, and I told him that I had never been able to have all trucks hauling timber on any day because one truck would be sent after gas and rations, one truck was usually being repaired, and the one which went after prisoners didn't haul any timber. My reports showed the number of trucks hauling each day. Col. White begged leave to testify in my behalf. I had a hard time keeping a straight face at his testimony! I was an angel who, only under the greatest stress, used the word "damn". I never failed to be most soldierly to any officer to whom I was speaking. He had known me for nine months and in that time had found that I had done my work excellently. My reports had been checked several times and were found to be surprisingly correct. In the end, all charges were dismissed and the lieutenant called in. I was asked if I wished to prefer charges against him, to which I answered, *"No, I think he misunderstood a lot of what I said or attached a significance to it which I did not intend."* The president remarked that I was being very generous, and the lieutenant should apologize. I spent that night in Conches, mostly in the Officers' Mess, and returned to camp the next day with the two Canadian trucks.

Black Market on the Western Front

When the ties were all hauled and shipped, one of our sources of income was cut off. We had an arrangement with a French sawmill by which we got 50 francs for a load of standard gauge ties (30 ties).

With no more ties we had to depend on gasoline sales, most of which we got by putting in extra mileage for the trucks. We got 100 francs for eight gallons from the French people who had cars but were rationed by the government. We did make one big haul of 400 gallons by lifting 50 cases from a big gas dump of the American Army at **Le Mans**, 50 or 60 kilometres south of us. Three of us had gone down there just to see new country and we passed these dumps which must have covered several acres. All the gasoline was in cases which held four two-gallon cans. The single sentry at the gate was easily bribed to go get himself a drink or two at a café down the street. We backed the truck in, loaded it with 50 cases and put a tarp over them. Then we went to the café to pay the guy the balance of his money.

We had a few other little sidelines when the chance came. Sometimes we could get sugar or cigarettes out of the QM stores, and both paid well. When the crew left and there were only the five of us in camp, French civilians began to come to me to ask permission to cut up some of the limbs, etc. for wood. I had been told that after we left prisoners would be brought in to cut wood for sale and no one was to get free wood. The first to ask me were an old couple who brought a basket containing a roasted chicken, a bottle of wine and one of brandy. I explained to them that officers would soon be out to look the place over, but if they would come to a small gate in the back wall the next day they could have a cartload. I took them down to show them the gate, and a treetop they could have. I got them out of camp just a few minutes before the officers arrived. They stayed only a short time, but brought orders about shipping all the slabs. They were gone only about half an hour when two women arrived with a three-horse cart. The older woman said she need a three-horse load of slabs to fence a pigpen. She showed me a couple of bottles of liquor and then, pointing to the girl, said something of which the only word I understood was "couche". I took them down to the last pile and told them they could take a load from there. When I left them they were already loading slabs. I started to cook supper for myself and the four drivers. After we had eaten and cleaned up I was in my office shack working on my reports when the girl who had been with the pig woman rode up on a bicycle. She told me that she could stay all night. I didn't send her away, but asked if she had eaten, then I took her to the kitchen where I warmed up a steak and potatoes for her, and made some coffee. She cleaned up everything and drank three cups of coffee. She liked the army bread, and asked if she could have two slices for breakfast in the morning as she had to leave early to get back to the farm. Instead I gave her half a loaf, a small can of jam and another of butter, both of which could be opened with a key. Next morning she left a little after five, but was back again that night. She stayed with me for two or three weeks, and during that time other civilians found out that a couple of bottles of liquor would get a load of wood. When Marie didn't return, another girl showed up.

Celebrating the Armistice in Paris

Saturday, November 9th, we were sitting in the café having a few drinks when the girl who was assistant to the station master came running down the road yelling, *"Le armistice is signed,"* in French. She came into the café where we gave her a glass of cognac, and finally got out of her the news which had come over the telegraph wire. Madame of the café ordered us out, saying that she would make us a dinner of hare with all the liquor we could drink. We were to be back at eight o'clock and at that time had a wonderful meal. Our dispatch rider found us there just as we finished. He had orders for us to report to HQ next day. He also brought word that the armistice was not yet signed, but would be on Monday. We went into Conches next morning and reported. We were told that we would be reassigned in a few days.

Monday morning we started up town for a drink and heard that the armistice had been signed. We were passing HQ and the OC's car was standing just ahead of us. Corkery suggested that we take off for Paris. The key was in the lock, and we were in Paris in an hour. That day no Canadian could spend any money in the city. We pulled into the driveway of a big hotel and the doorman escorted us into the lobby while another man took our car to park it. We were asked to register, and the manager gave an order to the clerk, and he himself showed us to a suite of three bedrooms with baths and a living room. When we protested that it was too expensive for us, he said that he was honoured that we had chosen his hotel and not to worry about the expense. A bellboy came in with a bottle of champagne in a bucket of ice, and six glasses. The manager filled all glasses and gave us a toast before he left. I left the others to hunt up a girl I had met before, but just got on the street when I was surrounded by a bunch of French munitions workers. They picked me up and carried me to a café where I think each of the 50 or so of them wanted to buy me a drink. I escaped after a while by asking where the toilet was. From it I got out by another door and went to the Place de Republic where my girlfriend was usually to be found.

When we got back to camp we parked the car where we had found it, and were unloading cases of champagne when the OC came along. He asked what was in the cases, and when we told him, he said, *"Where are you taking it?"* We told him *"To camp,"* and asked if he would care for a case. He was delighted, and said that there was an empty locked closet in the orderly room where we could keep it. We took all five in, put one in his closet, and the six of us emptied another before he led us away. All he ever said about our absence was to ask if we had had a good time.

I stayed in **Conches** about three weeks more and during that time Corkery and his partner and I made our spending money by taking trucks and cars when we could get them to a machine shop where we got from 10 to 25 thousand francs for them.

*Étaples Mutiny, France

I was given five days' leave and ordered to report to HQ when it was over. I spent four days in Paris; on day with Marie, and another day with Helene. I got back to Conches and was put in a draft returning to England. There were Canadians, Aussies, and English there, and for a wonder, the Canucks and Aussies got along fine. Across a gully from our camp was Paris Plage, which was officers' territory. No other ranks were allowed except on special pass. An armed Red Cap guarded the bridge across the gully. I don't know what his orders were, but an Aussie with too much liquor aboard started to cross the bridge and was shot. His companions immediately sent out their trouble call, *"Coo-ee"*, and you could hear it answered all over the camp and town. We knew that there was trouble and we were on the Aussies' side. We got there just in time to see the Red Cap taken by a bunch of Aussies and tossed over the railing of the bridge with a rope around his neck, the other end tied to the rail. Then about four or five thousand started through town cleaning out the Red Caps. I don't know how many were killed, but saw three as we went towards their HQ. We were just in time to see a car with four or five pull away in a hurry. After the riot there were no more Red Caps; all military police wore just a red armband with a black MP on it.

*Kinmel Park Mutiny

The draft I was in and more Canucks were loaded on a boat for England and sent to Seaford. We were there only long enough to get a pay and five days' leave. I went to London where I went first to the hospital I had been in to find only one nurse and a VAD I knew in the ward. I was told that Sister Stewart had volunteered for duty in France and had been killed when a shell landed on the casualty clearing station where she had been sent. I met the girl I had spent time with when I had my pass cancelled in hospital. She was quite happy as she had just had a letter from her husband saying that he would soon be home. I took her out to dinner and spent two days with her. I was back in Seaford on time and was in the first bunch sent to Rhyl in Wales, the embarkation camp for Canadians. Soon after I got there, trouble began brewing because some of the troops had been there a month or more. They were not allowed to leave camp and were paid only half a pound every two weeks. I don't know what caused the riot, but it wound up setting the camp HQ on fire, and I heard that the OC was killed. Several canteens were broken into and wrecked. It wasn't long after that we were told that there would be several boats in Liverpool to take us home. I had pulled off my stripes when I got my first pay in Rhyl because, as acting sergeant I was not entitled to working pay and wouldn't act as sergeant without the pay.

Going Home

I was in the first trainload to Liverpool, and we went on board the **RMS *Caronia***. The voyage to Halifax was uneventful except that we were paid $5 each, the day before we reached port. I made a few more dollars gambling as that was all there was to do except to get our meals. At Halifax we were loaded onto a train according to where we were going. I think there were three cars for B.C. Those of us going to Victoria were taken to the CPR station and told that we were too late for the midnight boat and would have to wait for the morning boat. Half an hour later we were told that the SS *Northland* would make a special trip with us. I don't remember how we got to Willows camp in the old Willows racetrack, but we were given a pass for two or three hours when we should report for discharge. My parents were in Victoria now, and while I knew the address I didn't know its location, so I stayed in camp until the discharge proceedings started. We had to turn in all our equipment except our uniforms and greatcoats. Then we went to the paymaster who paid us all our back pay, plus so much for the time we had been overseas. I got nearly a thousand dollars and my discharge just four years after I joined up. I then worked in a mine and got married to a woman called Lil, who was a cook on the CN car ferry.

Note: Don Dunwoodie died in the Veteran's Hospital in Victoria on February 15, 1990 at the age of 96.

* The Étaples Mutiny, France, September 9, 1917
Disturbances, which involved thousands of British soldiers, New Zealanders and Canadians, started on September 9, 1917 and continued for the following week at the Étaples military base. The Australians were not involved as they had left the camp four months earlier. The annoyance which started the Étaples mutiny was caused by an order which kept the ordinary rank and file in camp and prevented them from drinking at a nearby fishing village. To prevent the men leaving, pickets were thrown around the camp, however, soldiers found ways to circumvent them – one way was to cross the estuary at low tide.

On September 9, 1917, Gunner A. J. Healey, a New Zealander (camp rumour: Australian), on his return to camp, found the tide had cut him off. As he did not want to be charged as a deserter, he crossed a bridge manned by Red Corps and was arrested. The numbers of soldiers charged reflect the involvement of the various troops: 1 New Zealander, 1 Australian, 10 Canadians, and 37 British soldiers.

* Kinmel Park Mutiny, Wales, March 4-5, 1919
15,000 Canadian troops, while waiting to be shipped to Canada, were kept for four months after the end of WWI, in appalling conditions: unheated huts, overcrowding (some sleeping on dirt floors), half rations, reduced pay, and lack of information about the strikes which caused the holdup in shipping. Five men were killed and over 20 wounded. Of the 78 arrested, 25 Canadians were convicted of mutiny.

Don Dunwoodie (1894-1990), a logger from Stillwater
who volunteered to join the CEF in 1914.
Left: Don Dunwoodie (1970s) Right: 1914 Don Dunwoodie CEF Victoria, B.C.
Don worked on the supply line on the Western Front; he later wrote
his memoirs of life on the Western Front.
Photo: Harold Hardman collection

Harold Hardman, nephew of Donald Miller Dunwoodie CEF, Reg. # 629869,
with his uncle's broad axe, Lang Bay Hall, 2011.
Photo: Harold Hardman collection

Photos 1942-50
The Lloyd family of Stillwater—a patriotic family.
James Lloyd a veteran of WWI volunteered for WWII.
Four sons and daughter Belle volunteered for the
Canadian services in WWII; Jean Lloyd joined after WWII.
Top row: Kate (mother) and Albert Row 2: Billy, Jean and Roy
Row 3: James (father) and Andy Row 4: Archie, Belle and Ted
James died of natural causes while in training; all five Lloyd siblings survived WWII.
Photo: Ted Lloyd collection

World War II 1939-45 Service Men & Women
Stillwater, Lang Bay, Kelly Creek and Douglas Bay

Area	Name (* - killed)	Military Rank/Branch
Stillwater	Carpendale, L. (Leo)	Pte CITC
Stillwater	Cote, F.P. (Fred)	PO RCAF Overseas
Lang Bay	*Dickson, W.R.	LAC RCAF
Douglas Bay/Powell River	*Donkersley, Harry (DFC)	RCAF Overseas
Lang Bay	Kennedy, E.A. (Ernie)	RCAF
Lang Bay	Kennedy, G.A. (Gordon)	CAO
Stillwater	Lee, Alfreda (Freda)	LAW RCAF WD
Stillwater	Lee, Cpl John	(WWI CEF) WWII VGC
Stillwater	*Lloyd, James (WWI British Navy) WWII CA	
Stillwater	Lloyd, Albert	CAO
Stillwater	Lloyd, Archie	CAO
Stillwater	Lloyd, Billy	CAO
Stillwater	Lloyd, Andy	RCAF Overseas
Stillwater	Lloyd, Belle	RCAF WD
Stillwater	Lloyd, C.E. (Ted)	RCN
Lang Bay	Long, H.E. (Harold) **Long, Margaret**	CQMS CAO **WWII war bride**
Lang Bay	Long, Hibbert	CQMS CAO
Lang Bay	Long, J.E. (Jack)	LAC RCAF

Lang Bay	Long, Ken	Cpl	CAO
Lang Bay/Vancouver	*Maitland, William John	RCAF Overseas	
Lang Bay/Vancouver	Maitland, Robert Reid	RCNVR	
Kelly Creek	Martinuk, A. (Alex)	Sgm	CAO
Stillwater	Mckay, E. (Eddie)	Cpl	Iris Fusiliers
Stillwater	McNair, A.N. (Almer)	PO	RCAF
Stillwater	*Mullen, J.W. (Jack)	Pte	CAO
Lang Bay	Mullen, Bob	CAO	
Lang Bay	Mullen, Patrick	CAO	
Lang Bay	Mullen, Billy	RCN	
Lang Bay	Norden, R.	LAC	RCAF Overseas
Stillwater	Olsen, Henry	RCAF	
Stillwater	Palliser, Gordon	RCN	
Lang Bay	Palmer, Bob	CAO	
Douglas Bay	Patrick, Walter	RCAF Overseas	
	Patrick, Joan	**WWII war bride**	
Lang Bay	Phillips, Don	CAO	
Lang Bay	Phillips, Eddie	RCN	
Stillwater	Thompson, G.W. (Bill)	Cpl	RCAF
Kelly Creek	Zilnic, C.Y. (Cy) (change of name to Andrews)	Cpl	CAO
Kelly Creek	*Zilnic, Serge	Pte	CAO

A reception was held by the Lang Bay, Douglas Bay and Stillwater communities for Mr. and Mrs. Harold Long on April 21, 1945 at the Lang Bay School (2011 Lang Bay Community Hall). Margaret Long (Kemp) was an overseas war bride from Scotland. Harold Long was the first veteran to be discharged after being wounded twice.

The Stillwater Ladies' Club hosted a Welcome Home Party for the returning servicemen and women on April 5, 1946 at the Stillwater Hall, Stillwater. In attendance were John Lee, a veteran of WWI and WWII, and his wife Barbara Lee, a WWI war bride; the five Lloyd brothers: Albert, Archie, Bill, Andy and Ted and their sister Belle; and the two WWII war brides Margaret Long and Joan Patrick.

Six of "our boys" died in WWII: W.R. Dickson, Harry Donkersley DFC, James Lloyd, William John Maitland, J.W. Mullen and Serge Zilnic.

W.R. Dickson RCAF
A well-known and liked Lang Bay resident.

Harry Donkersley DFC, RCAF Overseas
Killed January 1944, B.C. Canada

Powell River Company Monthly Newsletter 1946:

"This fine lad returned to Powell River in June 1943, and was posted to duty in Canada. On January 9, 1944, he was piloting a Ventura plane on a flight from Lethbridge (Alberta) to Patricia Bay (British Columbia). Somewhere in the mountains of B.C. the plane was lost — and another of our splendid young men had answered his last roll call."

The Donkersley family lived in Powell River; however, they owned a summer cottage near the beach at Douglas Bay (Brew Bay). This cottage was later moved to the back of the property, and is still standing at the back of Bob and Jackie Durling's property.

Douglas Bay residents looked upon Harry as one of "our boys". Donkersley Road is named after the Donkersley family. Today the beach at Douglas Bay is referred to as the Donkersley Road beach.

James Lloyd CA
A patriotic man who fought in the British Navy in WWI and volunteered to fight in the Canadian Army for "King & Country" in WWII. He died of natural causes while in training in Canada.

William John Maitland RCAFO

The Maitland family lived in Vancouver; however they enjoyed a summer home at Lang Bay since 1913 when Robert M. Maitland had purchased an 8.58 acre lot in Wolfsohn Bay. William John Maitland, while on his first tour, was hit by shrapnel, however his life was saved by a cigarette case his girlfriend had given him. On his second tour, after a bombing raid over Germany, his plane went down in the English Channel.

Jack Mullen CAO

A well-known local athlete.

Serge (Steve) Zilnic CAO

One of the first Canadians to land in the invasion of Sicily. He was killed in the Italian campaign. Serge Zilnic was the first Powell River casualty in the overseas land campaign.

CO (Conscientious Objector) Forestry Camp
Between Nanton and Lewis Lake

The Militia Act of 1793 and Orders in Council of 1873 and 1898 allowed certain religious groups (known as peace groups), Mennonites, Quakers, Doukhobors, and Hutterites, exemption from bearing arms in times of war. These groups had been encouraged by the Canadian Government to come and settle in Canada.

During WWI individuals from these groups could apply for an exemption from military service. Exemptions were decided by local tribunals.

In WWII members of the peace churches plus a small number of Jehovah's Witnesses, Plymouth Brethren and Christadelphians were granted a postponement of training, not an exemption from military service. They became non-combatants and from 1941 served the country by working on roads, national parks and forestry projects. Approximately 11,000 COs were enrolled in this program and were paid 50 cents a day.

Nineteen forestry camps for COs were opened in British Columbia between 1941 and 1942 in remote communities. **A Conscientious Objector forestry camp was opened between Nanton and Lewis Lake, in the present Powell River Regional District.** A 1941 map (published in *Rusty Nails & Ration Books* B.A. Lambert 2002) shows the location of the camp plus the area of the spring and fall plantings.

Old timer, Roy Leibenschel, whose family owned City Transfer in Powell River, recalled delivering goods there during WWII. According to Roy, the CO camp was a temporary camp, the buildings were framed in and had canvas tarps over the top.

Stuart Lambert, owner of Lambert's farm in Paradise Valley, Powell River, recalled driving his truck to the CO camp near the Gordon Pasha Lakes. He picked up the kitchen waste and fed it to the pigs on the farm.

One time the COs came down to the docks at Stillwater to collect freight for the camp; they were met with hostility by the people at the dock. Many of the young people from Stillwater were overseas in the Armed Forces; COs were generally regarded as shirkers. After a cool reception they never came down to the docks again.

Towards the end of the war the CO camp at the Gordon Pasha Lake was closed and the men moved to work on farms, in another location in B.C., where there was a shortage of labour.

Japanese "enemy aliens" WWII
Exodus from McNair Shingle Bolt camp, Stillwater

The bombing of the U.S. base at Pearl Harbour on Sunday, December 7, 1941 by Japan, not only brought the United States into WWII but had a direct impact on immigrants of Japanese ancestry who lived on North American's West Coast. The U.S.A. and Canada registered all persons of Japanese ancestry (men, women and children) and placed them in camps for the duration of the war. All Japanese fishing boats were seized and sold.

On December 8, 1941 the U.S.A and Great Britain declared war on Japan. On December 11, 1941, Germany and Italy declared war on the U.S.A.

After declaring war on Japan, the Canadian Government used the War Measures Act to pass an Order in Council, designating all Japanese persons in Canada as "enemy aliens". Everyone, men, women and children were to be removed from within a 100-mile radius of the B.C. coast.

Prior to 1942, Canadians of Japanese ancestry worked in the shingle bolt industry at the McNair Company camp at **Khartoum Lake**.

McNair employed both Japanese and Chinese workers. They lived in separate camps. The Chinese were located in a camp near Dodd Lake. It was comprised of single men. During the winter shut-in they returned to Vancouver.

The Japanese camps were located at Khartoum Lake. The biggest camp, at the head of the lake, consisted of two adjacent camps with Sazuki in charge of one, and Tara in charge of the other. Japanese workers were paid $1.50 a day while non-Asians, working for McNair were paid $2.50 a day. Wives and children also lived in the camp. During the winter shut-down the Japanese families stayed in the camps.

Almer McNair (2001) Douglas Bay, Powell River, B.C.
"In 1941, after Pearl Harbour, the RCMP asked my father Nat McNair to bring out the Japanese to the coast. My father was pretty much in tears at having to do this, as he was on very good terms with his employees. Many of the Japanese were third and fourth generation Canadians. They had to leave everything behind them in the shingle bolt camps. About 250 Japanese (men, women and children) were escorted to Vancouver and later placed in camps, in the interior of B.C. for the duration of the war." (*Rusty Nails and Ration Books* 2002 Barbara Ann Lambert)

March 1942 all Japanese employees and families were removed from the McNair camp at Stillwater. The *Powell River News* announced "Jap Exodus Completed," March 19, 1942.

At the end of the war McNair's Japanese employees never returned to Stillwater. They were not allowed to return to the coast and were given a choice by the Canadian Government: return to Japan, or live east of the Rockies.

War Brides of Stillwater, Lang Bay and Douglas Bay

WWI war bride: Barbara Lee of Stillwater (see Chapter 8 WWI War Brides of Western Canada)

WWII war brides:
Margaret Long "Lang Bay Lad Marries Scottish Lassie"
Joan Alice Patrick of Douglas Bay
        (See Chapter 5 WWII War Brides)

Children having fun on the speeder—logging railroad tracks, Stillwater, B.C. 1930s.
Photo: Violet Woodman

Stillwater United School 1962-63 Grades 3, 4, & 5.
Stillwater United was a "modern" school, built on land donated by the Powell River Company,
with electricity and indoor toilets in 1937. The new school united three one-room schools:
Annie Bay, Lang Bay and Kelly Creek. Note: left of the door the Stillwater railroad bell.
The bell was stolen when the school closed. Its' whereabouts continue to remain a mystery.
Photo: Powell River Museum

8

World War I Brides in Western Canada

Of the 600,000+ men of the Canadian Expeditionary Forces, many were of British ancestry. Two-thirds of the soldiers in the CEF went overseas. They were based in army bases in Britain for the duration of the war. The wounded spent months in hospitals and recuperation centres. At teas, dances and pubs, CEF soldiers met young British women; romances blossomed, and many ended in marriage. By the end of the war, there were thousands of war brides and a large number of children.

Approximately 25,000+ brides and children travelled to Canada between 1917 and 1919. This number included two groups of women: war brides, and wives who had travelled to Britain to be near their husbands for the duration of the war. Some fiancés (numbers unknown) came over to Canada between 1918 and 1920 at their own expense.

In order to receive free travel, paid for the Canadian government, war brides had to fill in an Application for Repatriation form. The arrangements, made by the Canadian Government for shipping WWI war brides and their dependents from Britain to Canada, set a precedent for travel arrangements for WWII war brides.

War brides arriving in Canada in 1919 received a helpful booklet *Information for Wives of Soldiers Coming from Overseas* published by the Repatriation Committee. This is a small booklet 5x3 inches, with a total of 20 pages. It could easily be kept in a purse for reference.

The Repatriation Committee welcomed returning British brides, and gave a warm welcome to new brides:

*"To those who are coming to Canada for the first time Canada offers you a sincere and friendly welcome. **We are delighted to receive you as citizens.** Just as the whole country appreciated the sacrifice and service of our men, so do we realize that with you, the future homemakers of this new land, rest tremendous possibilities of ennobling our National life. As a part of the beloved Commonwealth for which our soldiers have fought and died, we look to you to stand for democracy and freedom, the heritage of the British people."*

The booklet gave practical information about clothing, travel arrangements, reception committees, and the estimation of travel time on the train to the various major Canadian cities from the port of entry. It stated that all 3rd class travel was free, however, it was possible to upgrade to a better class of travel:

"The Government (Canadian) pays the expense of the wife, and children under 18 years of age, of any member of the Canadian military and naval forces, sailing after November 11, 1918. The passage consists of 3rd class accommodation on ship, with corresponding rail fare from your present address in the United Kingdom or Europe to the port of sailing and from the port of landing to destination in Canada. You may, if you desire and if space is available on board, secure accommodation in a better class either on the ship or on the train by paying the difference."

War brides had to pay for their own food and other expenses on the train. The booklet explained travel in Canada could take several days to reach one's destination, and the traveller had to make their own arrangements for the purchase of food on the journey. Lunch boxes, with sufficient food for two persons for two days, could be purchased at the Immigration buildings for $2. Meal tickets, for the train restaurants, were available at 75 cents. Food was also available at station restaurants for a fast purchase.

Women's reception committees from patriotic organizations were waiting at the dock to help: the Red Cross, Canadian Patriotic Fund, YWCA (Young Women's Christian Association), IODE (Imperial Order of the Daughters of the Empire), and others. At various stations on route were organizations with gifts of fresh fruit.

There are few published personal accounts of WWI war brides in Western Canada. Arriving after WWI, war brides lived in an era where few people owned a telephone, many could not afford a newspaper, and mail between England and Canada could take months. After surviving the 1918 pandemic Flu epidemic, brides witnessed the 1929 Stock Market Crash, and hard times during the "Dirty Thirties". Some WWI brides lived to see their husbands, and children fighting for "King & Country" in WWII.

Many brides had large families, and they were busy raising them. There was no spare time, with household tasks: cooking, canning, washing, ironing, dressmaking, mending, and child rearing, taking up every waking hour. Few households owned telephones or cars. Brides socialized by walking to the nearest neighbour, general store, and church. Sharing information became easier in the Information Age, during the last half of the 20th Century. Thus accounts and photographs of Canadian WWI war brides are exceptionally rare.

In contrast, WWII war brides lived in a different economic era, and enjoyed household appliances which were mass-produced in the postwar era: refrigerators, freezers, dishwashers, vacuum cleaners, electric washing machines and dryers. These appliances helped brides with food preparation and household tasks; they cut down on the amount of time devoted to maintaining a household and gave women leisure time, and an opportunity to take a part-time job. Some women learned to drive during WWII, and others learned in the postwar era. At first, women were driving the family car; from the 1960s many Canadian households owned a second car.

With more leisure time and mobility, WWII war brides were able to travel longer distances to meet friends, and attend War Bride Association functions. The Associations became a focal point for the researching of war bride stories. The Information Age, which included the telephone (now in every household), computer, and email, social networking, and self-publishing, made it possible for collections of WWII war bride stories to be published.

Accounts of World War I war brides in Western Canada

Our knowledge of the life of WWI war brides in Western Canada is limited by the relative small number of published war bride stories. The few WWI war bride stories known in Western Canada can be discovered in rare 2nd hand books, family histories, and historical society publications.

The only WWI war bride book published in British Columbia was a journal of life on the rugged west coast by Dorothy Abraham.

Book publication:
Lone Cone: A Journal of Life on the West Coast of Vancouver Island by Dorothy Abraham, self-published during WWII.

Family histories:
Barbara Lee, WWI war bride, Stillwater, Powell River Regional District, B.C. Researched by Barbara Ann Lambert 2011.

Alice May Sikstrom, WWI war bride, Hay Lake, Alberta. (Alice Sikstrom was a summer resident in Powell River from the late 1950s to 1970s.) Researched by Barbara Ann Lambert 2011.

Charlotte Simister   Belgian WWI war bride
Family history researched by J.F. Bosher. "Our Roots the Families of Bosher, Marsden, Readings and Simister" February 2000.

Historical Society publications:
Aline Machell a Belgian WWI war bride – *"A history of Vancouver's 29th Regiment".*

A War Bride's Journey in 1917 by Flora Gould published by the Okanagan Historical Society November 1973. Transcribed tapes by the Summerland Museum of a historic road journey of the Gould family from Saskatchewan to British Columbia.

Mary Jane Yates, WWI war bride published by the Crowsnest Pass Historical Society, 1979.

WWI war brides from Belgium

The majority of soldiers in the CEF married British girls; however, some married Belgian girls (unknown number). The CEF spent months, after the war was over, in Belgium waiting for troop ships to take them back to Britain. There was a feeling of great joy that the Great War was over. Belgian families were grateful for the sacrifices made by the CEF. It is not surprising that romances flourished in the relaxed postwar atmosphere; however, there are few records of Belgian war brides.

Recent research accounts for two Belgian WWI war brides: a short reference is made to a charming Belgian girl, who married Lt. Machell CEF of Vancouver in "A history of Vancouver's 29th Regiment", and a family research project "Our Roots – The Families of Bosher, Marsden, Readings, and Simister" by John Bosher in 2000 includes a reference to his aunt Charlotte Simister, a WWI war bride from Belgium.

Charlotte Simister (Bary) 1894-1970 WWI war bride from Belgium

"The following summary of Norman Simister's life says nothing of what was certainly the principal event in it, the Great War of 1914-18. He was 21 years old when it broke out and soon joined the 48th Battalion of the Canadian Army, which sent him overseas. Once is northern France, he transferred to the Motor Transport service which entailed driving high-ranking officers about in a staff car and other such work.

At the same time, he applied himself to improving the French that he had learned as a school boy in England. Surviving postcards and family recollections tell us that he had visited France at least once before immigrating to Victoria. Among the wartime letters he wrote back to various members of his family were some in French to his sister Margaret. They show he was already writing fluent, wide-ranging, almost correct pages, drawing on a remarkably large vocabulary.

Norman was expected home in 1919. On 25th January that year his mother wrote to his sister Margaret, teaching on Salt Spring Island, "Did you wish to be in Victoria to welcome the heroes home? The Women's Institute are going to give a welcome supper when all the boys get back, a real jolly time. We had a letter from Norman yesterday written Christmas Day. He's still in Germany at a place called Bonn."

The crowning event in his French adventure came on Armistice Day, 11th November 1918, when at Mons in Belgium, he met Charlotte Aurelie Desiree Bary, a Belgian school teacher living with her parents. They married three months later, on 15th February 1919, and he brought her home to Canada on the troop ship the SS Metagama, which landed at Quebec in June 1919.

Our Aunt Charlotte, a lively, pretty pink-cheeked lady with a fascinating French accent in English, was one of the wonders of the Simister clan. She spoke little English for several years, partly because Norman's French was so fluent. On 15th August 1920 she had a daughter, our cousin Francine, the second in age among 16 cousins, as vivacious and pretty as her mother and eventually the best pianist in the family.

In 1923 Aunt Charlotte's parents "Monsieur and Madam Bary of Mons, Belgium", came out to Canada and late in May settled in Beach House for what "The Review" (24th May 1923) announced as "an extended stay to Sidney with a view to making their future home here." Monsieur Bary then advertised himself in "The Review" as a "general gardener — day or week — terms reasonable", giving his address as Beach House. They were still there in August 1924, but for some reason — possibly a difficulty in finding employment — the Barys later returned to Belgium. My mother believed that they soon tired of living in Canada, and found the problems of adaptation too discouraging.

The Norman Simisters lived in a series of houses in or near Victoria. Each of these houses was beautifully furnished with Aunt Charlotte's unerring continental taste and with many objects made by Uncle Norman, who was a skilled metal worker. What I remember best is an item they must have brought from Europe, a mantel clock that rocked back and forth suspended from a bronze female figure in a swirling gown, looking much like the symbolic French Marianne.

Norman Simister was a lively person, a joker who loved to make people laugh by playing the fool, capering about in a light-hearted way. As well as a sense of humour, he had a wonderful sense of the ridiculous which enlightens so much of the English. Tom Anstey remembers a typical Sunday in Grandpa's Simister's shop where Uncle Norman tried on a series of ladies' hats, acting various parts to suit each one. All who knew him can recall his songs, comic verses, and jolly ways."

Researched by John Bosher February 2000

Aline Machell born in Belgium 1898, married Lt. Frank Walter Machell CEF (Reg #75537) in Belgium, after the Great War, in 1919.

Lt. Frank Machell CEF of Vancouver's 29th Regiment (known as Tobin's Tigers) was with his regiment in Belgium, at the end of the Great War. It was a time of relaxation, fun and hope for the future. Officers played badminton, went to the theatre, and visited Belgian friends. It was in this relaxing, postwar atmosphere that Lt. Frank Machell met, and fell in love with Aline, "a charming Belgian girl". This event is documented in the regimental history of Vancouver's 29th Regiment. Lt. Machell returned to England where he was given special permission to leave the army, return to Belgium, and marry the girl he had fallen in love with.

Mrs. Aline Machell, a Belgian WWI war bride, sailed on the *S.S. Canada* with her husband, from Liverpool, England, August 1919, arriving in Quebec, Canada, on August 7, 1919; their destination Matsqui (Abbotsford), British Columbia.

WWI war brides from Britain

The majority of WWI war brides, married to soldiers in the CEF, came from Britain. The CEF forces were located in Britain and the troops during and after the war socialized with the British girls in pubs, parks, tea dances etc. Some met their war brides as nurses in hospitals and convalescent homes. By the time the troops went home, thousands of Canadian soldiers had married British girls.

Although many war brides came to Western Canada, there are few published accounts. *Lone Cone* by **Dorothy Abraham** is the self-published story of a British war bride living in an isolated area of the British Columbia coast; it portrays courage, endurance and fortitude. *Lone Cone* gives a glimpse into the life of a well-educated, articulate, middle class woman, who adjusted to the rugged life on B.C.'s West Coast.

The four WWI war brides: Barbara Lee, Alice May Sikstrom, Flora Gould, and Mary Jane Yates married men in the Canadian Expeditionary Force from "other ranks". They experienced a different economic and social life compared to war brides who married well-educated officers with financial means. With courage, and determination, they worked hard to provide the necessities of life for their families: food, clothing and shelter.

Barbara Lee, the resilient daughter of a Scottish sea captain, made a home for her family on B.C.'s West Coast. Originally from the Orkney Islands, Barbara Lee had no difficulty in adjusting to life in the isolated logging community of Stillwater (1941 population 317). Due to the Halifax explosion, December 6, 1917, a pregnant and penniless **Flora Gould** was forced to change her travel arrangements, and travel from New York to Saskatchewan. The account of her journey showed great personal courage, self-reliance, and a natural curiosity about her environment. In 1919 Flora made a historic journey by road to Summerland, B.C. **Mary Jane Yates** was shocked on her arrival in Michel, B.C. to find snow and a temperature of 50 degrees below zero. As a miner's wife, she struggled financially to provide for her family during various strikes. **Alice May Sikstrom** lived in Hay Lake, Alberta (population 300). Her husband, Private Ingve Sikstrom, was employed as a labourer by CNR. Alice May brought up her family in modest circumstances, and was well known for her generosity to others.

Dorothy Abraham (1894-1990)

Dorothy, an educated young woman, from a middle-class British background, came out to British Columbia, Canada with her officer husband, Ted Abraham in the spring of 1919. Ted, British by birth, took part in the Great War as part of the Canadian Expeditionary Force. Dorothy, as part of the war effort, had joined the Voluntary Aid Detachment, and worked as a nurse at a hospital in Wales.

No matter how much Ted had told her about life on Vargas Island (a remote island off the wild, stormy west coast of Vancouver Island), nothing could have prepared her for a way of life so different to the one she had left behind.

Dorothy's most important advice to WWII war brides was to learn to cook before leaving England! With loaves of bread like lead, and mince pies like bullets, Dorothy's cooking was to be endured by her loving husband.

The Journey

Dorothy and her officer husband, Ted Abraham, travelled 1st class on the RMS *Olympic* to Halifax, Nova Scotia. It was the *Olympic's* last voyage as a troop ship. There was a huge crowd at the dock to give the troops a send-off, a band playing and people singing.

.... *"We took six days to cross, and saw some icebergs enroute. On the last day excitement ran high, and much fun was had tossing everyone in a blanket on deck. Finally we arrived in Halifax — miles of people waving and cheering, sirens going, people yelling and singing and bands playing.*

After purchasing a delicious ice cream sundae in Halifax, Dorothy and Ted boarded the train for their journey west. The length of the train to Montreal was impressive. Beds were made up at night by "coloured porters who were most attentive". On the journey, when passing Lake Ontario, fresh trout was on the breakfast menu.

Home on the West Coast: Vargas Island and Tofino

"...My husband's place was on the open beach — beautiful, rugged, terrifying lonely, with a little shack on the beach, about two miles through the bush from my in-laws.
    No fields! No grass! No people! — The awful loneliness of it all frightened me. — We decided right away to build a house on the other side of the island next to my in-laws.

Our first home was a two-roomed shack. It was quite close to the beach and Lone Cone (an extinct volcano) looked down upon us."

After Vargas Island, came a move to Tofino (a small village of 300 people), and later a move to Victoria, where Ted Abraham had accepted an appointment as Magistrate. For Dorothy Abraham, the 11 years in Tofino were the best years of her life.

Flora Gould

Flora set off on her journey to Canada, as a war bride, when she was four-months pregnant. Her husband Arthur Gould, was expected to be invalided home sometime during the winter of 1917-18. She was advised by her family doctor to travel when she was pregnant because it would be easier than travelling with a baby!

Flora travelled steerage on the *Justica*, with other war brides. Flora had little money with her because she expected to stay with Arthur's grandmother in Halifax, until Arthur joined her later. All plans were changed with the news of a huge explosion in Halifax harbour on December 6, 1917; the *Justica's* destination was now New York. Flora had no money to pay for new travel expenses. Not knowing what had happened to relatives in the Halifax explosion, Flora's destination was now Saskatchewan where her father-in-law Allan Gould lived.

It was the kindness of strangers that helped her out. Nurse Gladys Black, a friend she had made on board the *Justica*, invited Flora to accompany her on a visit to an aunt and uncle, a Mr. and Mrs. Corbett, in New Jersey. Flora sent off a wire to Saskatchewan asking her father-in-law for money for the train journey. On December 25, 1917, now five months pregnant, Flora was on her way.

Flora:

"This was my first Christmas in a strange land and I spent it travelling and never missed the traditional Christmas meal, so busy was I taking in all the new scenes from the train. I travelled in a Pullman car, and the black porter was another novelty, as well as sleeping on the train."

Flora eventually arrived at her destination in Saskatchewan. The Gould family gave Flora "a very hearty and affectionate welcome".

"My daughter (Dorothy) was born in May 1918. Arthur got home in February, also via New York, on the Olympic. My in-laws in Halifax had lost the ceiling in their house from the explosion but were otherwise alright. Nurse Black had been transferred to an American hospital in France. My stay in Saskatchewan was short. The Gould clan moved to Summerland, B.C. in 1919."

The decision by the Gould family to move from Saskatchewan to British Columbia by car was certainly an ambitious one, probably foolhardy. For Flora, the war bride from Wales, it must have been an exciting adventure. The entire town of Valparaiso came to see them off. A banner on the back of one of the cars told all and sundry that their destination was – British Columbia! They travelled in two 1919 Model T Fords, and a 1916 McLaughlin Buick.

Les Gould:

"There were no road maps in those days, no road signs, and very little assistance as most folks had never been more than a few miles from home. It was simply a case of pointing the car west and keep going. There was no speedometer on those cars, so any time mileage is mentioned, it is not necessarily correct."

They had to detour down through the U.S. in order to reach their destination in B.C. It certainly had been a great adventure which involved numerous car repairs, changing of tires, cars going off the road, and pushing cars up steep grades. Some roadhouses had tobacco-stained sheets and bed bugs! Gasoline averaged 40 cents a gallon and the mileage worked out at 20 miles per gallon.

Mary Jane Yates

In 1916, while working in an ammunitions factory in Lancashire, England, Mary Jane met a young Canadian soldier, Sapper James Yates. James was on leave, while serving with the Canadian Expeditionary Force in France. The Canadian soldier and the young English girl kept "company" while he served in the army for two more years.

Mary Jane and James Yates were married in Tyldesley, Lancashire on September 28, 1918. The couple left Liverpool on February 28, 1919 on the *SS Melita*. They landed in St. John, New Brunswick. From there, they travelled west by train to James' hometown of Michel, British Columbia.

What a shock for Mary Jane, on arriving at Michel, British Columbia, there was deep snow and the temperature was 50 degrees below zero. She had never seen conditions like this, ever before, in England.

James found work with a mining company at Michel. He rented a house from the company which Mary Jane furnished with 2nd hand furniture. The couple moved from Michel to Coleman because the mine at Coleman offered better wages. Mary Jane worked hard, keeping house for her husband, brother-in-law, and a bachelor friend. Ella, Mary Jane's daughter, was born in 1920.

Life was difficult with a baby to care for, and frozen pipes in winter. Mary Jane was "thrifty" but unable to save anything for miners' strikes. They moved to another house in the same company town. Here, Mary Jane found the place overrun with mice! For a small amount of money the couple bought a lot in the town. They worked hard together, dismantling two houses which they had bought for $135 in the ghost town of Hosmer. Mary Jane, wearing shirt and trousers, helped her husband dismantle them, while living in a tent. Mary Jane and James built a new house on their purchased lot. In 1924 they moved into their new home. Soon they had electricity and running water.

Mary Jane:
> *"It was like Heaven to have a home of our own, garden and all."*

After the McGillivray mine explosion, James went to work for the International Mining Company. In 1968 James died. Mary Jane continued to live in the house they built together. She felt lonely, but had no regrets at coming as a war bride to Canada.

Mary Jane:

"I never did regret coming to this area in the great country Canada, the best (country) in the world. I had several trips to England but the way of life in Canada is the way of life for me."

Barbara Lee WWI war bride from Scotland

John Lee Jr. (79) 2011

"My Lee grandparents Charles and Helen (Ellen) Lee and their children emigrated from Scotland in 1907 to Canada.

My father, John Findlay Lee Sr. was born in 1890 on the Orkney Islands at Deepdale Hobbister, Orphir. He was one of ten children. There were five boys: Charles, James, William, Henry and John, and five girls: Susan, Margaret, Robina, Elizabeth and Lillian. Apart from the two youngest children, William and Lily, all the other children were adults when they left Scotland.

As soon as the First World War broke out, my father and his brothers Henry, James and Charles all volunteered to join the Army and serve overseas. My father revisited the Orkney Islands when he was overseas. It was here he met my mother Barbara Gray (Gunn). They fell in love and married in Scotland. My mother came as a war bride to Canada.

Amazingly, the four Lee brothers survived the bloody trench war in France."

Barbara Lee (Gray)

John Lee Jr.:

*"My mother **Barbara Lee** (Gray) was born in 1889 at Stromness, Orkney Islands, Scotland. She was a World War I war bride.*

As a young child, my mother sailed with my grandfather, William Alexander Gray, on the "Loch Tay" and "Loch Torridon". He was a deep sea captain and sailed from Scotland to Brisbane, Australia. My grandmother, Dolly Gray, died soon after her youngest child, James Alexander Gray was born; the baby was raised by a Mrs. Knight in Stromness. Grandfather Gray called my mother Dolly, after his wife Dolly. My mother had long, blonde hair; she was small, about five feet in height.

My mother had little formal education as she spent her childhood on the high seas. My grandfather Gray taught her to read and encouraged her to read from the library of books in the Captain's cabin. All her life she was an avid reader. My mother, while on the high seas, was taught how to knit. She was a great knitter all her life.

Grandfather gave my mother a parrot for companionship. The parrot was a great talker and, one time, my grandfather had to give strict orders to the crew, "No more bad language!"

Before Dolly Gray married, she worked in a jewellery store in Stromness. My father, John Lee Sr. CEF (originally from the Orkney Islands) met my mother in Stromness when he was on leave in Scotland during WWI. They married on January 21, 1919 in the Temperance Hall in Stromness. My mother sailed as a war bride on the S.S. Pretorian from Glasgow, for Canada, on January 23, 1920.

Five Lee children were born in Canada. I was the youngest, and the only one born in Stillwater. I was born in 1932 on my parents' 13th wedding anniversary. James (Jim), Margaret, Barbara and Alfreda (Freda) were born in Vancouver.

My father first came to Powell River with James Omand (brother-in-law) in 1930 looking for work. My dad first found work, shoeing horses, for Bloedel, Stewart and Welch at Myrtle Point. He then found work as a blacksmith at Stillwater. Later he worked for Kelly Spruce, a division of the Powell River Company, until he volunteered in 1939 for the Canadian Veterans Guard.

My mother never learned to cook while she was growing up because her mother (deceased) was not there to teach her, and the cooking aboard the ship was done by a male galley crew. After she married, mother learned to be a good, basic cook. My memories of my mother are of always wearing an apron, except when she had a photograph taken! Occasionally, my father made a meal.

My mother loved to dance the old Scottish dances. She sang and recited Scottish ballads at the old Stillwater hall. Mother was a great friend of Mrs. McNair. The McNairs and Lees lived next door to each other. The kids played together. The two families were very close. My mother and Ina Lloyd were good friends. All the kids loved to go swimming; to get us out of the water my mother blew a police whistle! All the Lee and McNair kids attended Annie Bay School. I was only there for six months before it closed. I attended Stillwater United from 1937-1946.

We had a radio. Every year on Remembrance Day, 11th November, my father made the kids be quiet. We had to listen respectfully to the service for all who died in WWI.

For Christmas we always had a turkey. Christmas Eve we'd get together with the McNairs. On Christmas Day we were not allowed to open our presents until after breakfast. Everybody had to be there for the present opening. Dad always had duck eggs as a special treat at Christmas. Alec

Stoddard or Sammy Lamont played bagpipes from the hotel at Stillwater, all the way up the railroad tracks to our house.

My father used to go grouse and deer hunting with a slingshot in his back pocket and a 30-30 rifle over his shoulder. He always came home with something. There was only one shot to the head, so as not to spoil the meat.

Dad had fought in WWI with the CEF and he wanted to fight again for "King & Country" in WWII. He lied about his age, and was assigned to the Canadian Veterans Guards. Dad was sent to Medicine Hat to help with the basic training of new soldiers, and to guard German P.O.Ws. After the war, he brought back to Stillwater some German war souvenirs.

My brother was a logger; he was not allowed to join up because he worked in a restricted trade. My sister, Alfreda, joined the Canadian Air Force and served back east in general service. She left home about the same time as my father. After the war she married Roy Smith, a WWII veteran from Vancouver. I was only 7 years of age when war was declared. I was the only one at home living with my mother. She was a great knitter, knitting socks and scarves for the boys overseas. She taught me how to knit socks.

My Uncle James ran a pool hall in Stromness. He never married. In 1946 he died and left some money. The money was sent to Canada and divided between myself, and my sister Alfreda. My mother died in 1961 in the Powell River hospital. My parents are buried side-by-side in Cranberry cemetery, Powell River, B.C.

I worked in the woods all my working life (50 years). I retired in January 1996."

Ina Lloyd (McNair) – Stillwater old-timer (90) 2011

Ina:

"Mrs. Lee was a very nice person. The Lees came to Stillwater after WWI. They were here before John Lee was born, and he was born in 1932. On their second visit to Stillwater they lived in Norden's house, and later, they moved up the tracks (railroad). Mr. Lee was a blacksmith when he first came to Stillwater.

Mrs. Lee was a small, stout Scottish lady. She was my mother's age. We were all good friends. As a young girl she had lived on a ship. Her father was a sea captain. Her mother died when Barbara was quite young. Barbara Lee had no formal schooling, her father taught her how to read and write when they were at sea.

My mother had lots of teas and (bridal & baby) showers at our house. Mrs. Lee always came. When we had social events at Stillwater Hall, Mrs. Lee used to make a great big pile of sandwiches. Mrs. Lee was a card player, and a good dancer. Mr. and Mrs. Lee taught some of the Scottish dances when we had dances in the hall. Old Mrs. Runnells and Mrs. Lee were very good friends. Mrs. Runnells was very deaf, and we used to visit her almost every day. Mrs. White lived near the Runnells' place; when Japan entered the war in WWII, Mrs. White broke every dish in her house that was made in Japan!

We (the kids) used to go over the bank for a swim to the wharf. Mrs. Lee had a police whistle, and she would blow it, to get us out of the water!"

Alice May Sikstrom (Latchford) (1902-1989)
WWI engaged war bride from Wales

Alice Sikstrom was a WWI engaged war bride. Alice came out to Canada in 1920 to marry Ingve Sikstrom, a Canadian soldier she had met in her hometown of Colwyn Bay, Wales in 1918.

Ingve had given Alice a diamond ring before leaving with the troops for Canada. They corresponded for two years while Ingve worked hard to save up the $200 for Alice's fare. Alice and Ingve Sikstrom were married on 16th August 1920 in Edmonton, Alberta. They had four children, three boys and a girl: Clifford, Harold, Fred and Evelyn.

In 1957 Evelyn Sikstrom came to Powell River with her husband Henry, and their two children Duane and Jerry. Henry worked in the Powell River mill on the clothing crew, employed first by the Powell River Company and later by MacMillan Bloedel. Alice and Ingve Sikstrom were frequent visitors to Powell River for many years.

Evelyn's Memories (age 81) Powell River 2011
My Father's Story

Private Ingve Sikstrom CEF

"My Swedish grandparents, Karl Petter (1860-1934) and Johanna Sikstrom (1855-1932), emigrated from Sweden to Canada, after selling their farm in Ledningsmark, Lycksele. They sailed from Stockholm to Halifax in 1903 with a large family. Many Swedes came to Canada at this time

due to bad harvests in Sweden. My father Ingve Sikstrom (1896-1978), age 7, was seasick during the voyage, he could only eat oranges! A decade passed before he ate another orange!

After crossing Canada by train, the Sikstrom family homesteaded a quarter-section (160 acres) in Hay Lake, Alberta. Their homestead was in the German section. In Hay Lake the homesteads were in three sections: Ukrainian, Scandinavian and German. The entire journey from Sweden to Alberta took two months.

It was difficult to get started on the homestead but other Swedes helped the family out. The first couple of years they relied on a plentiful supply of rabbits to feed their large family of eight boys and one girl: Hilmer, John Sigurd, Hugo Valfrid, Arvid, Fred, Sten, Vivian, Ingve and Astrid.

My father Ingve was called up in WWI. He went overseas to England and trained at Aldershot. He never made it to France because the war ended while he was in training. My uncle Arvid went into the American Army; he made it to France and then died of the flu in 1918.

After the war, my father and many other Canadian soldiers had to wait many months before being repatriated to Canada. It was during these months that my father started to seriously court my mother, Alice Latchford, with the intention of marrying her and bringing her out to Canada."

My Mother's story:

Alice May Sikstrom (Latchford)

"My mother was born in Manchester, England in 1902. Sometime later the family moved to Colwyn Bay, Wales. I am not sure exactly what my grandfather did for a living; I think he was into photography, and possibly framed pictures. Mother had two brothers: Harold and Stan and two sisters: Nellie and Elsie. Elsie died of consumption (tuberculosis of the lungs).

My grandmother was very strict. She would not allow my mother to wear lipstick, so my mother kept a lipstick in her coat pocket and secretly put it on when she was out with her friends, then rubbed it off before arriving home.

It was while walking with a friend on the Promenade at Colwyn Bay, on their way to church, that my mother met up with a couple of Canadian soldiers in 1918. On one occasion, Ingve met her family and had tea with them. Before he left England, he gave my mother a beautiful diamond ring. Alice was reluctant to tell her mother that she had accepted her Canadian boyfriend's ring; in the end, it was one of my uncles who let out the secret.

Ingve and Alice corresponded by letter. My father was a polite man, he wrote to Alice's father for permission to marry his daughter. My grandparents were not happy at their daughter marrying a

Canadian and leaving Wales. They were concerned they would never see their daughter again. They also felt Alice was too young, at age 18 to travel to Canada and start married life.

My mother found life at home restrictive. She wanted to leave, and marrying my father gave her that opportunity.

My father worked hard and saved up my mother's fare which was over $200; that was a lot of money in those days. The Canadian Government did not pay her fare; they would have if my parents had married overseas. My mother came out to Canada as an engaged war bride. She sailed on S.S. Metegama, with $40 in her purse, arriving in Quebec August 8, 1920.

Alice boarded the train at Quebec; however, instead of staying on the train all the way to Alberta, she decides to make a stopover at Winnipeg. My mother was impulsive by nature. This delay caused a great deal of confusion for Ingve, who was waiting for her in Edmonton. Finally, after making inquiries at immigration, he found Alice in a boarding house in Edmonton!

Alice married Private Ingve Sikstrom on the 16ᵗʰ August in Edmonton; my mother wore a long dress and flat canvas shoes. At first they stayed on the Sikstrom homestead near Hay Lake. The family was welcoming. One relative, however, was critical of my mother's accent – even though the same person had a Swedish accent! My parents stayed for only one year on the farm. My mother was glad to leave. Dad found a permanent job working as a labourer repairing the track for CNR. This was a job with steady pay, unlike farming – dependent on the weather, and one main cash crop. Dad was not a tall man but he was strong. He kept his job at CNR throughout the Great Depression, when jobs were hard to come by.

Dad bought four lots in Hay Lake, and built a house on one of them. Mum enjoyed living in Hay Lake. Our house was just one block from the main street. We had a garden behind the house. Hay Lake had a population of about 300-350 people. There was a dance hall, garage, barber's shop, hotel, post office, two cafes, school, railway station, two grain elevators, and a Lutheran church.

My mother did not know how to cook when she married my father because her mother would never let her in the kitchen. It was my father who taught her to cook. Mum became a very good cook. One dish she did not like cooking, and that was liver and onions. So, if she was away for some reason, that's what we had for supper! Whenever my cousins from the farm came into town, they would call at our place. Mum made them coffee, and shared meals with them. Mum was generous in sharing whatever we had with anyone who ever came through the door. One time my dad brought home for lunch a young man who was "riding the rods". Because it was wash day, Mum had a simple meal in the oven. She apologized to the stranger when she served him macaroni and cheese, with tomatoes on the top. The young man was overcome with gratitude, and said it was the best meal he had ever tasted!

My mother only went back to England once with my two older brothers, Clifford and Harold. My mother was not a disciplinarian, and at the end of the visit my grandmother said to my mother:

"… take those two savages back to Canada!"

My mother never wanted to go again, even though my father said he would pay for her fare. I have never been to England.

Mum liked to read, especially "True Stories". She would hide them under a cushion if she went out. I would find them and, of course, read them! She dressed smartly – her clothes were always in fashion. She liked stylish shoes – just like me. Mum was always losing either her false teeth, glasses or watch! I would find them under a cushion. We'd often chat about her life in the "old country" while we were doing the dishes in the kitchen.

Mum loved dancing. My parents went dancing at the local dance hall about once a month. When I was small, they would take me with them. The girls would sit at one side of the hall on a bench, and the boys on the opposite side. Before a dance, my cousins from the farm would arrive two days ahead of time, and they spent the time doing up their hair with curling irons, putting on makeup and trying on dresses. The band had a break at midnight for coffee, and then it would start up again at 1a.m. and last until 2 or 3 a.m.

We had an old record player which had to be wound up and cranked to play a record. We also had a radio. The only phone available was at the post office.

My mother liked going to the movies. Because my father worked on the railways we had free travel passes. We would go together for the weekend to Edmonton and stay at a hotel for $1.50 a night. Mother knew how to stretch a $10 bill. Sometimes we stayed in a rooming house run by a Ukrainian lady who only charged $1 a night for the two of us. Mum would say, "Shall we take a taxi to the station or stop at the bake shop?" I always chose the bake shop.

Mum was fun to be with. She encouraged me to wear lipstick when I was in my teens. We had day trips on the train to Camrose. Here we would take in a matinee performance of the latest film at the movie palace. Admission price was 25 cents.

My mother and father were good parents. They looked after us, fed us and clothed us in very difficult times, the Great Depression. In Hay Lake everyone was in the same boat financially. We were never rich but we had a good life.

During WWII we were supposed to get a British Evacuee; she was an English cousin. The cousin was supposed to come out on a government program (CORB) but after the sinking of the

295

"City of Benares" with evacuees on, my aunt Nellie changed her mind. She said it was safer for children to stay in Britain with the bombing, than being torpedoed and drowned at sea.

During WWII my brother Clifford was an engineer in Bermuda with the Air Force. My brother Harold was overseas in Italy. He was wounded during the war. He ended up in a hospital in Holland. After the war, my brothers married local girls I went to school with.

I married Henry, a local Hay Lake boy. We were married in Vancouver. We spent four years in Ocean Falls, and six years in Rossland. In 1957 my husband found work with the Powell River Company. When I first came here, my husband drove me up the cut to the mill. He asked me, "What do you think of the place?" I replied, "I feel I have died and gone to heaven!" I have loved living here ever since.

My parents frequently came to visit our family in Powell River. They travelled from Edmonton to Vancouver by train, using the free passes Dad had for working on the railroad. Mum and Dad were good grandparents.

Mum died in a nursing home in Edmonton in 1989. I remember her telling me that she was pretty lucky to have met and married my dad. She was a good mum."

Norman Simister CEF (1893-1970)
From 1915-18 Norman was overseas in France and Belgium. His duties in the Motor Transport
division included driving high-ranking officers. On Armistice Day 11th November 1918
at Mons, Belgium, Norman met Charlotte Bary, a Belgian school teacher;
they fell in love and married on 15th February 1919 in Belgium.
Photo: Elisabeth Bosher collection

1943 Sidney, B.C.
Elisabeth Bosher (L) and her aunt (R) Charlotte Simister (Bary) a Belgian WWI war bride,
wife, of Norman Simister CEF. Photo: Elisabeth Bosher collection

1918—the Canadian Expeditionary Force entered Mons, Belgium.
(Centre) Brigadier-General Clark of Vancouver. Norman Simister,
a driver in the Motor Transport division, witnessed this jubilant scene.
Photo: Powell River Digester May 1940 contributed by Charles McLean CEF

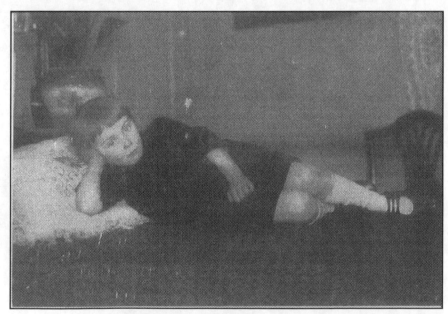

1896 Barbara Gray on the ocean going ship the Loch Tay.
Most of her childhood was spent on board the ship with her father, Captain William Alexander
Gray (a widower) sailing between Scotland and Brisbane, Australia.
Photo: John Lee Jr. collection

John Lee CEF and Barbara Lee WWI war bride, Stromness,
Orkney Island, Scotland (January 21, 1919).
Barbara Lee boarded the S.S. Pretorian of the Canadian Pacific Line,
at the Port of Glasgow, for Canada on January 23, 1920.
After landing at St. John, New Brunswick, she travelled to Vancouver, B.C.
Photo: John Lee Jr. collection

1918 Captain Gray (retired) on his ship the Loch Tay.
Photo: John Lee Jr. collection

1945 Stillwater, B.C. The Lee Family
Back row: John Lee (Canadian Veteran Guard WWII), Barbara Lee (daughter),
Margaret Lee, Alfreda Lee (RCAF WD), Jim Lee,
Front row: John Lee Jr., Barbara Lee (WWI war bride).
Photo: John Lee Jr. collection

1947 Stillwater, B.C. The Lee Family
Back row: Barbara Carpendale (Lee), Margaret Mckay (Lee), Eddy McKay, Alfreda Lee
Middle row: John Lee, Barbara Lee WWI war bride, Lil Lee (Jim's wife)
Front row: Leo Carpendale and baby Victor, John Lee Jr., Jim Lee and baby Alex
Photo: John Lee Jr. collection

Private Ingve Sikstrom CEF from Hay Lake, Alberta, was conscripted in 1917.
He trained at Aldershot in England, however the war was over before he saw action in France.
During the months of waiting to be shipped back to Canada,
Ingve Sikstrom, met and courted Alice May Latchford
Of Colwyn Bay, Wales. They became engaged before Ingve left for Canada.
Photo: Evelyn Sikstrom collection

Alice May Sikstrom (Latchford) at Hay Lake, Alberta, 1921 (age 19 years).
As an engaged WWI war bride, Alice May Latchford travelled to Canada on the S.S.
Metegama with $40 in her purse, arriving in Quebec on August 8, 1920.
Her fare was paid for by Ingve Sikstrom CEF.
Photo: Evelyn Sikstrom collection

1926 Hay Lake, Alberta
Ingve and Alice May Sikstrom with their children Clifford and Harold.
Photo: Evelyn Sikstrom collection

1938 Evelyn Sikstrom age 7 years, outside the family home,
one block from the main street of Hay Lake, Alberta.
Photo: Evelyn Sikstrom collection

1934 on Main Street, Hay Lake, Alberta.
(L) Evelyn Sikstrom (4 years) and Harvey Grahn, playing on the
sidewalk outside the Economy shop.
Photo: Evelyn Sikstrom collection.

September 1940: Evelyn Sikstrom (10) and
her mother Alice May Sikstrom in Edmonton, after seeing a movie.
Photo: Evelyn Sikstrom collection

1953 Rossland, B.C. Alice and Ingve Sikstrom with their grandchildren Duane and Jerry. Alice and Ingve were frequent summer residents in Powell River, B.C. from the late 1950s to the early 1970s, visiting their daughter Evelyn. Evelyn's husband worked at the Powell River Company mill.
Photo: Evelyn Sikstrom collection

1970 Alice (WWI engaged war bride) and Ingve Sikstroms' 50th wedding anniversary. Alice and Ingve (centre of photo), with their adult children. (L to R) The Sikstrom family: Harold, Evelyn, Alice, Ingve, Fred and Clifford. Photo: Evelyn Sikstrom collection.

9
Memories

Halifax Explosion 1917
Ida Osborn (nee Wells)

In 1912 Robert Wells came to Canada from England to join his brother William in Montreal. In 1914, after the declaration of World War I, Robert joined the navy and was sent to Halifax.

Robert's wife Annie with Ida, aged 5, and baby Bobby, joined Robert in Halifax. The Wells family rented an apartment halfway up on Russell Street, not far from the dockyard in the north end.

On December 6, 1917 the **Imo** of Oslo collided with the French munitions ship, **Mont Blanc**. This impact caused an immense explosion in the Halifax dockyards. Ida Wells, as a small child, remembers this tragic event.

Ida:

"The day before the Halifax explosion I was standing on the kitchen table and my mother was measuring me for a pair of serge bloomers. In those days girls wore serge bloomers (like plus fours) and a white middy-blouse (blouse with sailor collar). I remember looking up at the ceiling, and wondering to myself what would happen if it ever fell down.

The next day, when I woke up, I thought I was dreaming; the roof had fallen down! I forced my eyes open, in order to wake up. Plaster, from the ceiling, was in my eyes and I couldn't see. There was dust everywhere. I opened my eyes periodically.

In the meantime, my father was in the dockyard. After the explosion, he looked up and saw lumber flying through the air like matchwood! As soon as he could, my father raced up the street to our apartment.

By this time I was out of bed as our house had collapsed. All the north end of the city of Halifax was flattened. I crawled out from underneath the collapsed building, and I stood on what was left of the roof of the house. My father came up and saw me. He later said, "I saw this little old white-haired lady standing on the roof of the house." It was me, of course, covered in plaster!

He was beside himself and started to pull away the shingles; he then realized it was useless, the task was too enormous. He asked me how I had managed to get out, so I pointed to an opening (I was unable to speak).

My father went inside to help my mother. My mother had been saved by the iron canopy of the bed. It had bent over and saved her life when the building collapsed.

My mother wrapped the baby in a blanket. My father took his overcoat and put it around my mother. He gave my mother his boots. Together we made our way to the Commons, a flat open space.

It seemed a long walk to the Commons. People were crying and shouting. On the way there I remember a woman pulling on my dad's jacket; she had nothing on, not a stitch on, she was naked, everything she'd had on had been blown off in the explosion. She cried, "Come up and save my baby!" She pointed up to the third floor. I have no idea what happened to her or her baby. Everybody was looking for help. Everything had collapsed. It was chaos and confusion everywhere.

There was dust and plaster in the air. Eventually we arrived at the Commons. I still couldn't see. My brother and I were given blankets by the Red Cross. There was no water so my father licked the plaster out of our eyes, so we could finally see again.

Another English couple invited us into their house; it was still standing in a different part of the town. I was quickly put to bed. I remember feeling cold. My mother filled a rum bottle with hot water. Just as mum was going to put it at the bottom, I called out, "Mum what if it breaks?" So she took it out, and I lost my bottle!

The next day father brought back biscuits, with whole peanuts on top. I saw some the other day, and memories of the Halifax explosion came flooding back.

Many countries sent clothing and household goods to help out those who had suffered in the Halifax explosion. My mother was given a new home sewing peddle machine. Mum used it for years. Years later, she passed it on to me. With regret, I later traded it in on a modern electric sewing machine.

The Depression and World War II

My father stayed in the Halifax shipyard, as a carpenter, during the 1930s. For a short time he was unemployed when the dockyard shut down. We left the city and stayed with friends on their farm for the duration of the shutdown. I can remember going to a small country school.

During World War II, I worked for the Department of Agriculture (federal government) in Halifax. I met my husband, Erik Revfem, a naval officer, in Halifax in the summer of '41. We were married in December 1941.

My husband was Norwegian and had been caught in the Panama when war was declared. He came up to Toronto, Canada, to the "Little Norway" community. He was given a commission in the Canadian Navy as he was a trained engineer.

During the war he worked on convoys. He told me, when they were escorting merchant vessels, no one had a chance to change their clothes. They were too busy watching out for enemy submarines.

After the war, my husband remained in the navy. We later moved from Halifax, Nova Scotia to Victoria, British Columbia with our two children.

Erik passed away in 1975. In 1991 I married my second husband, Russell Osborn. After his death in the year 2000, I moved to Powell River, British Columbia.

Note: Ida Osborn was interviewed in 2001 by Barbara Ann Lambert and her memories of the Halifax Explosion were first published in *Rusty Nails & Ration Books* (2002).

Ration Books (1940-1954)

Barbara Ann Lambert

My childhood memories are of World War II. The day I was born my father was digging an Anderson bomb shelter in the back garden. The year was 1939 and the storm clouds over Europe were gathering. For me, growing up in wartime was everyday life. I lived in Guiseley, a small Yorkshire village in northern England.

A building site at the top of our road remained at the excavation stage for the duration of the war. A big pile of rubble remained there until years after the war was over. As a child I played wonderful games of imagination on that abandoned site.

I played all the traditional games that my older sister Joyce, and my mother, had played as children: singing games such as "Ring around the Roses", and other games including whip and top, marbles, hopscotch, hide-and-seek, skipping and kite flying.

My father continued to work on the railways as a signalman during the war; he worked 12-hour shifts as there was a severe shortage of qualified men. Dad was often called out for duty to work the big signal boxes in the industrial cities of Bradford and Leeds. The bombers often came over our house and targeted the railway depots there. On one occasion, on hearing the bombers go overhead, my father and his mate flung themselves down to one side of the signal box; they were lucky, after the raid they found it was the only part standing!

Dad planted a Victory garden and, as children, it was our job to help with the weeding, watering and harvesting. We kept chickens; eggs were put down in water glass for winter use. If we ran out of eggs, Mother made a wartime "no egg" cake! We also kept rabbits for meat. It was my job, after school, to walk along the hedgerows and collect grass and dandelions for their feed. We kept about 30 rabbits, and Dad traded the meat for anything else that was in short supply. Mother made a delicious rabbit pie with a flaky crust and mouth-watering gravy; I can still smell it cooking, to this day, in the coal-fired back oven.

Everything was rationed. The average weekly ration, per person, was half a pound of sugar, six ounces of margarine, two ounces preserves (jam), four ounces sweets or chocolate, meat valued at one shilling, and powdered egg.

Everyone had ration books. We spent hours lining up at small village shops for supplies which quickly ran out. On one occasion the shopkeeper told my mother that he was out of sugar. My sister, peeked around the counter, and called out, "Mum, there's lots back here!"

We shopped every day as no one had refrigeration, and food quickly spoiled. It was a mile to walk to the village, and we had no car. No one I knew owned a car, no relative or friend. Everything was carried in shopping bags, even the library books! We were healthy because we walked everywhere.

I called at the sweet shop once a week for my sweet ration. The shop was full of empty candy jars, and chocolate bars were kept under the counter. I usually bought a twist of lemonade powder and a black licorice stick, with three copper pennies.

The Nestlé's chocolate machines on the big railway stations were all empty. I dreamed of the day I would be able to put in a coin and take out a real chocolate bar. It was not until many years later, after the war, that the machines operated again.

The milkman came early, every morning. The glass bottles, with cream at the top, and a cardboard top, sat on the doorstep until retrieved. The bottles were kept in a cool larder, on a marble slab. Butter was not available during the war, instead we had margarine; it came in hard blocks and was difficult to spread. I remember collecting the cream off the top of the milk, and shaking it forever in a glass jar to make a small, soft blob of pale yellow butter.

Our sugar ration was kept entirely for baking and jam making. Blackberries, found in the hedgerows, provided free and readily available fruit for jam making. I never had sugar in tea or coffee (Camp chicory). We usually drank water or milk. Sometimes, in summer, we had homemade lemonade; our next door neighbour made a home brew of nettle beer.

Mother was a good cook. I was sent to the butcher's shop to ask for bones with scrapings of meat on them, and beef dripping. The bones provided the base for a vegetable soup, and the dripping tasted fantastic, spread on newly baked bread.

Our family weekly ration consisted of 4 shillings (50 cents) worth of meat: a pound of meat and a couple of cans of corned beef. The stew meat was made into a delicious meat and potato pie; the canned corned beef was mashed and became a meat base for a shepherd's pie. Lots of vegetables and gravy, made with OXO cubes, stretched the meagre meat supply.

Once a month we boarded the bus to Bradford. The city had been badly bombed but there was always a chance we could find goods (like wooden pegs, buttons, spools of thread and zippers) on the stalls in the open market. Most of the bombed buildings were boarded up but I used to find a crack to look through; all I could see were deep, dark cavernous holes with rubble in them. The highlight of the trip to town was having a dish of hot, mushy green peas (made from dried peas) with a dash of vinegar, at a market stall.

Harry Ramsden had a fish and chip shop nearby on the main road. We could never afford to eat there, and when I was a child, we never ate out.

I was lucky to have an older sister as I wore all her hand-me-downs. Clothes rationing was introduced in 1940 and ended in 1954. I was 11 years of age when I had my first coat made by a neighbour. Mother was a great knitter. We went to jumble sales and bought sweaters for a few pennies; the wool was unravelled, washed and stretched, and then reused.

Dad was a skilled rug maker. Again jumble sales came into good use. Old coats were cut up and made into peg rugs. Dad sorted out the colours, and pegged the three by one inch woollen strips, into the canvas to make an attractive pattern.

I was only four when I attended Infant's school. Once a week, all the children were given a spoonful of thick orange juice and cod liver oil. In our morning break we had a small bottle of milk which we drank with a straw. On cold winter days the teacher made hot cocoa, a real treat. For lunch we had school dinners, a hot meal delivered to the school premises. School dinners were, for most children in Britain, the main meal of the day. The government did everything it could to make sure that all the nation's children had one basic meal a day. After school we had teatime at home, consisting of bread and jam, and a glass of milk.

I never ate a banana as a small child; they were not available until 1946. At Christmastime I was lucky to get an apple, a handful of nuts, and one book (Rupert the Bear Annual) in my stocking. The sweet coupon allowance, for children, was doubled to 4 ounces of chocolate in the month of December.

The teachers at our small village school had been brought out of retirement due to a shortage of teachers. They were very strict and their methods were old-fashioned, having been trained in the previous century when Queen Victoria was on the throne. It was a basic three R's education: reading, writing and arithmetic. Classes were often disrupted by air raid sirens. The classes left the building in orderly lines, in quick march time, to the underground shelter at the bottom of the school playing field. After the "All Clear" siren it was quick march, and back to classes.

We all were issued with Mickey Mouse gas masks. I was glad we never had to use them as the masks were suffocating to wear. At night we had a complete blackout as all windows had to be covered with blackout curtains; show one bit of light and the bobby (police) was knocking on the door!

Every Sunday I attended Sunday school at the Methodist chapel in the village. Dad was Church of England but it was a two-mile walking distance to the church; we became Methodists as it was half the walking distance! Sunday evenings we dined with friends a bus ride away. Mrs. Dimelow always made an English trifle with real sherry; after the meal, both families played card games. My favourite game was betting pennies on "horses" (Kings, Queens and Jacks). Methodists did not drink or gamble. I often wondered, as a small child, if God would ever forgive me for eating sherry trifle and playing cards on a Sunday!

Every evening we listened to the news of the war on the radio. Gracie Fields and Vera Lynn sang patriotic songs like, "There will always be an England". Winston Churchill inspired us with his speeches to the nation. We admired King George VI and Queen Elizabeth for staying in London with Princess Elizabeth and Princess Margaret.

V-E Day (May 8, 1945) – I walked for miles with my family to a huge bonfire burning on Otley Moor. Bonfires were lit all over England to celebrate the end of the war in Europe. It was a centuries' old tradition to signal, around the country, news of invasion or victory.

The wedding of Princess Elizabeth and Prince Phillip Mountbatten, in 1947, was a highlight in the postwar years. Clothing was still on ration, however, the government allowed extra coupons for her wedding dress but not her trousseau; the public responded by sending their clothing coupons to Buckingham Palace! In 1952 a princess became the Queen, as the nation mourned the death of King George VI.

In postwar Britain, there was an economic depression, as the nation struggled to find the money and resources to rebuild the bombed-out towns and factories. Food shortages continued after the war. From 1946-47 bread was rationed; jam came off ration in 1948; tea came off in 1952; sugar, sweets and eggs came off in 1953; butter, margarine, cooking fat and meat came off in 1954. Rationing in Britain lasted 14 long years.

Apart from the fear I felt during bombing raids, I had a happy, secure childhood with simple pleasures. In postwar Britain I missed the routine of daily life which had evolved during the war. I was afraid of change, going from the known to the unknown. Looking back, I regretted not being old enough to join the WRAF and fight for Britain.

During the war, a Coalition Government under Winston Church directed the affairs of the nation. In the summer of 1945 the Labour Government swept to office with Clement Atlee as the Prime Minister.

With political change came education change. Entrance to previous fee-paying Grammar schools became based on merit (known as the 11+ exam). The entry into a Grammar school allowed thousands of blue collar, working class children to train for a white collar, middle class job (such as bank clerks, teachers, librarians, etc.) I was lucky to be one of them.

Author: Barbara Ann Lambert

Barbara Ann Lambert was born in Yorkshire, England at the beginning of World War II. She lived with her parents, Ernest and Margaret Rathbone, and older sister, Joyce. She attended elementary school at St. Oswald's Church of England Junior School, Guiseley and Prince Henry's Grammar School, Otley, Yorkshire. In 1952 the family moved to Lancaster, Lancashire where relatives on both sides of the family lived.

After attending Lancaster Girls' Grammar School, Barbara trained as a teacher at Wentworth Castle Training College, near Barnsley, in Yorkshire. She completed her education at Liverpool University, England and the University of British Columbia (UBC) in Vancouver, British Columbia, Canada. In 1975 Barbara received her Bachelor of Education degree in History and Special Education from UBC.

In 1966 Barbara immigrated to Canada. After accepting a teaching position in Powell River in 1968, Barbara met and later married Stuart Lambert. They have a daughter, Ann.

Barbara Lambert's teaching career covered 35 years in England, Germany and British Columbia, Canada. She retired in 1997 from the Powell River School District.

In 1998 Barbara self-published her first book on local history: *In Paradise: West Coast Short Stories, 1890 – 1960.*

In December 2000 Barbara self-published her second book: *Chalkdust & Outhouses: West Coast Schools, 1893 – 1950.*

In 2001 Stuart Lambert died at age 87. In 2002, in memory of her husband, Barbara published through Trafford Publishing, her third book: *Rusty Nails & Ration Books: Great Depression & WWII Memories, 1929 – 1945.*

In 2006 Barbara published through Trafford Publishing her fourth local history book: *Old Time Stories: Billy-Goat Smith, Powell River Co. Xmas, Mr. Dippie & others.*

To celebrate the centennial of the Powell River Townsite, Barbara published in 2009, through Trafford Publishing, her fifth local history book, *Powell River 100: The Largest Single Site Newsprint Manufacturer in the World.*

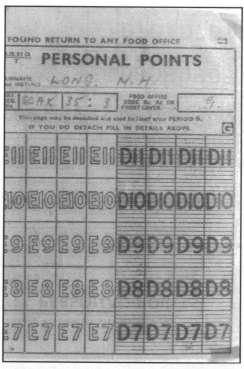

A page of Margaret Long's (WWII war bride) WWII ration book.
Photo: Margaret Long collection

1945 Morecambe Promenade, Lancashire, England.
Margaret Rathbone with her two daughters (L) Barbara Ann (R)
Joyce Barbara Ann's hair in fashionable ringlets.
Photo: Barbara Ann Lambert (Rathbone) collection

1918 Ida Wells enjoying the Halifax Parade seated on a gun mount, Halifax, Nova Scotia.
(L to R) Bobby Wells, Betty Betterson, Mrs. Cheeseman and Ida Wells.
All survivors of the 1917 Halifax Explosion.
Photo: Ida Osborn (Wells) collection

Centennial Tea at Dwight Hall, Powell River, B.C. 2010.
Dwight Hall: a historic hall built by the Powell River Company
in 1927 for the use of Powell River Townsite employees and families.
(L to R) Barbara Ann Lambert and her daughter Ann Bonkowski
Photo: Ann Bonkowski collection

Bibliography

Books

Abraham, Dorothy. *Lone Cone: A Journal of Life on the West Coast of Vancouver Island, B.C.* Victoria, B.C.: Tiritea, 1945.

Bilson, Geoffrey. *The Guest Children: The Story of the British Child Evacuees Sent to Canada During WWII.* Fifth House, 1988.

Boyer, Karen R., Powell River Economic Study Adjustment Committee. *An Economic Base Study of the Powell River Region.* Powell River, B.C.: Powell River Progress, 1977.

Buckton, Henry. *Friendly Invasion Memories of Operation Bolero – The American Occupation of Britain 1942-1945.* The History Press, 2006.

The Canadian Encyclopedia. Hurtig Publishers, Edmonton, 1985.

Carlson, Linda. *Company Towns of the Pacific Northwest.* University of Washington Press, 2003.

D-Day: 24 Hours That Saved the World. Time Books, 2004.

Day, Frances Martin, Phyllis Spence, and Barbara Ladouceur, eds. *Women Overseas: Memoirs of Canadian Red Cross Corps.* Ronsdale Press, 1998.

Downing, Taylor. *Churchill's War Lab: Codebreakers, Scientists and the Mavericks Churchill Led to Victory.* New York: Overlook Press, 2011.

Farrington, Karen. *An Illustrated Chronicle of the Struggle for Victory.* Abbeydale, 2001.

Fethney, Michael. *The Absurd and the Brave: CORB – The True Account of the British Government's World War II Evacuation of Children Overseas.* Book Guild Ltd., 1990.

Goddard, Lance. *Canada and the Liberation of the Netherlands, May 1945.* Dundurn Press, 2005.

Gossage, Carolyn. *Greatcoats and Glamour Boots: Canadian Women at War (1939-1945).* Dundurn Press, 2001.

Granfield, Linda. *Brass Buttons and Silver Horseshoes: Stories from Canada's War Brides.* McClelland & Stewart, 2002.

Jarratt, Melynda. *War Brides: The Stories of the Women Who Left Everything Behind to Follow the Men They Loved.* Dundurn Press, 2009.

Knight, Katherine. *Spuds, Spam and Eating for Victory: Rationing in the Second World War.* The History Press Ltd., 2007.

Kozar, Judy. *Canada's War Grooms and the Girls Who Stole Their Hearts.* General Store Publishing House, 2007.

Ladouceur, Barbara and Phyllis Spence, *eds. Blackouts to Bright Lights: Canadian War Bride Stories.* Vancouver: Ronsdale Press, 1995.

Lambert, B.A. *Chalkdust & Outhouses: West Coast Schools, 1893-1950.* Friesens Printers, 2000.

Lambert, B.A. *Rusty Nails & Ration Books: Great Depression & WWII Memories 1929-1945.* Trafford Publishing, 2002.

Lambert, B.A. *Powell River 100: The Largest Single Site Newsprint Manufacturer in the World.* Trafford Publishing, 2009.

Levez, Emma. *People of the White City: Stories from the Powell River Mill.* Powell River, B.C.: Norske Canada, Powell River Division, 2002.

Lyster, Eswyn. *Most Excellent Citizens: Canada's War Brides of World War II.* Trafford Publishing, 2009.

The New Encyclopedia Britannica 15th edition. Encyclopedia Britannica Inc., 2010.

Nicholson, Virginia. *Millions Like Us: Women's Lives During the Second World War.* Penguin Books, 2002.

Powell River's First 50 Years: Powell River, B.C. Golden Jubilee 1910-1960. Powell River News, 1960.

Southern, Karen and Peggy Bird. *Pulp, Paper and People: 75 Years of Powell River.* Powell River, B.C.: Powell River Heritage Research Association, 1988.

Strange, Kathleen. *With the West in Her Eyes.* MacMillan Co. of Canada, 1945.

Thompson, Bill. *Once Upon a Stump.* Powell River, B.C.: Powell River Heritage Research Association, 1988.

Thompson, Bill. *Boats, Bucksaws and Blisters.* Powell River, B.C.: Powell River Heritage Research Association, 1990.

Articles & Periodicals
"1912-1987 MacMillan Bloedel: 75 Years of Papermaking." *Powell River News* (April 10, 1987)
Powell River Company WWII Newsletters to Servicemen & Women
Powell River *Digester*, Powell River Company
Powell River News & Town Crier, Glacier Ventures
"The Second World War" *The Vancouver Province* (August 27, 1989)

Booklets
"Information for Wives of Soldiers Coming from Overseas (WWI)." Repatriation Committee, Library and
    Archives Canada.
"Welcome to War Brides (WWII)." Archives: Canadian Museum of Immigration at Pier 21.

Publications by Societies & Associations
Gould, Florence E. "A War Bride Journey in 1917." Okanagan History: The Thirty-seventh report of the
    Okanagan Historical Society, 1974.
Transcribed tapes of a historic road journey 1918 by the Gould family from Saskatchewan to B.C.
    Summerland Museum
"Mary Jane Yates, WWI War Bride." Crowsnest Pass Historical Society
History of the Vancouver 29th, Tobin's Tigers Association, 1964. Captain W.D.M. Sage M.A. Regimental
    Historian and H.R.N. Clyne, M.C. Vancouver, B.C.

Private Publications
Bosher, John. "Our Roots: The Families of Bosher, Marsden, Readings and Simister." 2000.
Entwisle, Rosemary, M.ED. "War Child: Memoirs, 1939-1945".
Falconer, Bev. "Our Evacuee Cousins." 2011
von Holst, Elisabeth. "Childhood Memories: Evacuee and Refugee."

Scrapbook
"Powell River During WWII" compiled from copies of the Powell River *Digester* 1938-46 by Chuck and
    Karen Crashley (March 1996) Dedicated to Branch #164 of the Royal Canadian Legion.

Websites
Ancestry.ca: Canadian shipping records
Library & Archives Canada: Soldiers of the First World War records
Powell River Museum & Archives: A Record of Service (WWII) October 19, 2010. Scanned by volunteer
    researcher Lee Coultor.

Documentary Films
3D Spies of WWII – RAF Medmenham (air photo intelligence) BBC/WGBH co-production. 2011.
Canada Remembers: Women Who Have Served and Sacrificed. Thomega Entertainment Inc. 2010.
The First World War From Above. BBC Wales. 2010.
Home by Christmas. Gaylene Preston Productions in association with Midnight Film Productions Ltd., Motion
    Pictures, New Zealand Film Commission, New Zealand On Air, TVNZ. 2010.
John McCrae's War - in Flander's Field. National Film Board of Canada. 1998.
Operation Mincemeat – a deception which changed the course of history. Walker George Films. 2010.
Passchendaele: The Underground War. Cream Productions. 2009.
Powell River Overseas Reunion film 1944, January 23rd, Beaver Club, London, England.
Rosies of the North. National Film Board of Canada. 1999.

Men and Women from Powell River & District
Serving in the Canadian Armed Forces WWII (1939-1945)

(Powell River News Publication, "Welcome Home" July 1, 1946)

† Killed in Action
*Prisoner of War

A
Abbott, John
Adams, Albert
Ahola, A. E.
Alexander, John
Allan, A.
Allen, W.
Allan, J. B. †
Allan, Robt.
Allman, R. P.
Almond, A. A.
Alsgard, F.
Alton, H. S.
Amato, E. J.
Amos, N. P.
Andersen, Alton
Anderson, Manfred
Andersen, Bertram
Andersen, Olaf
Andersen, N. M.
Anderson, Harold G.
Andersen, S. B. J.
Angell, Harry
Anglin, J. A. †
Anchor, W.
Anchor, H.
Appleby, John
Aprilis, D.
Aquilin, Evelyn
Arnold, V. R.
Anderson, Norman E.
Auline, Arthur
Aune, L. R.
B
Bachen, H.
Bagley, J. M.
Bailey, D. E. M.

Bailey, L. W.
Baker, Jos.
Baker, John
Baker, R. C. †
Baker, Ron
Banham, Jean
Barlow, Eric
Barnes, Irving
Barnes, John
Bartfai, A. W.
Barton, Alan
Barton, K. F.
Batterham, W. C.
Baum, C. V.
Baum, William G. R. †
Baxter, Geo.
Bayer, H. C.
Beattie, W.
Begley, W. R.
Behan, E. T.
Bell, W.
Bell, John M. †
Belyea, H. T.
Bellamy, H. L.
Belyk, John N.
Belyk, M. M.
Belyk, R.
Bentham, T. J.
Berglund, W. E.
Bernier, R.
Bethune, Angus C.
Bichard, J.
Bernier, A.
Bird, C. D.
Blacklock, J.
Black, Doreen
Blondin, S.
Boida, Fred
Bond, J.
Borden, C. I.

Bordenuk, J.
Borer, F.
Bizovie, G
Bigold, A. J.
Bortolussi, G.
Bortolussi, Aldo †
Bowers, H. J.
Bowman, P.
Brand, G.
Branter, J. A.
Brinkman, C.
Brooks, F. W. S.
Brooks, Lucien †
Brooks, A. S.
Brown, E. R.
Brown, S. T.
Brown, M. J.
Brown, W. R.
Bryan, Betty
Bryce, R.
Buchanan, Harry
Bull, W. C.
Burgess, W. N.
Burke, T. S.
Buse, Chester F.
Buse, Irvine A.
Butler, Bruce
Butler, Leo
Button, Arthur R.
Bye, A. O.
C
Cadwallader, E.
Cadwallader, J. L.
Carney, H.
Calder, W. R.
Caldicott, James
Callegari, A.
Cameron, Robt.
Cairney, Jas.
Campbell, A. D.

Campbell, E.
Campbell, Jock M.
Carey, A. M. †
Carlsen, A. B.
Carpendale, L.
Carr, Jack
Carrie, James B.
Carrott, B.
Carroll, P. J.
Carruthers, J.
Carruthers, H.
Carter, N.
Carter, W. D.
Casey, Ranie
Cattermole, M. R.
Cattermole, N.
Challis, Jack
Chalmers, T. D.
Chandler, D. W.
Chapman, Harold
Chase, R. D.
Chiarcossi, G.
Christiansen, Lloyd
Christiansen, A. J.
Christie, R. J.
Christie, T. S.
Clapp, Hazel
Clapp, Don
Clarke, L. F.
Clayton, D. H.
Clayton, H. F.
Clough, W.
Clark, Zella I.
Clutterbuck, W.
Coe, Stanley
Cofield, Russell
Commo, K.
Condon, C. P.
Connelly, J.
Coomber, H. S.
Coomber, R. B.
Collette, F. A.
Cooper, Harry
Cooper, T.
Cormier, Ray
Cormier, Stanley
Cornwall, J.
Courte, J. E.

Cote, F. P.
Couvelier, C. A.
Coweley, J. A.
Cowley, J.
Cowley, V. D.
Craig, R. R.
Cramb, Henry
Crawford, A. B.
Craigen, Louise C.
Crilly, M.
Crockett, Geo.
Crockett, J. W.
Cyr, R. J.
D
Dalla, Pria, P.
Daly, R. H.
Dalzell, G. W.
Dalzell, N. J.
Dalzell, W. E.
Daniel, F. W.
Daubner, J. W. †
Daubner, H. A. Jr. †
Davenport, J. *
Davies, F. W.
Davies, H. L.
Davies, R. B.
Davis, Wilfred
Dawson, Henry
Dawson, Donald
Dawson, W. G.
DeGroot, Peter
Deakin, A. K. †
DeLisle, W.
Denton, B.
DeWynter, E.
DeWynter, L.
Dickson, W. R. †
Dittloff, W. †
Dodsworth, F.
Dolan, D. J.
Dolan, T. E.
Dolan, T. W.
Donkersley, W. R.
Donkersley, E. B.
Donkersley, Harry † **DFC**
Donnelly, Frank
Doran, G. F.
Dore, Alice

Dore, E. J. C.
Draper, W. H.
Drayton, G.
Drayton, T. E.
Drayton, W.
Drayton, H. †
Drury, Roy
Duffield, V. H.
Duke, J.
Dunlop, Alex
Dunlop, Jean V.
Dunn, Robert
Dykes, G. S.
Dykes, Jack
Dykes, Ray
E
Eckman, G. †
Eckstrand, L.
Eckstrand, N.
Edwards, W. A.
Egan, J. F.
Elly, J.
Elly, Walter
Emerson, W. H.
Eno, Floyd
Eno, L. R.
Enquist, R.
Ethofer, Anthony
Ethofer, G. †
Erickson, E. M.
Evans, Eric S.
Evans, R. B.
Ewing, G.
Ewing (Jr.), Geo.
Erickson, Edward J.
F
Fairgrieve, W. C. †
Fairgrieve, M. K.
Farnden, A. J.
Farquharson, Ian
Fee, E. L.
Fidler, R. G.
Finlay, G. M.
Fishleigh, J. F.
Fitch, R. C.
Fleming, E. R.
Foisy, C. A.
Forbes, Vincent

Foster, Elsie
Fox, C. R.
Foxall, R. A. L.
Fox, A. W.
Foyston, F. S.
Frame, M. H.
Fraser, R. J.
Fraser, M. D.
Fraser, S. A.
Fredrickson, A. A.
Freeman, H. †
Fullerton, G.
Furness, J.
Furness, Ronald
Furnival, W. E.

G

Gaganoff, Wesley
Gairns, Bob *
Gairns, G. A.
Callicano, W. B.
Gann, H. T.
Gardiner, T. H. *
Gardner, R. W.
Gartlan, J. J.
Gaudet, B. A.
Gaudet, Reg †
Gauthier, F.
Gebbie, J.
Gensiorowski, J.
Gibson, F. G.
Gibson, Garnet
Gibson, H. C.
Gibson, J. W.
Gibson, Ronald P.
Gibson, Wilfred
Gillis, Jas.
Gilmour, W. †
Goddard, A. E.
Goldsmith, J. K.
Golley, Merton E.
Golley, W. S.
Gorbatuk, S.
Gornall, R. J.
Goulding, J. R.
Gowdyk, Chas.
Gowdyk
Graham, J. M.
Graft, Alex

Graham, J. R.
Graham, Jos. A.
Graham, Ronald
Grain, Peter
Gramberg, A.
Granger, F. D. *
Green, D.
Gribble, H. L.
Grundle, A. E.
Grundle, J. L.
Gustafson, K. M.

H

Haddock, Geo.
Haddon, B. W.
Haigh, Frances
Hall, C. J.
Hamilton, Tom
Hammer, H. B.
Hamelin, A.
Hancock, R. N.
Hansen, E. Ivan
Hardie, A. N.
Harding, F. E.
Hardy, R.
Harper, H. L.
Harper, H. R.
Harper, W. R.
Harrett, R.
Harris, G. W.
Harris, H.
Hartley, John
Haskell, M.
Hassell, E. †
Hastings, Norman
Hatch, A. E.
Hatch, C. O.
Hatton, James
Hawkins, Bert
Hayes, R.
Heaton, J.
Heavenor, Douglas
Heavenor, Elaine
Heisterman, H. R.
Helland, N.
Hembroff, Margaret
Hembroff, L. W.
Henderson, Eric
Heritage, G. W.

Heward, A.
Heyes, W. A.
Hicks, Ralph A.
Hill, Norman J.
Hobson, L. H.
Holborne, A. P.
Holden, W.
Holyoke, V.
Hopkins, Bruce †
Hopkins, D. C.
Hopkins, R. T.
Hopkins, W. J.
Howell, R. B.
Hughes, David
Hughes, P.
Hughes, W. G.
Humphrey, Doris
Hunter, Brisbane
Hunter, G. A.
Hunter, J. C.
Hunter, T. R.
Hutchison, L.
Hutchison, K. L.
Hutton, J. C.
Husar, N.

I

Imerson, J. K.
Ingram, Doug
Ingram, Joyce
Ingram, Ray
Ingram, G.
Innes, A.
Irwin, Gordon B.
Irwin, Jean

J

Jack, Dave
Jackson, J. M.
Jacob, Phil
Jackson, Norman
Jackson, T. S.
Jacobs, R. A.
Jacob, J.
Jacob, W. H.
Jamieson, L. A.
Jamieson, L. D.
Jamieson, Wm. M.
Johnston, J. S. †
Johnston, N. †

319

Jensin, J.
Johns, W. H.
Johnson, R. G.
Johnson, J. R.
Jones, C. A.
Jones, D. M.
Jorgenson, C.
Jones, Wyville
K
Keaist, R. †
Keenan, R. A.
Keeling, C. H.
Keith, A. C.
Kennedy, E. A.
Kennedy, G. A.
Kenny, Ralph
Kielty, M.
King, F. G.
Killen, H. E.
Killen, R. J.
King, G. W.
Kipp, Gordon C.
Kipp, Wilfred *
Knowles, Ben
Kohut, M.
Kram, W. H.
Kyles, J. A.
L
Lambert, T. R.
Lanyon, Arthur
Lasser, Bob †
Lawrence, R. C. M.
Lawson, C.
Lawson, R. W.
Lawson, J. B.
Layton, T. A.
Leask, J. I.
LeClair, Louis M.
LeClair Raymond L.
LeClair, Ted
Lee, C. D.
Lee, Don †
Lee, Freda
Lee, Norma
Lee, Jack F.
Leese, R. †
Leese, W. H. †
Leese, Robin

Leighton, J.
Leitch, Kenneth B.
Lennox, T. H.
LeVae, Gray
Lewis, E. A.
Lewis, Ray
Lewis, Ray
Lewis, Reg
Leyland, V. H.
Lightfoot, J.
Linder, T. W.
Lingdren, C. V.
Liney, W. E.
Lloyd, C. A.
Lloyd, J. A. †
Lloyd, W.
Long, H. E.
Long, J. E.
Long, K.
Lorenson, R. J.
Loukes, Mary
Loukes, J.
Lund, Roy
Lye, R. A.
Lyle, Arthur †
Lyons, Ormond
Lyons, Warwick
M
McAuley, Allister
McAskell, A. R.
McCartney, Wm.
McBurnie, F. M.
McCartney, John
MacCullough, I. S.
McCracken, John
McDonald, Frank
MacDonald, D. L.
MacDonald, G. A.
MacDonald, J. C.
MacDonald, B. W.
MacDonald, J. W.
MacDonald, Ken
MacGregor, James
McGregor, A. J.
Macgregor, John
McGuffie, James
McGuffie, Julia
McGuffie, Gwen

MacIntosh, Chas.
MacIntyre, B. M.
McIsaac, E. J.
McIsaac, J. F.
McKay, D.
McKay, E.
McKenzie, A. T.
McKenzie, J. G.
McKenzie, Gordon
MacKenzie, D. R.
MacKenzie, P. W. A.
MacKenzie, R. C.
McKie, Hugh
McKnight, D. E.
McKinley, H.
MacKinnon, J. R.
McKissock, T.
McKnight, Watson
MacLachlan, H.
MacLauchlin, C.
MacLean, Neil
McLean, Ada
MacLean, K.
McLean, A. L. †
McLeod, Alex
McLeod, E.
McLeod, E. V. Y.
McLeod, Hugh
McLeod, J. B.
McLeod, John Wm.
McMaster, D. H.
McMullen, F. †
McNair, A. M.
McNair, D. S.
McNair, R. L.
McNair, R. L.
MacNeil, G. F.
McPhalen, C. G.
McPherson, A. G.
McRae, H.
McVicker, John
McWhinney, J.
Macken, D. K.
Maguire, Jack
Magson, Phil †
Malyea, H. E.
Mannion, F.
Maple, J.

320

Marchant, A.
Marcoux, Wm. F.
Marlatt, S. P. †
Marrs, G. A.
Marshall, Ronald
Marshall, W. K. †
Martin, Ian
Martinuk, A.
Maslin, G. E. H.
Matheson, C. D.
Matheson, Ken
Matheson, N. P.
Matheson, R. A.
Mathews, A. M.
Mathews, Peter M.
Mawn, Art
Mayo, J.
Medforth, J.
Midelto, P.
Menzies, Gordon
Messmer, E. S.
Miller, Joe A.
Miller, I. D.
Miller, W. N. F.
Milne, W.
Mitchell, Albert
Mitchell, Fred
Mitchell, M.
Mitchell, W.
Mitten, J. R.
Mitten, Louis J.
Mitten, Chas. I.
Monsell, D. E.
Monsell, D. L.
Monsell, P. E.
Monsell, R. L.
Mooney, J. A.
Moore, W. A.
Morfitt, W. A.
Morin, D. P.
Morgenthaler, Geo.
Morris, Andy †
Morris, Ralph C.
Morris, I. R.
Morris, John †
Morrissey, G. M.
Morrissey, Joe
Moss, L. W.

Morrow, Fred
Mowbray, Fred
Mowbray, Geo.
Muir, F. W.
Mullen, W. P. R.
Mullen, R.
Mullen, J. †
Mumford, A. R.
Murray, Chas.

N

Naylor, Martin A.
Nello (Sr.), F.
Nello, F. (Jr.) †
Nelson, K. R.
Nelson, N.
Nicholson, J. H.
Norden, R.
Nutchey, Tom
Nuttall, D.

O

O'Byrne, E. W.
Oldale, T.
Oliver, Frank
Olsen, H.
Olsen, Leo. D.
O'Neil, Frank
Oram, D. H.
Oldenburg, Herman L.
Owen, W.
Oxbury, R.
Oxbury, W. A.
Ozavitsky, J. *

P

Palmer, J. M.
Palmer, W. B.
Parker, Harold G.
Parkin, T. R.
Parkin, J. W.
Parkin, R. W.
Parish, W. K.
Parry, John
Parson, C. S.
Parsons, Lyonel M.
Paterson, A. D.
Paterson, R. B.
Patrick, W. J.
Patrucco, A. J.
Patton, W. K.

Peck, Eric
Peebles, W. E.
Pelly, Jack
Perry, Camille
Peter, Albert F.
Peterson, F. D.
Peteske, Nancy
Peteske, Geo. H.
Petrie, A. G.
Petty, Robert
Phillip, G. A.
Phillips, S. R.
Phillip, D. N.
Phillips, E. C.
Phillips, R. D.
Phipps, Isaac H.
Phipps, B.
Piccinato, Luigi
Pickering, Alonzo
Pickles, A. C.
Pickles, H. W.
Pickles, T. M.
Pidcock, T. †
Piper, Gordon G.
Piper, James
Pirie, Dawson
Pitt-Cross, F. R.
Pitton, P. A.
Plaskett, J.
Poole, C. P. R.
Poole, Victor H.
Powell, C. H.
Powell, George
Powell, T. C.
Price, Wm.
Price, Ernestine
Price, Max
Price, P. M.
Price, W. R.
Plisson, S. N.

Q

Quinn, J. A.
Quinn, E.

R

Raimondo, C.
Raimondo, R.
Razzo, Geo.
Razzo, Paul

Redhead, J.
Redhead, Robt.
Reed, W. G.
Rees, S. S.
Regan, B. A.
Rennie, D. W.
Rennie, G.
Reynolds, A. E. L.
Rice, Leslie
Richards, Stan
Richardson, Stan
Richardson, T.
Richmond, H. B.
Ridge, Keith
Riley, E.
Riley, Harry
Ritchie, W. R.
Robbins, Vincent
Roberts, Aleda
Roberts, A.
Roberts, F. M.
Roberts, Owen
Robertson, I. B.
Robertson, A. H.
Robson, J. L.
Robson, O. Charles
Rochat, Chas
Rolandi, Violet
Rolandi, R.
Roland, Donald B.
Rorke, Lionel †
Rose, Andrew H.
Roslinsky, F. E.
Ross, Benny
Ross, Delbert
Ross, Arthur
Rowe, H. F.
Royce, H.
Rumley, L. R.
Runnells, W.
Rud, E.
Russell, H. B.
Russell, H. R.
Russell, Ronald
S
Salmon, R. A.
Sample, J. G.
Savage, W. A.

Savory, H. L.
Scarlett, J. H.
Schaffer, F.
Schon, L. A.
Scott, Bob
Scott, Beverley
Scott, Dennis I.
Scott, Frank
Scott, J. N.
Scott, Grace
Scott, Melvin E.
Scriven, G. H. L. †
Sekulitch, F. N.
Serle, Wm. C.
Shaw, R. W. †
Silvester, E. A.
Simard, R. D.
Simonetta, D.
Simonetta, J.
Simmons, P. E.
Skorberg, Gunnar
Simpson, Frank
Sivertson, E. S.
Skorey, Joe
Sleigh, Dudley
Smith, Gordon J.
Smith, Harvey F.
Smith, W. A.
Smith, Walter
Smythe, M. C. L.
Snihur, F.
Snow, B. E.
Somerville, S. Don
Sopit, M.
Southcott, R. H.
Southcott, S.
Srigley, R. G.
Spackman, N.
Spratt, F. †
Spence, J. E.
Srigley, R. G. †
Stapleton, A. B.
Stapleton, A. E.
Stasuick, M.
Stevenson, O. J.
Stinson, W. E.
Staniford, Hilda
Stephen, A. F.

Stapleton, J. R.
Stevens, R. A.
Strachan, A.
Stricker, Fred
Stusiak, N. †
Stutt, R. J.
Summers, S. J.
Sutherland, D.
Sutherland, E.
Sutherland, J. D.
Sutherland, P. M.
Sutton, H. M. B.
Swanson, A.
Sutton, E.
T
Tanton, T. D.
Tapp, G. A. M.
Tartaglia, Ralph
Tate, Ernie
Tate, Alfred
Tauber, A.
Taulbut, W. A.
Taylor, Edith M.
Taylor, Len M.
Taylor, Ken
Taylor, R. L.
Taylor, P. V.
Taylor, T.
Tearle, T. E.
Teteranko, J.
Teteranko, P.
Templeton, W.
Thompson, E. L.
Thompson, G. W.
Thomson, James
Thorburn, G. H.
Thorpe, P. V.
Thomson, N. L.
Timothy, W. J.
Todd, Alan
Tomado, J.
Tomlinson, Joan F.
Tomlinson, Pat M.
Tosh, J.
Toth, Alec
Trembley, P. W.
Trevison, R.
Trombley, R. J.

Tull, Harold
Turnbull, Bob
Tweed, G. B.
Tweed, J. H.
V
Vandervoort, H.
Vandervoort, W. D.
Verdiel, L.
Vanichuk, Fred
Vanichuk, Pete
Vanichuk, Mike
Vincent, E.
Virag, J. E. †
Vizzutti, D. G.
Vizzutti, G. E.
Vogler, G. W.
Vonarx, R. C.
W
Walker, E. N.
Walker, Cliff

Walker, W. E.
Wallace, Dan
Warman, J. E.
Warr, J. G.
Warris, Colin
Wasp, G. Godfrey
Waugh, J.
Weber, Clarence
Wells, E. Gordon
Wells, Robert
Wheeler, G. E.
Whipple, A. R.
White, Allistair
Whitley, E. C.
Wilcox, J. B.
Williams, A. F.
Williams, C. E.
Williams, J. H.
Williams, J. H. (Mrs.)
Willis, J. W.

Wilshire, Sid
Wilshire, Morris †
Wilshire, Thora
Wilson, E.
Wilson, M.
Winter, F. G.
Wilson, Edward H.
Wood, Nelson E.
Woodruff, Don
Woodruff, R. J. †
Worth, John
Wright, Graham
Wright, Walter
Wright, Chas.
Y
Young, J. L.
Young, Ronald W.
Z
Zilnic, C. Y.
Zilnic, S. †

Note: This list is incomplete. The names of some men and women, from Powell River & District, who served in the Canadian Armed Forces during WWII, are not recorded on this list.

WWII Powell River & District P.O.W.s
(as listed by the Ex-Service Men's Association)

P.O.W.s in Germany – released 1945:

Cooper, Gordon L. RCAF   Stalag Luft III Germany
Davenport, J. CA   Germany
Gairns, R. RCAF   Stalag Luft III Germany
Gardiner, T. RCAF   Stalag Luft III Germany
Granger, F. D. RCAF   Stalag Luft 6 Germany
Johnson, Oliver M. CA   Lager-Bezeichnung, Germany
Kipp, Wilfred RCAF   Stalag Luft III, Germany
Osavitsky, J. CA   Germany

Powell River & District Roll of Honour
Those who gave their lives during Two World Wars

1914-1918

Birkenshaw, Ralph
Black, Alex
Bryanton, R.
Carter, E. A. (Harry)
Cole, Gordon
Lant, Tommy
Moodie, C.
Simmons, Tommy
Stanley, W. (Bill)
Stewart, S.
Washington, George
Welch, R. (Dick)

1939-1945

Allan, J. B.
Anglin, James A.
Baker, Ronald C.
Baum, William G. R.
Bell, John M.
Bortolussi, Aldo
Brooks, Lucien
Carey, A. M.
Daubner, H. A. Jr.
Daubner, J. W.
Deakin, Arthur
Dickson, William R.
Dittloff, William
Donkersley, Harry W. **DFC**
Drayton, Henry S.
Eckman, August J.
Ethofer, George P.
Fairgrieve, William C.
Freeman, Henry G.
Gaudet, Reginal C.
Gilmour, William
Gribble, Ernest
Hassell, Ewart
Hopkins, Bruce
Hughes, Gordon B.
Johnston, John S.
Johnston, Norman
Keaist, Richard P.
Lasser, Robert A.
Lee, Don
Leese, R. G.
Leese, W. H.
Lloyd, James
Lyle, A. J.

McLean, A. L.
McMullin, Frank
Magson, Phillip J. A.
Marlatt, Sholto P.
Marshall, William K.
Morris, Andrew
Morris, John
Mullen, John W.
Nello, Frank R. V.
Pidcock, Charles T. L.
Rorke, Albert L.
Scriven, Gilbert L.
Shaw, Robert
Smith, Bernard
Spratt, Frederick
Srigley, Ralph G.
Stusiak, Nicholas
Virag, James E.
Wilshire, Maurice
Woodruff, Richard J.
Zilnic, Sergie

"All these boys were intimately known to almost everyone in the community. These boys – those killed, the missing, and the prisoners of war – were all Bill and Harry and George and Dick to us."

Powell River Digester June 1945

Glossary

Canadian Services
CA – Canadian Army   CAO – Canadian Army Overseas
CEF – Canadian Expeditionary Force – WWI field force created by Canada for overseas service.
CITC – Canadian Infantry Training Centre
CWAC – Canadian Women's Army Corps
RCAF – Royal Canadian Air Force
RCAFO – Royal Canadian Air Force Overseas
RCAF WD – Women's Division of the RCAF
RCN – Royal Canadian Navy
RCNVR - Royal Canadian Naval Volunteer Reserve
RCOC – Royal Canadian Ordnance Corps
WRCNS (Wrens) - Women's Royal Canadian Naval Service

British Services
ATS – Auxiliary Territorial Service (Women's Division of the British Army)
BA – British Army
BEF – British Expeditionary Force
FANY – First Aid Nursing Yeomanry (British women's ambulance unit)
RAF – Royal Air Force
RN – Royal Navy
WAAF – Women's Army Auxiliary Corps
WLA – Women's Land Army (assisted farmers in food production)
WRNS (Wrens) – Women's Royal Naval Service
WTC – Women's Timber Corps
WVS – Women's Voluntary Service (British women not in the services due to age, health, in care of young children etc.: volunteering for work in canteens, driving ambulances, clothing centres, etc.)

Medals
DCM – Distinguished Conduct Medal
DFC – Distinguished Flying Cross
ED – Efficiency Decoration
MC – Military Cross   BAR – Second awarding of the Military Cross
MM – Military Medal
VC – Victoria Cross

Other Military Terms
AEF – Allied Expeditionary Forces
ARP – Air Raid Precautions (men and women on patrol in towns and factories – enforcing blackout regulations, rescuing people after air raids, issuing gasmasks and shelters, putting out small fires, etc.)
AW1 – Aircraftwoman 1st class
AW2 – Aircraftwoman 2nd class
CMF – Central Med Forces
CQMS Company Quartermaster Sergeant
CSM – Company Sergeant Major
LAC – Leading Aircraftman (Air Force)

LAW – Leading Aircraft Woman (Air Force)
OC – Officer Commanding or Officer Cadet
PO – Petty Officer (Naval Rank equal to Warrant Officer)
Pte - Private
QM – Quarter Master
SGM – Sergeant-Major

Other Terms

Anderson shelter – small air raid shelter made of corrugated metal, built in backyards in Britain.
Blighty – England
Boche – derogatory slang (esp. in WWI & WWII) for German
Bully beef – term for canned corned beef in U.K.
COs – Conscientious Objectors to military service
DP – Displaced person. Displaced from home country due to war.
Enemy Alien – person living in a country with which his own country is at war.
Jerry/Jerries – slang for Germans
IODE – Imperial Order of the Daughters of the Empire. They knitted sweaters for seaman, scarves and socks for those in the services, stitched clothing for bombed-out women and children in Britain.
Morrison shelter – a shelter (big enough to sleep in), used inside British homes, with heavy mesh sides and a metal table top
Victory Gardens – due to the shortage of food during the war, governments in Britain and Canada encouraged everyone to plant a vegetable garden.

Index

Wedding photo of WWII war bride **Violet Woodley (Fitch)** *and* **Harold Woodley CAO CVSM,**
Lancaster Priory, England Sept. 22, 1945; they stayed with relatives in Manchester for their honeymoon.

On leave from the Artillery Regiment in 1944, Harold met Vi while playing the piano in the Silver Keys Cross pub, Lancaster when Vi came over to sing. Vi was working in the wing department of an aircraft factory, building mosquito bombers. They corresponded, met on leaves, and fell in love. Vi's father was a Cockney and her mother a real Lancashire lass. Vi's paternal grandmother's house was bombed in the Blitz, the house was lost and her grandmother was buried for 24 hours in the debris — she later died of her injuries. Vi's mother was a cleaner at Lancaster Castle, she damp-mopped the stairs to the dungeon where no one else would go. In June 1946 Vi Woodley left Southampton on a war bride ship, the Aquatania. A band was playing on the ship's arrival in Halifax; the war brides threw English money to the crowd below! After receiving a basket of fruit, she travelled to Edmonton on a war bride train. What a shock to arrive in Hinton, Alberta: one hotel, one garage and one store! Vi and Harold lived in Hinton for 17 years; they had eight children: Rose, Alfred, Brenda, Mona, Rocky, Frank, Frances and Helen. In 1970 Vi and Harold moved to Powell River, B.C.; they both worked in the Rodmay Hotel until they retired.
Vi (age 85) Woodley interviewed Powell River August 2012